Brilliant ITQ

PEARSON EDUCATION HIGHER EDUCATION DIVISION

We work with leading authors to develop the strongest educational materials in computing, bringing cutting-edge thinking and best learning practice to a global market.

Under a range of well-known imprints, including Prentice Hall, we craft high quality print and electronic publications which help readers to understand and apply their content, whether studying or at work.

To find out more about the complete range of our publishing, please visit us on the World Wide Web at: www.pearsoned.co.uk

Brilliant ITQ

Nik Taylor
Catherine Jones

PEARSON
Prentice
Hall

Harlow, England • London • New York • Boston • San Francisco • Toronto
Sydney • Tokyo • Singapore • Hong Kong • Seoul • Taipei • New Delhi
Cape Town • Madrid • Mexico City • Amsterdam • Munich • Paris • Milan

Pearson Education Limited
Edinburgh Gate
Harlow
Essex CM20 2JE
England

and Associated Companies throughout the world

Visit us on the World Wide Web at:
www.pearsoned.co.uk

First published 2008

ISBN: 978-0-13-615758-8

British Library Cataloguing-in-Publication Data
A catalogue record for this book is available from the British Library

Library of Congress Cataloging-in-Publication Data

Taylor, Nik.
  Brilliant ITQ / Nik Taylor, Catherine Jones. - - 1st ed.
      p. cm.
  "National Vocational Qualification (NVQ) for IT."
  Includes index.
  ISBN 978-0-13-615758-8 (pbk.)
  1. Electronic data processing personnel--Certification--Great Britain. 2.
Information technology--Great Britain--Study guides. 3.   National Vocational
Qualifications (Great Britain)--Study guides. I. Jones, Catherine. II. Title.
  QA76.3.T38 2007
  004.0941--dc22

                                                                    2007039843

10 9 8 7 6 5 4 3 2 1
11 10 09 08 07

Typeset in Helvetica Roman 9pt on 12pt by 30
Printed by Ashford Colour Press Ltd., Gosport

The publisher's policy is to use paper manufactured from sustainable forests.

Contents

Introduction

Using This Book

ITQ is the National Vocational Qualification (NVQ) for IT users. It is designed to help you develop your IT skills around your current job – so you learn more about the aspects of IT that you need during your working day.

You get to choose which units of ITQ you want to take, and for this your supervisor at work should be able to help. The purpose of this book is to act as a guide once you have decided on your units. While you are completing the work, you can use this book to help you through any difficulties you may come across.

The book is intended for those aiming to complete ITQ at Level 2.

At the end of each chapter is a short quiz designed to test how you are doing on the knowledge and understanding areas of the unit.

Also at the end of each chapter is a list of suggested tasks for you to complete as evidence of your competency in the unit. These are just suggestions, and you may well have to adapt them in order to make them fit your own work. However, they should give you some idea of the sort of work required.

ITQ Level 1

You can also use this book for guidance if you are taking a unit at Level 1 (or perhaps taking the whole ITQ at this level). Level 1 covers similar ground, but does not require you to go into so much depth either in your task work or your knowledge and understanding. Before starting work on a Level 1 unit, you should discuss the requirements with your supervisor.

Real Advice from Real ITQ Assessors

In writing this book, the authors have drawn on the extensive experience of actual ITQ assessors.

Rudy Bagot, Sheena Smith, Lynne Pearce and Georgie Trehan are all qualified ITQ assessors at training company Happy Computers (www.happycomputers.co.uk).

Between them they have trained and assessed hundreds of ITQ students. Look out for their advice in the 'Assessor's tips' boxes you'll see dotted throughout the book.

Choosing Your Units

There are 17 units from which you can choose to make up your ITQ qualification. One of these units is mandatory – Make selective use of IT. From the rest, you have a completely free choice.

To reach Level 1:

- You must achieve a total of 40 points.

- 15 points must come from the mandatory unit.

- The additional 25 points come from optional units.

To reach Level 2:

- You must achieve a total of 100 points.

- 25 points must come from the mandatory unit.

- The additional 75 points come from the optional units. Of those 75, at least 40 must be achieved at Level 2.

Below is a table which shows the values you can gain by completing each unit.

Unit name	Unit values	
	Level 1	Level 2
Make selective use of IT (mandatory unit)	15	25
Operate a computer	10	20
IT maintenance for users	5	15
IT troubleshooting for users	5	15
IT security for users	5	15
Artwork and imaging software	10	20
Internet and intranets	5	15
Email	5	15
Word-processing software	10	20
Spreadsheet software	10	20
Database software	10	20
Website software	10	20
Presentation software	10	20
Specialist or bespoke software	10	20
Evaluate the impact of IT	5	15
Use IT systems	5	15
Use IT to exchange information	5	15

Note: the Use IT systems unit is a general unit that covers much of the same ground as Operate a computer, IT troubleshooting for users, IT maintenance for users and IT security for users. If you intend to include any of those units in your ITQ portfolio, it is not recommended that you also include the Use IT systems unit.

Note: the Use IT to exchange information unit is a general unit that covers much of the same ground as the Internet and Intranets and Email units. If you intend to include either of those units in your ITQ portfolio, it is not recommended that you also include the Use IT to exchange information unit.

Software Used

When completing a software-based unit in ITQ, you are free to use any suitable software package.

For example, if you choose to take on the Word processing software unit, you can use any current word processing package.

For the purposes of this book, we have concentrated on the commonly used packages for each unit.

Hence, the software-based chapters use the following software…

Chapter	Software used
Internet and Intranets	Internet Explorer 6
Email	Microsoft Outlook 2002
Word processing software	Microsoft Word 2002
Spreadsheet software	Microsoft Excel 2002
Database software	Microsoft Access 2002
Website software	Microsoft FrontPage 2002
Artwork and imaging software	Adobe Photoshop CS2
Presentation software	Microsoft PowerPoint 2002

As you can see, the Microsoft programs referred to are all from the Microsoft Office 2002 package (also known as Office XP).

If you are using Microsoft Office 2003, you will find the instructions are the same – although the screenshots will look slightly different from the software you are running.

Throughout the book, the operating system shown is Microsoft Windows XP.

Creating Evidence

Much of your evidence will be made up of the files created when using the software relevant to your unit. However, it's often a good idea to take screenshots of what you are doing, so you can further back up your evidence by showing the steps you took.

There are many software packages you can use to take screenshots. Free packages (or free trials) include ScreenHunter and HyperSnap.

However, you can easily take screenshots without the need for any specialist software.

To take a screenshot of the entire screen…

Press the Print Scrn button on your keyboard.

To take a screenshot of the active window (e.g. just the application you are working in)…

Press the Alt + Print Scrn buttons on your keyboard.

Both actions will make a copy of the chosen area to your computer's clipboard. You can then open a new document in your word-processing package and paste in the screenshot (press Ctrl + V).

About the Authors

Nik Taylor and Catherine Jones know a thing or two about teaching people to use computers – by day they both create courses for the online training company Happy eLearning.

This innovative company considers its mission to be training people in the use of computer software without the need for mounds of jargon.

It's an approach the authors have used in this book, so you can learn what you need to know without feeling overwhelmed by technobabble.

Happy eLearning has courses on all kinds of software, and you can try them for free. Just visit www.happyelearning.com/freestuff to find out more.

A Free Gift for You, Dear Reader

We're delighted you've chosen to buy this book and we're sure it will give you everything you need to complete your ITQ qualification.

As a thank you, we'd like to offer you the chance to accompany your learning with free trial access to any of our online courses in Microsoft Office.

Simply visit www.happyelearning.com/freestuff and sign up for the free trial, where we'll give you the opportunity to try out a selection of our existing online lessons.

If you like what you see, why not contact us to get a licence to access the whole course? Should you decide to purchase one licence, we'll also throw in three months' access to another course of your choice, absolutely free!*

To purchase your licence, please contact our booking team on 020 7375 7300.

* Offer ends September 2008

Training managers!

Do you manage the IT training for your company? If so, you can take advantage of Happy eLearning's unique approach and gain access to the latest courses for free.

We all know how email has taken over our lives. Let our *Email Exemplar* course guide your staff towards a more streamlined, efficient and time-saving way of dealing with their email. You'll be amazed at the time they save!

Most of us spend our working week at a computer desk. Our *Office Sense* course helps your staff ensure that time is spent working safely. The course guides them through the correct set-up of their desk, chair and computer, so they can minimise common complaints such as back, neck and wrist pain.

As a special offer to IT managers, if you book 50 or more licences on any of our IT courses, we will give each of your licence holders three months' free access to either our *Email Exemplar* or *Office Sense* courses.

If you buy licences in bulk, we can also offer special price reductions – please contact our booking team for details on 020 7375 7300.

Happy eLearning can also offer special discounts for either online or classroom-based ITQ training, led by the ITQ trainers who helped compile this book. Call the number above to find out what deals are available.

Thanks to...

If we'd put the name of everyone who helped create this book on the front cover, there would have been no space left for the title. As it is, we'd like to take this opportunity to say a hearty 'ta very much' to all those who helped with everything on the following pages. In particular...

Victoria Hull, Dominic Riches, Lucy Blake, James Moran (for his words and pics), Adam Taylor (for being a general Photoshop guru), Sheena Smith (for bundles of help throughout the project), Rudy Bagot, Lynne Pearce and Georgie Trehan.

Thanks go to them and everybody else at Happy.

CHAPTER 1

Make Selective Use of IT

1.1 About This Unit

What you need to know

To gain ITQ Level 2 in this unit, you should demonstrate the following competency:

Work out how to use IT effectively for more complex tasks and purposes, taking into account your own skills and capabilities.

To achieve this you should know:

1 What the purposes for using IT are and how appropriate they are.

2 How to produce information that is clear and appropriate.

3 What the appropriate terms that may be used for IT are and how to use them.

You should also be able to display the following skills and techniques:

1 Explain decisions and actions taken about using IT.

2 Find and evaluate information using appropriate methods.

3 Organise information.

4 Review your own use of IT and feedback from others.

How to prove your skills

This unit is first in the list, but you will generally complete it last. That's because you can re-use tasks you've completed for other units as evidence for this one.

The assessment for this unit must take place in the workplace, and your tasks have to be things you would naturally do as part of your job.

You have to provide at least four tasks, and these must come from at least two of the other units you have chosen. So you can't provide four spreadsheets or four Word documents as evidence, but you can provide two of each.

It's also a good idea to compile a personal statement for each task in which you discuss the work you have completed and explain how you did it.

1.2 Using IT

1.2.1 What Software to Use

This unit is all about choosing the correct software for a particular task and using its features to complete your task efficiently. You need to explain why you chose the software that you used and why it was particularly suited to the task. The table below shows the functions performed by some of the most popular programs.

Software type	Key functions	Common programs of this type
Word processing	Producing text-based documents such as letters, simple news-sheets	Microsoft Word Corel WordPerfect Lotus WordPro
Spreadsheet package	Making calculations on figures. Producing graphical charts from data	Microsoft Excel
Database software	Used to organise data so it can be searched and manipulated easily	Microsoft Access Lotus Approach
Presentation production	Used to create slide-show style presentations	Microsoft PowerPoint Apple Keynote
Website construction	Used to create websites	Microsoft FrontPage Adobe Dreamweaver
Photo editing	Used to view digital photographs and make editing changes to them	Adobe Photoshop Corel Paint Shop Pro
Desktop publishing	Used to create magazines, brochures and other publications	QuarkXPress Adobe InDesign
Web browser	Used to view pages from the World Wide Web	Microsoft Internet Explorer Mozilla Firefox
Email	Used to send and receive email messages	Microsoft Outlook Microsoft Outlook Express Mozilla Thunderbird
Compression software	Used to reduce the size of files by compressing them into a single folder	WinZip WinRAR

The table below gives examples of tasks you may complete using IT, as well as the software you would use to do so.

Task	Software required
Produce personalised letters for 100 people from your company's mailing list	Word processor
Create a file to keep track of a department's monthly spending	Spreadsheet
Create a file to list all employees in your company, along with their personal details and employment history	Database
Send a document file to a colleague in another city	Email
Search for available hotel accommodation in Brussels	Web browser

Of course, there are all sorts of tasks you can accomplish using IT. While you are working, think about what packages you are using to achieve your goals and ask yourself what made you choose that package.

Also consider why you have chosen to use a computer to complete the task. How does using a computer make it easier? Here are some examples:

- Writing a letter in Word. This is easier than writing a letter by hand because you can quickly make changes to what you've written. You can also use additional features, such as mail merge to personalise a number of letters.

- Creating a budget in Excel. This is easier than filling in a ledger by hand because the computer does all the calculations for you. You can also use more advanced features to link calculations together, quickly create charts from the data, and so on.

Practise this!

When you complete a task using IT, think about the following questions.

- How was using IT for this task better than using a non-IT-based approach?
- Why was the package you chose the best one for the job?
- What were the key features of the software package that helped you achieve your goal?
- How did these features make what you were doing easier?

1.3 Key Skills

There are four key skills you need to demonstrate when completing this unit and we take a look at each of these below. You should make sure the tasks you choose to supply give plenty of evidence of these skills. You can go into more detail by talking with your assessor or by compiling a short statement about the work you have done.

1.3.1 Understanding Software Functions

It's important not only that you are able to choose the correct software for the task, but also that you can explain *why* you made that choice.

Consider each piece of work you create and think about which of the software's features you found particularly useful.

For example, let's say you have been asked to produce a simple newsletter. You decide to use Microsoft Word for this task, as it gives you plenty of design options (different fonts, clipart, text colours and so on). You can also use additional features to put text into columns, use text styles and perhaps even personalise each newsletter (using mail merge).

Practise this!

Think about the piece of software you feel most confident using. What are the features you find most useful on this software? What can you do with this software that makes your job easier? These are the sorts of things you want to be able to point out when completing this unit.

1.3.2 Finding and Evaluating Information

This section of the unit tests your ability to use search features. That might make you think of web browsers and search engines – but there are plenty of other methods of searching. For instance, Microsoft Word's find and replace feature enables you to search a document for particular words and phrases. Microsoft Excel contains a clipart search which makes it possible to search for images to add to your spreadsheets.

To demonstrate your ability in this section of the unit...

- Choose a task where you need to find a significant amount of information.

- Ensure it is a task where you will actually find more information than you need.

This will ensure that you can show your ability to find information, and also that you can filter out irrelevant data.

Practise this!

Try one of the following:

- Use a search engine to find information on the Web.

- Use queries and criteria to find selected records in a database.

- Use the search facility of your email program to find emails from a particular sender.

1.3.3 Organising Your Work

Once you've chosen a software package and selected the data you will include, you need to put it all together to make a useful document.

Show that you have given consideration to the following:

- *Who will be accessing your work?* Think about whether your audience has any special requirements. Perhaps you are compiling a document on a technical subject that will be read by non-technical people? In this case you would need to show you have thought about the tone of the piece. Maybe you have created a presentation that needs to be small enough to be easily emailed? Here you could discuss how you kept the size of the file down by limiting images and additional content.

- *What content is required?* Consider the purpose of the document and ensure you have acquired enough content for it to meet this purpose. At the same time, ensure you haven't made things confusing by including too much data.

- *How should the document be formatted?* Perhaps your company has a standard template which should always be used when preparing Word documents. Maybe there is a house style that should be used when creating spreadsheets. Think about how your formatting choices affect the usefulness of your document.

Assessor's tip

Rudy says:

It's really important that you show you have considered your audience when creating your work. Think about your audience's specific needs and make lots of notes to show how you have accommodated these.

1.3.4 Reviewing Your Work

Think about your strengths when it comes to using IT. What programs do you feel most comfortable using? What features do you use regularly to save time? When have you been asked by colleagues to explain how something works?

Also, consider where you can improve your skills. Which programs do you find challenging? What are you doing to broaden your knowledge of these areas?

A crucial area in this unit is your ability to show a thorough awareness of your strengths and weaknesses in IT.

Think about features you have had trouble with. You don't necessarily need to have solved the problem – the most important thing is that you can display an awareness of your own limitations when it comes to IT. After all – none of us knows all there is to know!

Additionally, consider how you have responded to advice from others on your IT skills. For example, you might have been using a slow method to create calculations in Excel, before a colleague showed you how to use AutoSum. Think of similar examples from your own working life.

1.4 Techie Terms

You will be expected to understand common technical terms used in computing. Listed below is a selection of such terms. If you come across others that you don't understand, run a search for the word in a search engine to find an explanation.

Anti-virus	Software that protects your computer against viruses.
Attachment	A file that you attach to an email.
Base unit	Another word for your computer. This refers to the big box that contains all the electronics that make your computer work.
Boot up	Starting up your computer.
Browser	A program that enables you to view pages from the Internet.
Character	Any letter, number, punctuation mark, symbol or space in a written document.
Check box	A list of options may have check boxes next to each. You can click on as many of these as you like to select them.
Control key	There are two Control keys at the bottom left and right of the main keyboard. Normally, they are labelled with the letters Ctrl. Holding down one of these keys along with a combination of other keys enables you to perform keyboard shortcuts.
Control Panel	One of the options you'll see when you click on the Start button. The Control Panel enables you to make changes to how your computer works.
Crash	When a computer becomes overloaded with information and stops working.
Desktop	The background screen that you see when your computer has booted up.
Dialog box	A message box that appears to give you information about the program you are using. You have to click a button inside the dialog box before continuing.
Domain name	The unique name that identifies a website.

Download	The process of transferring data from another computer onto your own computer. Normally used to refer to transferring data from the Internet.
Drive	A device connected to your computer that is used to store data (such as your documents and other files). Most of your data will be stored on your hard drive.
Drop-down menu	A menu that appears when you click on its title.
Email	An electronic messaging system that enables you to instantly send a text-based message to anyone anywhere on the planet.
File	A document on your computer. For instance, when you save an email on your computer, it will be stored as a file.
Firewall	A type of program that prevents hackers from gaining access to your computer via the Internet.
Folder	An object used to contain files.
Hacker	Someone who gains unauthorised access to computer systems.
Hard drive	A device inside your computer that is used to store data.
Icon	A picture on your screen that symbolises an object, such as a folder, program or file.
Inbox	The folder in your email program which stores incoming mail.
Keyboard shortcut	A combination of keys that can be pressed to complete a task quickly. For instance, you can save a document by pressing the Ctrl and S keys at the same time.
Log off	The process of finishing your session on a computer without actually turning it off.
Log on	The process of typing in your name and password when you start using your computer. Logging on enables the computer to load up your personal settings.
Menu	A list of tasks and commands displayed on screen. You can choose one of the commands by clicking on it.
Menu bar	Usually found near the top of a program window, this contains a number of menus. Clicking on a menu name opens that menu.
Monitor	The screen that's attached to your computer.
Mouse	A hand-held device that enables you to move a pointer around on the screen. The buttons on a mouse enable you to interact with the items on the screen.
Netiquette	A term for being polite when communicating online. Common points for good netiquette include not writing entirely in capitals (it's considered shouting), not using too much text-speak in messages and not sending large attachments with emails without first checking it's OK with the recipient.

Operating system	The software that runs the computer. The most common type of operating system is Microsoft Windows.
PC	Stands for personal computer.
Peripheral	An additional item attached to your computer. Examples of peripherals include printers, scanners and speakers.
Pointer	A small image on the screen that moves as you move the mouse. The pointer will have a different shape depending on what you are doing.
Program	A tool that you open on your computer when you want to complete a particular task. For instance, if you wanted to type a letter, you would open a word-processing program.
Radio button	A list of options may have radio buttons next to each. You can click on one of the radio buttons to select it. If you then click on another to select it, the first is deselected.
Search engine	A type of website that is used to find other web pages.
Shift	This key changes what the other keys do while it is held down. For instance, press a letter key while holding down the Shift key and the letter will come out in upper case (capitals).
Shut down	Switching off your computer.
Spam	Unwanted email – typically marketing scams.
Start button	The button at the bottom left of the screen. Clicking on this opens all the options available to you on your computer.
Stop button	Used in a Web browser to stop any more data being downloaded.
Subfolder	A folder that is contained within another folder.
Submenu	A menu that is contained within another menu.
System tray	Located on the far right of the taskbar, this shows the programs running in the background on your computer.
Tab	Pressing this key moves the cursor along to the next tab point. This key is located directly to the left of the Q key.
Taskbar	The bar that stretches along the bottom of your screen. The taskbar lists the programs currently open, as well as other information such as the time.
Title bar	The bar at the top of a window that tells you the program and file you are working with.
Toolbar	A group of buttons, normally found at the top of a program window. Each button is associated with a different command. Clicking on the button activates that command.
URL	Uniform resource locator. Simply put, this is the address you will type in to get to a specific web page.

Virus	A malicious program that spreads from computer to computer. Viruses will often cause damage to data stored on computers they have infected.
Webcam	A camera attached to your computer which can be used to record video or broadcast live video on the World Wide Web.
Wizard	A program that guides you through the completion of a complicated process.
World Wide Web	Often known simply as 'the Web', this is a system that provides global access to all the data (such as web pages) that can be accessed by web browsers.

Can't find it?

If you're stuck on a techie term not listed above, try running a search for it on www.techterms.org

---

Also check...

For more on types of computer hardware, take a look at Chapter 2, Operate a computer.

1.5 Test Your Knowledge

The questions below will test what you know of the knowledge and understanding requirements of this unit. All the answers to these questions are referred to within this chapter, but you may have to check other chapters for full answers.

1 For what type of work would you be most likely to use Microsoft PowerPoint?

2 You have been asked to create a database of customers' names and telephone numbers. What Microsoft program would you use for this?

3 Name a program that would be useful for working with digital photos.

4 What type of program would you use if you wanted to book a European flight using your computer?

5 List three key advantages to writing a document in Word, as opposed to writing it by hand.

6 List two advantages to compiling a budget in Excel, rather than writing it out by hand.

7 List one way in which the content of a document you are creating might be affected by the needs of your intended audience.

8 What is netiquette?

9 What would you use a search engine for?

10 What is a base unit?

1.6 Evidence

For this unit, you can supply tasks you have completed for other units, and your supervisor at work should be able to give you guidance on the type of tasks to use. Below are some ideas. Consider how you can adapt these ideas to make them more relevant for your own workplace and to ensure you cover all the skills requirements.

- Select a task you have completed for another ITQ unit. Create a document that explains the software you used for this task and why you chose it. Why is the software you have chosen particularly suitable for the task? Contrast the software with any alternatives.

- Create a document that explains how you have searched the Internet to find help on a work-related query. Explain how you used search engine features such as keywords and Boolean searching to improve the number of relevant results.

- Create a presentation that is intended to be run by other users from their own desktops. Ensure the presentation is simple to run, that all the slides are in the correct order and that any included features are working properly.

- Create a document that lists any IT tasks that you have had difficulty with. Identify what you found challenging and then consider the possible reasons. Discuss which difficulties were caused by a lack of knowledge and which for other reasons. Also talk about instances when you have been given advice on your use of IT and show how you have acted upon that advice.

CHAPTER 2

Operate a Computer

2.1 About This Unit

What you need to know

To gain ITQ Level 2 in this unit, you should demonstrate the following competency:
Use most types of hardware, software and storage media effectively.
To achieve this you should know:

1 What most types of computer hardware are and how to use them.

2 What most software tools and functions can be used for and how to use them.

3 How to identify health and safety issues in using IT.

4 That it is essential to make sure that hardware and software are compatible.

5 How data transmission speeds vary.

You should also be able to display the following skills and techniques:

1 Setting up most types of hardware safely.

2 Accessing data.

3 Using common storage media.

4 Using common software tools and techniques.

How to prove your skills

You need to carry out at least two work-based tasks which demonstrate the skills and knowledge listed above. In order to show your competency, it may well be necessary for you to complete more tasks than this.

Make sure you have plenty of evidence that shows how you completed each task, such as a copy of the file you worked on, or a document with screenshots of the processes you followed. You can back this up by producing a report which shows your knowledge of the subjects covered within the unit.

2.2 What Your Computer's Made of

2.2.1 Parts of a Computer

At its most basic level, a computer is made up of just two parts: hardware and software.

All the physical, solid objects that make up your computer are pieces of hardware. If you can touch it or feel it or bang your head on it, it is hardware. Software is the name for programs you can use once your computer is up and running.

The outside:

- **Base unit**: this is the square box that all the other parts plug into. It contains all the components that make the PC work.

- **VDU**: the screen/monitor/visual display unit (VDU) is the part of the computer that shows you what is going on, and what you are doing. For example, in a word-processing program, you would see the letters you type appearing on the screen.

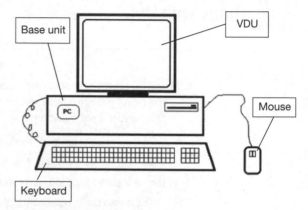

- **Keyboard**: this is what you use to type information into the computer.

- **Mouse**: the mouse is used to point and click on things on the screen – when you move the mouse, a pointer on the screen moves as well. If you press the mouse button while the pointer is on certain icons or buttons, you can run programs or give the computer commands.

The insides:

- **CPU**: the central processing unit is the brains of the computer. All the 'thinking', calculating and processing is done here. Its speed is measured in megahertz (MHz) or, more commonly, gigahertz (GHz). This figure measures the number of complete circuits a signal can travel around the processor in one second, or the millions of simple calculations it can make in a second. If a CPU has a speed of 600 MHz, this means it can do 600 million things in one second. If it has a speed of 2 GHz, then it can do 2000 million (or 2 billion) things in one second.

- **Hard disk**: the hard disk drive is used to store programs and information. When you save a file, it is saved onto your hard disk.

- **Memory**: when a program is run, it is loaded into the computer's memory. The more memory a PC has, the more things it can do at one time.

Different types of computers

The picture above shows a desktop computer. However there are other types of computer that you may use, for example:

Laptop: a portable version of a desktop computer. The keyboard and monitor screen are combined into one unit that can be folded away when not in use. Commonly seen on the 08:42 to London Bridge.

PDA: this stands for personal digital assistant, which is a rather grand way of describing a hand-held computer. These are capable of performing many of the functions that a full-size computer can do, but they're much easier to fit in your pocket.

2.3 Computer Accessories

2.3.1 Storage Devices

- **Floppy disks**: once the most common method of storing data, floppy disks are now becoming less popular as they can hold only 1.44 megabytes of data. These days, that's not a whole lot.

- **CDs**: by using a CD writer/burner, you can put files on a compact disk, which can hold over 400 floppies' worth of files. A DVD (digital versatile disk) looks just like a CD, but can hold six to seven times more information again.

- **Flash drive**: also known as thumb drives, pen drives and a million other names, these ingenious devices are small enough to fit on a keyring yet can hold several gigabytes of data. They plug directly into a USB port on your drive. Once plugged in, your flash drive will appear in My Computer as another disk drive.

- **Hard disk**: your hard disk drive is the place where most of your data will be stored. Advances in computer technology mean the capacity of hard drives is being increased all the time. It is common now for hard drives to have a capacity in excess of 200 gigabytes.

Practise this!

Make a list of the types of storage media available to you at work and which you use regularly.

2.3.2 Printers

Printers are used to transfer information from the computer onto paper. They come in many different shapes and sizes:

- **Laser**: these are large, expensive printers that work like a photocopier. They usually have very high-quality printouts and would normally be used in busy offices.

- **Inkjet**: these are smaller, cheaper printers that use a little cartridge to spray a jet of ink onto the paper. They are fairly quiet and of good quality, but are not as fast or good as lasers. Most home printers are inkjets.

- **Dot matrix/impact**: this old type of printer uses a ribbon and a print head, like a typewriter. They are very loud, extremely slow and virtually no one uses them any more. However, they are still used with pre-printed forms on continuous rolls of paper.

2.3.3 Modems

A modem is a device that allows a computer to connect to a telephone line or cable network and access the Internet. Most PCs have a modem built inside them, but external ones are also available.

2.3.4 Network Cards

A network card is used to link up to another PC or several PCs in a network.

2.3.5 Talking to the PC

Apart from the mouse and keyboard, there are other ways of communicating with your PC:

- **Trackball**: like an upside-down mouse – it sits on the desk, and you move the ball with your fingers to control the movement of the pointer on the screen.

- **Light pen**: a special pen that lets you draw directly onto the screen, or click on buttons and menus.

- **Touchscreen**: like a normal screen, but with a thin, transparent, touch-sensitive layer of plastic covering it. When you touch a part of the screen, it has the same effect as if you had clicked on that area with a mouse.

- **Joystick**: a knob that can be moved around in any direction. Used mainly for playing games.

2.3.6 Multimedia

Multimedia is a buzzword for something that uses sound, music, pictures, video and animation. Most modern PCs are multimedia machines, and need certain things to work:

- **Sound card**: a special controller inside the PC that translates sound into a form the computer can understand.

- **Microphone**: a device that lets you record your voice, or other sounds.

- **Speakers**: these plug into your sound card so you can hear the sounds and music playing.

- **Scanner**: a bit like a photocopier, this scans your own pictures or drawings into the computer so you can save them as digital copies.

- **Digital camera**: these have pretty much eclipsed film cameras now. A digital camera stores your photos on a memory card, so you can transfer your pics directly onto your PC.

2.3.7 Input and Output Devices

All the bits and pieces above are input and output devices. This means that they are used to get information into the PC, or take information out of it.

- An *input* device lets you put information *in* to a PC – a keyboard, mouse, microphone, scanner, digital camera, etc.

- An *output* device takes information *out* of the PC – a printer, a screen/VDU, speakers, etc.

Some items, like floppy disk drives, modems and touchscreens, are both input *and* output devices – they are used to get information in as well as out of a PC.

Practise this!

Take a look at your computer and list which hardware items are input devices and which are output devices.

2.3.8 What is a Peripheral Device?

A peripheral device is anything which you can attach to the main part of your computer. Some of the accessories we have looked at so far are peripheral devices, such as:

- Printers.

- Scanners.

- Modems.

- Speakers.

Assessor's tip

Georgie says:

To find out what printers you have access to, click on the Start button, then click on Printers and Faxes. The box that opens shows you all the printers you can use. The printer with a tick next to it is your default printer – this is the one your computer will use unless you tell it otherwise.

2.3.9 What is Software?

Software refers to the programs that are loaded onto a computer. Microsoft Word and Excel are software programs, as are Internet Explorer and Windows.

- **Systems software** is the software that runs the computer – this is usually called the operating system. Some common operating systems are Windows, Mac OS and Linux.

- **Application software** is the programs that run on the PC. Word and Excel are applications, for example.

2.3.10 Examples of Application Software

Type of software	What does it do?	Examples
Word processor	Has the same function as a typewriter – for producing letters, reports or other written documents	Word, WordPerfect
Spreadsheet	Used to perform calculations on a table containing text and figures. Spreadsheets are usually used for budgets, statistics, etc.	Excel, Lotus 1-2-3
Database	Stores information, e.g. the names and addresses of all your clients	Access, FileMaker Pro
Accounting	Used to analyse finances, do accounts, organise company payrolls, etc.	Sage, QuickBooks
Desktop publishing (DTP)	Used to produce magazines, newsletters, etc.	Quark, PageMaker, Publisher
Web browsing	Used for reading web pages on the Internet	Internet Explorer, Firefox, Safari, Opera

Practise this!

Make a list of the software you use most often at work. List also what you use the software to do, and which features you use most regularly.

2.3.11 What is a Network?

A computer network is two or more computers connected together. They could be in the same room, in the same building, or on opposite sides of the world. There are several reasons for using a network:

- If you have two PCs but only one printer, the PCs can both connect to the printer and share it. You could have a whole company full of computers but with only one printer, and everyone would be able to use it.

- As well as sharing things like printers, PCs on a network can share files and data. Instead of making lots of copies of a file, like a company letter, one copy could be stored on a particular PC, and everyone could read it. This can also work with software – you could have one copy of a piece of software, which is shared so that other people can run it or connect to it.

- To help people work together better, users can send messages to each other through their connected computers – this is called electronic mail, or email.

2.3.12 LANs and WANs

There are two main types of network:

- **LAN (Local Area Network)**: this is a small network, connecting computers spread out over a fairly small, local area – either in the same building or in a few buildings.
- **WAN (Wide Area Network)**: this is a larger network, connecting computers spread out over a wide area – usually around the whole country, or around the world.

2.3.13 Connecting Computers Together

LANs are connected by a system of cables that let the computers talk to each other. The computers must also have network cards installed in order to get them to connect to the network.

WANs use the telephone cables: the Public Switched Data Network (PSDN), as well as satellites and other clever bits and pieces. This saves companies having to lay loads of extra cable, but it means they have to use special equipment to send their information down the phone lines.

2.3.14 Clients and Servers

In a network, a server is the big, powerful PC that controls who logs in, what they can do, and where things go. A client is the PC that most people use to log into the network. Most critical data and software are stored on the server.

Practise this!

Look at your computer and name the various components in your set-up.

2.4 Getting Started

2.4.1 Connection Types

There are lots of different plugs used to connect various gadgets to your PC. Here are some of the most common:

- *USB* In recent years this has become the standard connection type for most types of peripheral. It's easy to use and has fast transfer speeds.
- *Parallel* The parallel port was generally used to plug a printer into your PC. Now superseded by USB and gradually becoming obsolete on home computers.
- *PS/2* Used to connect a keyboard and mouse to your computer. The keyboard and mouse plugs are physically identical, except they are colour-coded so you don't get them mixed up.

- *DB15* This 15-pin plug is used to connect your monitor to your computer's graphics card, so you can see information on the screen.

- *8P8C* Widely used on network cables. Also known (wrongly) as an RJ45 connector.

The pictures below show you the inputs where these plugs will fit.

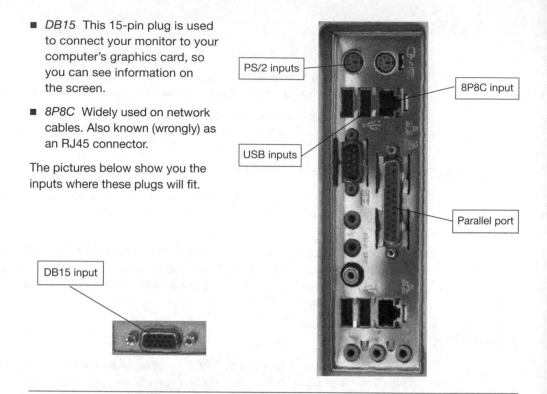

PS/2 inputs

8P8C input

USB inputs

Parallel port

DB15 input

The beauty of USB

USB connections have made adding extra devices to your computer really easy. There are three main benefits to using USB.

1 *Speed.* USB is a whole bunch faster than the older style of connections. At its quickest, USB is capable of transferring data at up to 60 MB per second.

2 *Hotswapping.* A real nerdy buzzword – hotswapping simply means you can connect and unplug USB devices from your computer while it's switched on. Before USB, it was often necessary to switch off your computer before plugging or unplugging anything.

3 *Connectability.* The real seller is the fact that USB connections have become so widespread. Before, additional devices came with all kinds of connections. Now, pretty much any peripheral you buy will plug into a USB port – making it really easy to set up your computer.

If you are connecting a newly bought peripheral to your computer, it is most likely to have a USB connection.

2.4.2 Plugging it all in

Plugging everything into your computer for the first time can seem a daunting task, but it's really very straightforward. There are only four things you need to plug in to get basic functionality from your computer. All of the inputs for these will be found on the back of your computer.

1 *Monitor*. The standard connector for monitors is a DB15 plug. There will be only one socket on the back of your computer where this plug will fit, so plug it into that. You will probably find there are two screws on either side of the plug that can be tightened by hand to secure it.

2 *Keyboard*. Most keyboards have a PS/2 connector, which is a small round plug. The casing on this plug is colour-coded, so you just need to match the plug to the correct colour input. Some keyboards have a USB connector instead. This is a flat rectangular plug. You will find several USB ports on the back of your computer and the keyboard can be plugged into any of them.

3 *Mouse*. Again, most mice have PS/2 connectors. Match the coloured plug to the correct input to plug it in. If your mouse has a USB plug, it can be plugged into any USB port.

4 *Power cable*. Once you've got everything else plugged in, you can plug in your computer's power cable. *This should be done last*, and only after you've checked that all the other connections are secure. The input for your power cable will be near a fan vent on the back of your computer and will be the only one that will fit the plug.

Practise this!

Look around the back of your computer and work out what is connected to each of the plugs.

2.4.3 Starting it up

Before you can do anything on your computer, you need to fire it up. You do that by giving a quick jab to the power switch you'll see on your computer's main box. Have a look at the front of your computer to find this. Power buttons will look different depending on which computer you have. However, they should all have the same symbol next to them. This is a circle with a vertical line running through it. Whenever you see this symbol on a computer, you're looking at a power button.

1 First, press the power button on your PC.

2 Press the power button on your monitor.

I can't see the symbol on any of the buttons!

Sometimes the power symbol might be printed on the actual casing of the computer, rather than on the button itself. Look around the buttons on the front of your computer if you're not sure which activates the power.

Considering compatibility

To achieve Level 2 in this unit, you need to understand the problems that can occur when hardware, software and operating systems are not compatible. For information on this subject, read the relevant section in Chapter 3, IT troubleshooting for users.

2.4.4 Logging on

Once you've started up your computer you will probably see a box asking you to log on. This is so the computer knows who's using it. It's a bit like typing a PIN number into a cash machine.

1 Click in the box next to user name.

2 Type in your user name.

3 Click in the box next to Password.

4 Type your password.

5 Click OK.

2.5 The Desktop

The desktop is the first screen you see when your computer has started. It can be customised to look how you want and make it easier for you to do your work. Here's a picture of the desktop screen. Each desktop will look a little different.

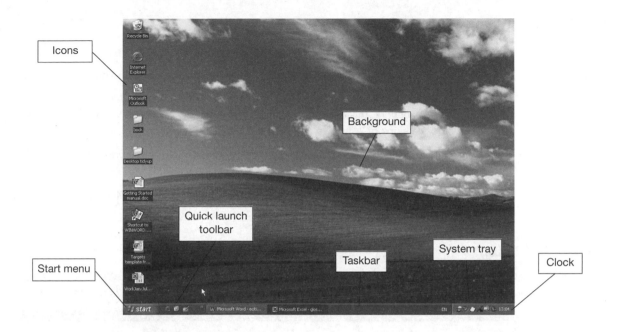

2.5.1 What is Each Part For?

The table below explains what the parts of the screen are for.

Part of the screen	What is it?
Icons	Pictures that represent a part of your computer, or applications or tools available on your computer. Double click on them to run programs.
Background	This is the main desk part. The picture can be changed to show whatever you like.
Start button/Start menu	The place that contains icons that link to all your programs and tools.
Taskbar	The bar that shows you what applications you have open. It also provides a way of switching between open applications.
Quick Launch toolbar	This is a toolbar that can be positioned anywhere but often sits somewhere on your taskbar. It provides quick access to applications on your computer.
System tray	A tool that can be used to change some of your computer's settings, and also provides information (such as whether you have certain software in use, or if you are low on battery if you are using a laptop computer).
Clock	A normal clock that tells the time (or at least the time your computer thinks it is).

2.5.2 Desktop Icons

The little pictures you have on your desktop are all for different things:

My Computer

This lets you get at the computer's filing system. It gives you access to the different parts of your computer where information is stored (drives).

My Network Places

If your PC is on a network, this contains a list of all the resources available to you, i.e. printers, folders. In older versions of Windows, this is called Network Neighborhood.

Recycle Bin

When you delete a document, it goes in here. You can then take it out if you didn't really mean to delete it.

My Documents

When you save a document, unless you instruct the machine otherwise, it will be saved in this folder.

2.5.3 The Taskbar

At the bottom of the screen there is a blue bar that runs from left to right. When you open a window a button for that window will appear on the bar. The Start button is on the far left…

Having more than one window open

You can work with a number of different windows at the same time. For example, you might have both Word and Internet Explorer open at the same time. To switch between the windows you have opened, just click on its button on the taskbar.

If you can't see the whole description on the taskbar…

As you open more windows or programs in Windows, the buttons that represent them on the taskbar become smaller. Just hold the mouse over the taskbar for a second or two, and a note will pop up with a full description.

2.5.4 The Start Button

Clicking on the Start button shows the Start menu. From here you can open applications, view files, get help, find files, access your favourite websites, run programs, change your settings and shut down or restart your computer.

Using software

If you are aiming to achieve Level 2 in this unit, you need to be able to demonstrate that you can use some of the more complex features found in common software. For instance, while a Level 1 student might be able to write a letter using Microsoft Word, a Level 2 student might be able to use the mail-merge feature in Word to produce a series of business letters.

For an in-depth look at the functions of a particular software package, take a look at the relevant chapter in this book.

2.5.5 Using the Start Menu

1 Click on the Start button.

2 Click on the option you require (see below) – a submenu may appear.

3 If necessary, click on the option you require in the submenu.

The icons on the left of the Start menu are your most recently used programs, and will be different for every user.

Your Internet and email programs will normally be kept at the top of this section, and any other recently used files, or important programs you haven't used yet, will be stored underneath.

All Programs	Shows more programs you can run.
My Documents	Takes you to your document files.
My Pictures	Takes you to your picture files.
My Music	Takes you to your music files.
My Computer	Takes you to My Computer, where you can open, copy, move or delete files.
My Network Places	If your PC is on a network, this contains a list of all the resources available to you, i.e. printers, folders.
Control Panel	Where you can change your system settings, e.g. the colour of your desktop.
Printers and Faxes	Where you can see what printers you have, and change their settings.
Help and Support	This starts Help. If you are stuck, this is where you go.
Search	Use this to search your computer for files and folders.
Run...	From here you can start a program, or install one from a CD-ROM or disk.
Log Off	If your computer is connected to a network, you can log off here, but keep your computer running. If you are at home and there is more than one user, you can switch users or log off.
Shut Down	Shuts down or restarts your computer.

When you click on the All Programs submenu, there are more programs to run, and these two extra options:

New Office Document	You can create a new Office document from here.
Open Office Document	You can open an existing Office document from here.

2.6 Desktop Icons

2.6.1 Selecting Icons

Click on the icon to select it – it will turn blue.

2.6.2 Deselecting Icons

Click away from the icon – it will no longer be blue.

2.6.3 Moving Desktop Icons

You can rearrange your computer's desktop, just as you might rearrange your desk at work.

1 Position your mouse over the icon you wish to move.

2 Click and drag to a new position.

3 Release the mouse.

My icons won't move!

Right click anywhere over the desktop and choose Arrange Icons. Make sure there is no tick next to Auto Arrange.

2.6.4 Arranging the Icons

You can let Windows tidy up your desktop by getting it to automatically arrange your icons.

1 Right click anywhere over the desktop.

2 Click on Arrange Icons By.

3 Click on Auto Arrange.

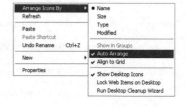

How do I know when it's on?

When Auto Arrange is on it will have a tick before it in the menu. Click it again to switch it off!

2.6.5 Opening a Desktop Icon

What happens when you open a desktop icon depends on the type of icon. Some, such as the My Computer and Recycle Bin icons, will open a window on your desktop showing files on your computer. Other icons may be shortcuts to programs. Opening these icons will start the program. To open the icon:

Double click on the icon.

2.6.6 What are Desktop Shortcuts?

- You can create shortcuts that allow you to open programs, folders or documents that you use frequently. You can put a shortcut onto your desktop.

- Shortcuts always have a little curly arrow in the bottom left corner of the icon.

Cat pictures

- Shortcuts are only a link to the folder, document or program. If you delete a shortcut, it does not delete the original object.

2.6.7 Creating a Shortcut on the Desktop

1 Open My Computer and find the icon for the program, folder or document.

2 Restore or resize the My Computer window so you can see the desktop as well.

3 Hold the mouse over the icon for which you wish to create a shortcut.

4 Click and drag the icon onto the desktop using the *right* mouse button.

5 Release the mouse button. A shortcut menu will appear.

6 Click Create Shortcut Here.

Or

1 Find the item that you want to create a shortcut for, using My Computer.

2 Right click on the item. A menu will pop up.

3 Click Send To.

4 Click Desktop (create shortcut).

Practise this!

Create a desktop shortcut to a document you use every day.

2.6.8 Renaming Shortcuts

Because a shortcut just points to a document, folder or program (and is not the actual thing) you can rename the shortcut without renaming the file. So you can call it whatever you like.

1 Position your mouse over the shortcut you wish to rename.

2 Right click on the shortcut. A menu will pop up.

3 Click Rename. The name of the shortcut is highlighted.

4 Type the new name for the shortcut.

5 Click away from the shortcut or press Return.

2.6.9 Deleting Shortcuts

You might wish to remove shortcuts you no longer require. Deleting shortcuts does not delete the item to which the shortcut is pointing.

1 Right click on the shortcut.

2 Click Delete.

3 Click Yes to confirm it.

2.7 The Desktop Settings

2.7.1 How Does my Computer Know the Date and Time?

The date and time is just one of your computer's settings, and you can change it if it's wrong. You may find your network (if you are connected to one) resets the date and time.

2.7.2 Viewing the Date and Time

The time is shown on your taskbar.

To view the date:

Hover your mouse over the clock – a label will pop up with the date.

2.7.3 Setting the Date and Time

If you need to adjust the date or time:

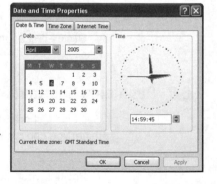

1 Double click on the clock in the System Tray on your taskbar. This will open the Date and Time Properties dialog box.

2 Click on the drop-down arrow at the end of the month.

3 Select the correct month.

4 Click on the up or down arrows to change the year.

Or

Click on the correct date from the calendar.

Or

Double click on the hour, minutes or seconds in the Time box to select it, then click the up or down arrow to change the hour, minutes or seconds.

5 Click OK.

2.7.4 Changing the Volume

If you have speakers for your computer, they probably have their own volume control. However, you can also change the master volume for your PC.

1 Click on the Volume icon in the System Tray on your taskbar.

2 When the volume control appears, click and drag the slider to adjust the volume.

3 Click in the box next to Mute to turn the sound on or off – it will appear ticked if on.

4 Click away from the volume control to make it disappear.

Or

1 Double click on the Volume icon in the System Tray.

2 Click and drag the sliders to adjust the volume settings.

Or

Click in the boxes before Mute to turn the volume settings on or off.

3 Click on the X at the top right of the Volume box to close it.

2.7.5 Changing the Regional Settings

Your regional settings affect the way that dates, numbers and times are displayed and which currency symbol is displayed in the programs you use.

1 Click on the Start button.

2 Click on Control Panel.

3 Click on the Date, Time, Language, and Regional Options icon.

4 Click on the Regional and Language Options icon.

5 Click on the Regional Options tab if necessary.

6 Click on the drop-down arrow at the end of the country.

Select an item to match its preferences, or click Customize to choose
your own formats:

English (United Kingdom) ▼ [Customize...]

7 Click on the country you are in.

8 Click OK.

9 Click on the X to close the Control Panel window.

2.8 | Working with Windows

2.8.1 What are Windows?

Every task you perform on your computer will open in a box called a window. For instance, when you open Word, a window appears on the screen containing the software. You then work inside the window. It is possible to have many windows open at once.

2.8.2 The Elements of Windows

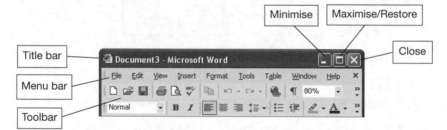

2.8.3 Minimising Windows

Minimising a window makes it temporarily disappear into the taskbar. Use it if you have to get a window out of the way so you can see something else. To minimise a window, click the Minimise button at the top right of the window.

To restore a window after it has been minimised, click the name of the window from the taskbar at the bottom of the screen.

2.8.4 Maximising/Restoring Windows

Maximise allows you to make a window fill the whole of the screen. Use it when you want to concentrate on just one window. Maximise is interchangeable with Restore. When you restore a window it is still visible, but will not fill the whole screen. You can change the restored shape to anything you want by resizing the window.

Maximising a window:

Click Maximise at the top right of the window.

The window will fill the screen, and the Maximise button will change to the Restore button.

Restoring a window:

Click Restore at the top right of the window.

The window will shrink, and the Restore button will change to the Maximise button.

2.8.5 Resizing Windows

1 Ensure the window is restored – if the window is maximised you can't resize it.

2 Position the mouse at the edge of a window – the mouse pointer will change to a double-headed arrow.

3 Click and drag to resize the window.

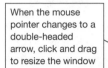

When the mouse pointer changes to a double-headed arrow, click and drag to resize the window

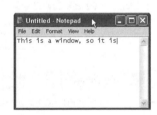

2.8.6 Moving Windows

1 Ensure the window is restored – if the window is maximised you can't move it.

2 Position the mouse on the blue title bar – the mouse pointer will change to a white arrow.

3 Click and drag to move the window to a new position.

2.8.7 Closing Windows

Click the X at the top right of the window.

2.8.8 Switching Between Windows

Click the window you require on the taskbar to make the window appear on the screen.

2.9 Finding Files

2.9.1 The Computer's Filing System

■ The computer's filing system is very much like an ordinary filing cabinet.

■ The whole of the filing cabinet is your computer.

■ The drawers in the filing cabinet are known as *drives*.

- *Drives* are represented by letters of the alphabet (see below).

- Inside the drawers are *folders* that hold your documents.

- Inside some of the folders may be *subfolders* to make things more organised.

- Inside the folders are the pieces of paper you have written on, known as *files*. Word files are known as *documents*.

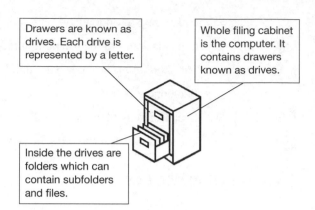

Drawers are known as drives. Each drive is represented by a letter.

Whole filing cabinet is the computer. It contains drawers known as drives.

Inside the drives are folders which can contain subfolders and files.

Imagine you are filing your work documents inside these drives. You may have a main folder which contains all your work. Inside that, you may have subfolders to contain your memos, reports and letters. Inside those subfolders are the actual files you have written on.

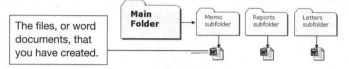

The files, or word documents, that you have created.

2.9.2 What Drives Do I Have?

The drives you have and the letters assigned to them can be different. The table below describes what you will find on most computers.

Letter	Drive	What do you use it for?
A:	Usually the floppy disk drive	■ Saving onto the floppy disk means you can take the document to another machine ■ It is also useful to make copies of documents onto the floppy disk as a back-up
C:	Usually the hard disk drive	■ The hard disk is your main disk drive ■ It is situated inside the box that makes up your PC ■ If you save onto the hard disk, you can only access that file from that machine, but there is much more space on the hard disk than on a floppy disk
D:	Usually the CD-ROM drive	■ Used for accessing files from CD ■ If your CD-ROM drive is capable of writing to CD, you can use this drive to copy files to CD
F:–Z:	Usually network drives, also used for storage devices such as flash drives	■ If you can see these drives you are probably connected to a network ■ A network is a group of computers connected to each other through a server. If you save onto a network drive, the information will go to the server and everyone else who is connected to the network will be able to access your document ■ If you plug a flash drive into your computer, it will probably also be assigned one of these letters

---

Practise this!

Open My Computer or Windows Explorer and work out how many drives you have on your system. How many of them are network drives?

2.9.3 What are Files?

All the information on your computer will be stored as some type of file. There will be lots of different files on your computer. For instance, if you write a letter in Microsoft Word it will then be stored as a Word document file.

2.9.4 File Icons

These are some of the file icons that you might see on your computer.

	Microsoft Word (word processing)		Microsoft Excel (spreadsheet)
	Microsoft PowerPoint (presentation)		Microsoft Access (database)
	Text		Pictures
	Movies		Sound/Music

2.9.5 What are Filename Extensions?

Each different type of file (e.g. Word document, Excel spreadsheet) has three letters stuck on the end of its name. This is called the file name extension. The extension for a type of file lets Windows know what type of file it is, so it knows which icon to display and which program to open the file in.

Underneath the icon for the file you will see the name of the file, sometimes followed by a full stop and then the filename extension. For example, this Word icon...

report.doc

has a filename of report, and an extension of .doc.

Some of the filename extensions you might see include:

.doc	Microsoft Word document	.xls	Microsoft Excel spreadsheet
.ppt	Microsoft PowerPoint presentation	.txt	Plain text (e.g. Notepad file)
.mdb	Microsoft Access database	.htm	Internet Explorer web page

---

View file extensions

If you can't see the file extensions:

1 Open My Computer.

2 Click on the Tools menu.

3 Click on Folder Options.

4 Click on the View tab.

5 Untick the box next to Hide extensions for known file types.

6 Click Apply.

7 Click OK.

2.9.6 Which Filing System?

There are two places where you can manage your files:

- Windows Explorer.

- My Computer.

Windows Explorer is more or less the same thing as My Computer. They both contain the same elements, they are just arranged slightly differently. You'll see the differences over the next few pages. It's up to you which one you use – they're both effectively the same program, so use the one you feel more comfortable with.

2.10 Windows Explorer

2.10.1 Starting Windows Explorer

1 Click on the Start button.

2 Click on All Programs.

3 Click on Accessories.

4 Click on Windows Explorer.

Shortcut

A quick way to open Windows Explorer is to hold down the Windows button on your keyboard, then press the E key.

2.10.2 What You See in Windows Explorer

- The screen is divided into two 'panes'.

- The left-hand side shows the hierarchical structure of your folders on your computer.

- The right-hand side represents the contents of the selected item in the left pane.

- If you click on a folder in the left pane, its contents will appear in the right pane.

2.10.3 Expanding and Collapsing

You can expand and collapse the hierarchical view of the left pane to see more or less detail.

Expanding   If you see a plus (+) by an item in the left pane then it has an additional folder within it. To display it, just click on the plus.

Collapsing   If you see a minus (–) by an object then you can hide its contents by clicking on the minus.

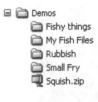

☐ 🗀 Demos

Click the plus next to the folder to open it and see what's inside.

Click the minus sign to 'close' the folder again.

2.10.4 Looking in a Drive or Folder

Click on the drive or folder in the left-hand pane.

The contents will be displayed in the right-hand pane.

2.10.5 Opening a Folder in the Right-hand Pane

Double click the folder you wish to open (in the right-hand pane).

2.11 My Computer

Windows organises all of your hard drives, floppy drives, network drives, settings and the rest into an area called My Computer.

2.11.1 Opening My Computer

My Computer

Double click the My Computer icon on the desktop.

Can't see the icon on your desktop?

If the icon isn't displayed, just click on the Start button on the taskbar, then click on the My Computer icon on that menu.

2.11.2 What You See in My Computer

The picture below shows the main drives and folders you might see in My Computer.

Hard disk drive

Floppy disk drive

CD-ROM drive

Control Panel

2.11.3 Opening a Drive

If you want to see what's inside a drive:

Double click on the drive icon. Local Disk (C:)

Is there a disk in the floppy disk drive?

You'll need to have a disk in your computer's floppy disk drive to be able to see what's in it! Otherwise you might hear a funny whirring noise and get the following message:

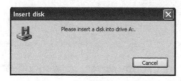

2.11.4 Opening a Folder

Double click on the folder icon to look inside.

2.11.5 Closing a Folder

Each time you double click on a folder, the contents are opened in a new window. To close it, click on the X at the top right of the folder window.

2.12 Changing the View

2.12.1 Showing the Standard Buttons Toolbar

This toolbar allows you to navigate around My Computer and Windows Explorer. To switch the toolbar on and off:

1 Open My Computer or Windows Explorer.

2 Click on the View menu.

3 Click on Toolbars.

4 Click on Standard Buttons – a tick appears next to it in the menu when it is displayed.

2.12.2 Changing the View of Your Files and Folders

To change the way you see your drive, folder and files displayed:

1 Click on the View menu.

Or

Click on the View button – if the toolbar is displayed, see above.

2 Click on the option you require (see below).

Thumbnails

Tiles

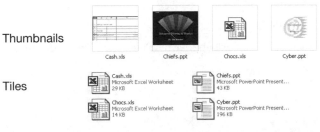

Icons				
	Cash.xls	Chiefs.ppt	Chocs.xls	Cyber.ppt

List	
	Cash.xls
	Chiefs.ppt
	Chocs.xls
	Cyber.ppt

Details				
	Cash.xls	29 KB	Microsoft Excel Worksheet	07/02/2000 12:45
	Chiefs.ppt	43 KB	Microsoft PowerPoint Presentation	04/04/2000 20:38
	Chocs.xls	14 KB	Microsoft Excel Worksheet	03/02/2000 15:11
	Cyber.ppt	196 KB	Microsoft PowerPoint Presentation	06/04/2000 16:46

2.12.3 Arranging Your Drives

In My Computer you can have your drives arranged by drive letter, type, size or free space.

1 Click on the View menu.

2 Click on Arrange Icons.

3 Click on the option you require.

Auto Arrange

To ensure all icons are evenly spaced you can choose Auto Arrange from the list.

2.12.4 Sorting Your Files and Folders

You can have your files and folders arranged by name, type, size or date.

1 Click on the View menu.

2 Click on Arrange Icons.

3 Click on the option you require.

Auto Arrange

To ensure all icons are evenly spaced you can choose Auto Arrange from the list.

2.12.5 Viewing the Properties of a File

By viewing the properties of a file, you can find out its size, when it was created, when it was modified and so on.

1 Click on the file to select it.

2 Click on the File menu.

3 Click on Properties. A box will appear displaying the file's properties.

4 Click on the General tab.

When you have finished looking:

Click OK to close the box.

2.12.6 Viewing the Properties of a Folder

If you want to find out the size of a folder, when it was created and how many files and other folders it contains:

1 Click on the folder to select it.

2 Click on the File menu.

3 Click on Properties. A box will appear displaying the folder's properties.

You can see how many files are in the folder, how many subfolders it contains, and the space it takes up. When you have finished looking:

Click OK to close the box.

2.12.7 Changing the Status of a File

Got an important file that you don't want to accidentally delete when it's Friday afternoon and you're not really concentrating? You can add a small level of protection by making a file Read-only. To do this:

1 Click on the file to select it.

2 Click on the File menu (or right click on the file).

3 Click on Properties.

4 Click on the General tab, if you are not there already.

Attributes: ☑ Read-only

5 Place a tick in the Read-only box to protect the file, or remove it to put it back to its normal (read-write) state.

6 Click OK.

When the file is Read-only, you will get a special message if you try to delete it:

Confirm File Delete

The file 'Agenda.doc' is a read-only file. Are you sure you want to move it to the Recycle Bin?

Yes   No

You can still say yes and delete it, but it will make you think twice. If you open the file, edit it, and try to save it, you will be forced to give it a different name – you will not be allowed to save the Read-only file over itself.

2.12.8 Opening a File

Double click the file to open it.

2.13 Navigating Your Folders

2.13.1 Going Back

If you want to move back through the drives and folders you have already looked at:

Click on the Back button.

Where was I?

If you want to know what the next folder 'back' is, hold the mouse pointer over the Back button for a second and a little yellow flag will pop up and tell you.

2.13.2 Going Forward

If you want to return to the drives and folders you have already looked at after going back:

Click on the Forward button.

What's next?

If you want to know what the next folder 'forward' is, hold the mouse pointer over the Forward button for a second and a little yellow flag will pop up and tell you.

2.13.3 Going up a Level

If you want to go up a level (e.g. if you look in a folder in the C drive and then want to go back again to see the other folders in the C drive):

Click on the Up button.

2.13.4 Creating a Folder

Once you start getting a lot of files you might want to create different folders to store them in so you can find them quickly.

1 Open My Computer or Windows Explorer.

2 Open the folder or drive where you would like this folder to be stored.

3 Click on the File menu.

4 Click New.

5 Click Folder. A new folder will appear.

6 Type the name for the new folder.

7 Press Enter to create the folder.

Subfolders

You can have folders inside other folders. Create them in exactly the same way.

2.13.5 Selecting a File or Folder

You may need to select files or folders if you want to delete, move or copy them.

Click on a file or folder to select it. It will appear blue.

2.13.6 Selecting Adjacent Files and Folders

If you want to select several files or folders that are next to each other:

1 Select the first file or folder.

2 Press and hold the Shift key on the keyboard.

3 Click on the last file or folder of the group you want to select.

4 Release the Shift key.

2.13.7 Selecting Non-adjacent Files and Folders

If you want to select several files or folders that are not next to each other:

1 Select the first file or folder.

2 Press and hold the Ctrl key on the keyboard.

3 Click on the next file or folder you want to select.

4 Continue clicking on files until all the files or folders you want are selected.

5 Release the Ctrl key.

2.13.8 Selecting all Files and Folders

1 Click on the Edit menu.

2 Click on Select All.

Shortcut

To select everything, press Ctrl + A.

2.13.9 Deselecting Files and Folders

Click into an empty space anywhere in the window.

2.13.10 Renaming a File or Folder

1 Right click the file.

2 Click on Rename.

3 Type a new name for the file.

4 Press Enter.

Not including the filename extension

If the filename extension is visible in your window and you don't include it at the end when you rename a file, you may see this error message:

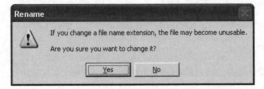

Click No and rename it again to include the existing filename extension. If you can't remember the original extension, press Escape (Esc) to go back to the original file name and start again.

2.13.11 Moving a File or Folder Using Cut and Paste

1 Select the file(s) or folder(s) you want to move.

2 Click on the Edit menu.

3 Click Cut.

4 Open the folder where you want to place the file(s) or folder(s).

5 Click on the Edit menu.

6 Click Paste.

2.13.12 Copying a File or Folder Using Copy and Paste

1 Select the file(s) or folder(s) you want to copy.

2 Click on the Edit menu.

3 Click Copy.

4 Open the folder where you want to place the file(s) or folder(s).

5 Click on the Edit menu.

6 Click Paste.

2.13.13 Printing Files from Folders

To quickly print a text file:

1 Right click on the text file you want to print.

2 Click on Print.

2.14 Storing Data

As well as saving files onto a hard disk, you can save onto other types of storage. This can be useful if you want to:

- Make copies of your files (in case something happens to your computer). These are called back-up copies, or back-ups, and are a good idea if your files are valuable or would take a long time to replace.

- Archive your files. If your hard drive is getting low on space, you can move files from your computer to another storage medium. This frees up space on your hard drive and keeps the files safe.

- Share files with friends and colleagues.

- Copy a file from one computer to another.

2.14.1 Copying a File to a Storage Disk

1 Ensure your storage disk is connected to your computer (either insert a disk into your floppy drive or plug a flash drive into a USB port).

2 Open My Computer or Windows Explorer.

3 Find the file you wish to copy.

4 Click on the file so it is selected.

5 Click on the Edit menu.

6 Click on Copy to Folder.

7 Click on the drive name of the disk to which you wish to copy the file.

8 Click on a subfolder if desired.

9 Click on the Copy button.

Moving instead of copying

If you want to move the file onto the disk – so it is no longer on your computer – just choose the Move to Folder option in step 6 instead.

Removing your flash drive properly

If you have saved files onto a flash drive, you must ensure you close down that drive properly before removing it. Otherwise, your data may become corrupted. Look for the Safely Remove Hardware icon in the System Tray of the task bar. Click on this icon, then click on the drive name of the disk you wish to remove. It is now safe to remove your flash drive from its USB port.

2.14.2 Copying Files to a CD

1 Insert a blank recordable CD into your CD-ROM drive.

2 Open My Computer or Windows Explorer.

3 Find the file you wish to copy.

4 Click on the file so it is selected.

5 Click on the Edit menu.

6 Click on Copy to Folder.

7 Click on the CD-ROM drive.

8 Click on the Copy button.

9 In My Computer or Windows Explorer, open the CD-ROM drive.

10 Click on the File menu.

11 Click on Write these files to CD.

2.14.3 Data Transmission Speeds

The time it takes to move or copy data depends on two key factors:

- The size of the file(s).

- The speed of the hardware involved.

Obviously, the larger the file, the longer it will take to move or copy. That's because large files contain lots of data. The more data a file contains, the more work your computer has to do when copying it to another drive.

Hardware speeds vary dramatically. When moving data around on your own PC, the slowest type of drive you are likely to encounter these days is a floppy disk drive. Saving to floppy disk used to be the most common way of making your data portable.

Nowadays, there are much faster options, such as CD-ROMs (which can store a lot more data than floppies too). The speed at which you can save to CD is determined by the speed to your CD drive. You also need software on your computer that is capable of 'burning' data onto CD.

An even quicker way is to save to a USB flash drive, or to your hard drive.

File compression

You can reduce the time it takes to move files by first compressing them. File compression software such as WinZip or WinRAR can reduce the size of files, thus making it quicker to move them around.

Practise this!

Copy one file from your hard drive to a floppy disk, CD-ROM or USB flash drive.

2.15 Working Safely with Computers

2.15.1 Common Sense

Computers are never going to rebel against humanity and attack you while you sleep. However, as with any objects that use electricity, or objects that you use a lot, you must use your common sense. Computers are usually safe to use, but there are some things you must look out for.

2.15.2 RSI

RSI stands for Repetitive Strain Injury. If you are typing and/or using the mouse a lot, you can strain the muscles in your hand, arm or back. Take a short break every 15 minutes, so that your muscles can relax. Do not go longer than an hour without a break. Try to arrange your day so that you break up your computer time by doing tasks away from the screen.

A wrist rest for your keyboard can also help reduce the strain on your wrists when typing. Mouse mats are also available with a built-in wrist rest.

2.15.3 Eyes

Like your hands and arms, your eyes can get strained if you have been working on a PC for a long time without taking a break. Look away from the screen whenever you can, focus on things further away, and remember to blink – it sounds silly, but when you get heavily involved with any screen (television included) you blink a lot less. You should have adjustable controls on your screen so you can change the brightness and contrast. If you have a CRT (cathode ray tube) monitor (the big, heavy ones with the glass screen), you might want to put a screen filter over it, to reduce glare. LCD (liquid crystal display) monitors (the thinner, lighter ones) are also easier on the eyes.

2.15.4 Lighting

It is very important that the lighting is correct when you look at your computer screen as this can help reduce eyestrain. It's a bit like when you're watching television inside on a bright sunny day and you have to draw the curtains. Light should be soft – so fit blinds on windows and diffusers over lights.

2.15.5 Sit Properly

You probably spend the bulk of your working week sat at your computer, so make sure you're sitting properly. If you don't, you risk all manner of back problems and shoulder pains.

To ensure you have the correct posture when working:

- Your PC screen should be at a distance where you can see it clearly without leaning forward or backward. It should be directly in front of you, so you don't have to twist to use it.

- You should have an adjustable chair that supports your back properly. Your seat should be at a height where your arms are parallel with the floor when typing, i.e. not raised or lowered.

- Your feet should be placed flat on the floor, with your knees at a 90 degree angle. If your feet don't reach the floor comfortably, get a footrest.

- Make sure you have enough space on your desk to have your mouse and keyboard directly in front of you.

2.15.6 Cables

With all the connections going into the back of your PC, it can quickly become a sea of cables. If someone trips over one of these cables they could easily hurt themselves or yank your computer off its desk. So, make sure your cables are all neatly tidied away.

Another thing worth mentioning is, try not to plug everything into one adapter. That goes for any electrical equipment, as you can overload your fuses or start a fire.

Health and safety – a legal requirement

There are several laws governing the health and safety of individuals working with computers. For more information, check Chapter 5, IT security for users.

Assessor's tip

Rudy says:

For more information on health and safety at work, take a look at the Government's website on the subject at www.hse.gov.uk.

2.15.7 Keeping Your Computer Safe

- Try not to eat or drink while using your PC – spilt drinks and dropped biscuit crumbs make your keyboard sticky and unusable, but if you spill them on your PC they can destroy it completely.

- Don't leave the PC in a place where it will get very hot or very cold.

- When you have finished using your PC, shut it down properly using the Turn Off Computer command on the Start menu. Don't pull the plug out or switch it off while it's still doing something. Lots of processes are always running in the background on your computer and if you turn it off when it's not expecting it you risk losing work or even damaging your hardware.

- Try to keep dust away from your PC – it clogs up the insides.

- See those air vents and holes in the case? They're there for a reason (to keep your PC cool while it works). Don't block vents. Keep at least a foot between them and any walls, shelves etc.

- Don't move the PC base unit while it is switched on. The hard disk is very delicate, and moving it can cause the read/write arms to come into contact with the disk surface. This will badly damage it.

- Keep floppy disks away from the screen, speakers, and magnets – any data on them can be erased. Similarly, keep magnets away from the base unit.

- Although this should go without saying, never ever hang clothes on a PC or monitor to dry. That's not a joke, some people actually do it.

2.16 Test Your Knowledge

The questions below will test what you know of the knowledge and understanding requirements of this unit. All the answers to these questions are contained or referred to within this chapter.

1 What is a modem? What does it do?

2 Name two types of printer.

3 How would you print a document in Microsoft Word?

4 What software would you be most likely to use if you wanted to work out a monthly company budget?

5 What software would you use if you wanted to send a personalised letter to a large number of people?

6 Why might the cables going into your computer represent a health and safety risk?

7 Name two other health and safety considerations in a computing environment.

8 Why is it important that all your software is compatible?

9 Which is quicker: saving a file to floppy disk or saving the same file to your hard drive?

2.17 Evidence

The tasks you undertake as evidence for your ITQ should be work-related. Therefore, your supervisor at work should be able to give you guidance on the type of tasks you should take on. Below are some ideas of possible tasks for this unit. Consider how you can adapt these ideas to make them more relevant for your own workplace and to ensure you cover all the skills requirements.

■ Write a set of instructions detailing how you would connect up your PC if you had to move it across the office. Include steps on how to safely connect any piece of hardware to your computer.

■ Transfer a file from your computer's hard drive (or from the network, if you are connected to one) onto a storage medium (such as a floppy disk or flash drive). Take screenshots that show how you accessed the file and write a brief report that discusses how you transferred the file and why you chose this method.

- Write a report on health and safety in your office. Highlight the steps that have been taken to ensure good health and safety and list ways in which things could be improved.

- Write a report on the piece of software you use most often at work. Describe what the software does and point out the features you find most useful. Illustrate your report with screenshots from the software.

2

CHAPTER 3

IT Troubleshooting for Users

3

3.1 About This Unit

What you need to know

To gain ITQ Level 2 in this unit, you should demonstrate the following competency:
Solve errors on most types of hardware and software using skills and experience.
To achieve this you should know:

1 What errors may happen on most types of hardware and software and with data.

2 What advice is available and how to get it.

3 What compatibility issues may occur.

You should also be able to display the following skills and techniques:

1 Restarting most hardware and software using manufacturers' guidelines.

2 Correcting errors by using methods that have worked in the past.

How to prove your skills

You need to carry out at least two work-based tasks which demonstrate the skills and knowledge listed above. In order to show your competency, it may well be necessary for you to complete more tasks than this.

Make sure you have plenty of evidence that shows how you completed each task, such as a copy of the file you worked on, or a document with screenshots of the processes you followed. You can back this up by producing a report which shows your knowledge of the subjects covered within the unit.

3.2 Spotting Errors

3.2.1 Oh no! My Computer's Gone Wrong!

When something goes wrong with your computer (and unfortunately it will), try not to worry about it. Just like cars, computers break down all the time. Fortunately, fixing a computer error is a lot easier and less mucky than changing the head gasket on your motor.

If there's a problem, it will fall into one of two camps. You will either have a helpful error message pop up on your screen, which will give you a rough idea of what's going on, or your computer will simply stop doing anything and not explain itself at all. The second scenario is known as freezing, and for ways around it you need to use the Task Manager (see Section 3.4, Dealing with a frozen computer).

The error message scenario is much more common, and most of the time you'll find the error is remarkably easy to remedy. Even if you don't know how to get around the error yourself, its message will give you all the detail you need to explain to someone else exactly what the issue is.

The main thing to remember is not to panic! You won't be expected to solve every problem that comes up on your work PC (unless you're head of IT, in which case you can probably skip this section). Just take a little time to work out what is happening and if you can't solve the problem on your own, get in touch with technical support.

Assessor's tip

Rudy says:

Completing this unit relies on you demonstrating how you deal with errors on your computer. Of course, you don't know when an error is going to crop up, so make sure you are aware of this unit while you are completing the others. Whenever an error pops up, take screenshots of it as well as notes detailing how you dealt with it.

3.2.2 Understanding Error Messages

When there is an error on your computer, a message should appear on your screen. It will open in a small box, like this:

Read the message carefully, so you know what's up. There may be an error code listed, which you can take note of. This will be helpful if you need to call technical support, as it will help them pinpoint the error quickly.

In the following sections are some error messages you may come across. However, bear in mind these are just a handful of the messages you could see. There are many thousands of programs out there, and each has its own way of working, so it is impossible to detail all the different types of error message you might find.

By reading the message carefully and following its instructions, you should be able to deal with the majority of everyday errors that crop up.

3.2.3 Software Errors

A software error means something has gone wrong with a program you're using. These errors are almost always the fault of the program's coders and developers, because the software is trying to perform a function which they did not foresee.

When an error message pops up, it will normally be nothing more than a brief explanation of what has gone wrong and what the result of the error is. Expect something along the lines of 'Due to an xyz error, the requested function could not be performed'. This type of error message is more for information than anything else. You are being told that what you tried to do has not been done, and you are normally given only one option – click OK to proceed.

Sometimes things go seriously screwy and your program will decide to close itself down. The slightly melodramatic name for this is a 'fatal error'. Realistically, it just means you need to start the program again. If this happens when you're using a Microsoft program, you will probably see an error message like this:

You don't have any options here other than choosing whether you want to allow the program to send Microsoft an error report. Make sure the tick box remains checked before you click on your choice and the program will restart automatically. If it crashes again soon after, try restarting your whole machine.

My computer is running slowly!

If your computer is running at a much slower speed than usual, check how many programs you have open. The more you have running, the more work your computer has to do. This can result in slow speeds, so try closing down some programs. If that makes little difference, save your work and restart your computer.

3.2.4 Hardware Errors

PCs are complicated pieces of kit, so if something goes wrong inside your computer it's normally best left to the techies to fix it.

However, if your computer won't start at all there are a few things you can check yourself. For a start, make sure all your computer's cables are properly connected. If your computer or monitor won't turn on, it's likely a power cable has dropped out, or the mains has been switched off.

If that doesn't help, check that the mains point you are using is OK. Plug something else into the same socket to make sure it works.

If the mains socket is OK, unplug any extra items from your PC so you have only the monitor connected. Any faulty peripherals that are attached could prevent your computer from booting up. If the PC then starts up OK, restart it with the peripherals reattached one by one until you isolate the problem.

Assessor's tip

Georgie says:

The key to this unit is to show that you are able to learn from your experience of computer errors. Whenever your PC throws a wobbly, make a note of what happened, what you did to resolve the problem, and how you would tackle it next time.

Missing drivers

Any peripheral plugged into your computer will run only if it has the necessary software installed. This software is known as a 'driver'.

So, if the driver goes missing or is corrupted or outdated, the peripheral will probably stop working. In this instance, you need to reinstall the drivers. At work, this is something your technical team would be responsible for doing. However, it is useful to be aware of this as it can often be the cause of hardware failures.

3.2.5 Data Errors

Some error messages will pop up if the user enters incorrect data. For example:

Microsoft Excel: in the cell shown, the formula **=12/0** has been entered. This formula is instructing Excel to divide a number by zero, which is not a valid function. As a result, the error message #DIV/0! is displayed. To correct this error, you would need to change the formula so it no longer divides by zero.

Microsoft Office Excel

Circular Reference Warning

One or more formulas contain a circular reference and may not calculate correctly. Circular references are any references within a formula that depend upon the results of that same formula. For example, a cell that refers to its own value or a cell that refers to another cell which depends on the original cell's value both contain circular references.

For more information about understanding, finding, and removing circular references, click OK. If you want to create a circular reference, click Cancel to continue.

[OK] [Cancel]

Microsoft Excel: this error message is displayed when a spreadsheet includes a circular reference. That means the result of a calculation has been included in the calculation itself –

making the program go round in circles. By clicking OK, you are guided to help on how to deal with circular references.

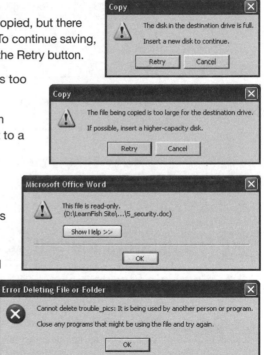

Microsoft Access: error messages will appear in Access if you enter data that does not fit into the required format. In this example, the user has attempted to leave a field blank. However, the field has been set to require data, so the error message appears. To solve this problem, you would click OK and then add data to the relevant field.

3.2.6 Storage Errors

Errors often pop up when you are saving files or moving them about. Below are some common examples.

- If you try to save a number of files onto a storage device that does not have enough space, you will get a message like this:

  This means some of the files have been copied, but there was not enough space to fit them all on. To continue saving, insert a new storage device and click on the Retry button.

- If you are copying one single file, and it is too big, you will get a message like this:

  In this instance the file will not have been copied at all and you will need to copy it to a drive with greater capacity.

- This message pops up when you try to save changes made to a read-only file:

  The file will have been made read-only as its author does not want it changed. To save the changes you have made, save the file with a different file name. You will also see this message if another user has the file open.

- If you attempt to delete a file which is currently open, you will see a message like this:

You need to make sure the file is closed. If you've already done that, close the file's application as well. You should now be able to delete the file. You'll see a similar message if you try to move a file that is already open.

3.2.7 Removing a Flash Drive

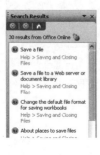

If you are using a flash drive to store files, you must remember to close it down properly before removing it from your system. If you don't, then you risk losing your saved files. Look for the small icon in the system tray with a green arrow on it.

To remove your drive, click on that, then click on the name of the drive. It is now safe to unplug the drive.

If you see the following error message, it means you have not closed down all the files contained on the drive.

Close down those files and you will then be able to close down the drive properly.

3.3 Fixing Errors Yourself

3.3.1 Use Help Menus

If you have a fairly basic question – or if you know exactly what you're looking for – the help files bundled with programs can be worth a look. Most programs will have a help menu which you can click on to access the help section.

In Office XP programs, there is a question box within the toolbars at the top of the screen. To search through Help using this:

1 Click inside the Help box at the top right of the screen.

2 Type your question, then press Return.

3 Click on the query that most closely matches your own.

3

Shortcut

To get to the Help section of any major program quickly, just press the F1 button.

3.3.2 Search the Net

If you're not sure how to solve a problem and Help has been no help, then you need to find someone who knows. The Internet is, of course, an excellent place to find answers to all kinds of geeky questions and there are loads of informative sites out there.

Beware though – none of the info you'll find on these comes with a guarantee, so if you're unsure about something, double-check it with your tech support folks before going any further.

Useful sites

Microsoft Help and Support: http://support.microsoft.com

Tech Support Guy: http://forums.techguy.org

Tech Support Forum: www.techsupportforum.com

Geeks to Go!: www.geekstogo.com

3.3.3 Update Your Operating System

Some problems can be caused by running an outdated version of Windows. Updates are released for Windows all the time, and you can download them for free from the Internet.

1 Open your web browser and go to http://update.microsoft.com.

2 Click on the Express button.

3 Follow the instructions to install the updates.

Assessor's tip

Lynne says:

Depending on the rules at your company, you may not be allowed to install updates on your machine. However, you can mention your knowledge of the process in your written tasks.

3.3.4 Detect and Repair

You will often find software comes bundled with repair tools, which you can use if it's playing up. Microsoft programs include a Detect and Repair tool. To run this:

1 Click on the Help menu.

2 Click on Detect and Repair.

3 Click on Start.

4 Follow the instructions to go through the process.

3.3.5 Ask for Advice

Don't put pressure on yourself to deal with every problem your computer throws at you. If you're feeling unsure then it's better to get advice from an experienced techie type. Indeed, for the purposes of this unit, assessors will be looking for evidence of your ability to find out information from other sources.

3.3.6 Working from Experience

As you become more experienced with computers, you'll come across different types of error messages.

Take note of the solutions to these errors – perhaps keep a spreadsheet. This will not only help you solve problems in the future, it will also be useful when you are assessed as you can use it to show how you have learned from various errors.

3.4 Dealing with a Frozen Computer

3.4.1 Using Task Manager

If you're facing a frozen screen on your computer, or things are moving at a snail's pace, Task Manager should be your first port of call. To access this utility, press the Ctrl, Alt and Delete buttons on your keyboard at the same time. Then:

1 Click on the Applications tab to see all the programs running at the moment. (If your mouse is not working, press Ctrl and Tab until the correct tab is selected.)

2 Look for any programs that are listed as 'Not responding'. These are the root of your problem.

3 Select the troublesome program in the list, then click on the End Task button. Do this for every program that isn't responding and your computer should perk up. (If your mouse isn't working, use the Tab key and cursor keys to move through the options and Return to select.)

What to do next

If you've had to close down programs, it's a good idea to restart your computer so it can tidy up any loose ends that might otherwise cause more problems. Save all your work, then restart to be sure everything is back to normal.

Escaping from the Task Manager

Don't worry about doing something catastrophic when you open the Task Manager utility. If you decide you don't need to make any changes, you can simply close it by clicking the Cancel button.

3.4.2 Logging Off

If closing down non-responsive programs doesn't bring about any improvement in your computer's slapdash attitude, you need to take things a step further. By logging off from your Windows XP session, you will automatically close down all open programs and processes.

1 Press Ctrl, Alt and Delete to open the Task Manager.

2 Click on the Shut Down menu.

3 Click on Log Off (your user name).

Once you have logged off, you can then log back in and start from scratch. Bear in mind that if you had any unsaved work, that may now be lost.

The keyboard option

It may be that your mouse has stopped working along with everything else. If so:

1 Press Ctrl, Alt and Delete to open the Task Manager.

2 Press the Alt key.

3 Press U.

4 Press L.

…and you will be logged off.

3.4.3 Restarting

If things look really bleak, then a restart is the best option to go for. This forces the computer to completely shut down everything it is doing and start afresh.

1 Press Ctrl, Alt and Delete to open the Task Manager.

2 Click on the Shut Down menu.

3 Click on Turn Off.

The keyboard option

You can do this with the keyboard too.

1 Press Ctrl, Alt and Delete to open the Task Manager.

2 Press the Alt key.

3 Press U.

4 Press U again.

3.4.4 The Last Resort!

If absolutely nothing else works and your computer is steadfastly refusing to even acknowledge your existence, you need to force it to restart. Look for the reboot button on the front of the PC casing. This will be a button that is recessed so it can't easily be pressed by accident. Press that and it will force your computer to reboot.

If that doesn't work – remove the power cable from the back of the computer, wait a few seconds, replace the cable, then restart the computer.

Note that neither of these methods is particularly desirable as they bypass your computer's normal shut-down procedures, during which time it does all sorts of important things to keep everything in order. However, sometimes you have no choice.

3.5 Getting Technical Support

3.5.1 Calling Technical Support

You won't always be able to solve everything by yourself. Computers can be tricky things, so sometimes you'll need a chat with an expert.

You may have a technical support department in your company which you can call, or you might be phoning an external support line. Either way, the first thing the person on the other end of the phone will do is ask you a bunch of questions to help them suss out what's causing your problem. These questions are all designed to establish what type of hardware and software you are using, and if you can supply this information it will be a whole lot easier for the techie to help you out.

3.5.2 Finding Out Your OS

Your operating system is responsible for pretty much everything that's going on with your computer, so any techie will want to know what version of Windows you are running. To find out:

1 Click on the Start menu.

2 Right click on the My Computer icon.

3 Click on Properties.

4 Click on the General tab if necessary.

5 Look at the details under System. This tells you the operating system being used on your computer.

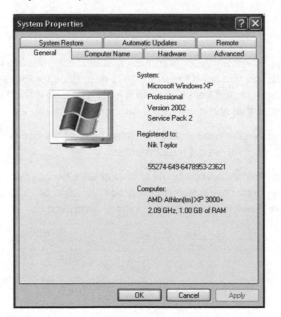

Other useful info you can find here

The System Properties box (which you have just opened) is full of useful info. Also on the General tab, look for the information under Computer. This tells you the type of CPU being used by your computer, and then how much RAM you have.

3.5.3 Finding Your Software Version

If you have a problem that is related to a specific program, you should determine which version of the program you are using before calling tech support.

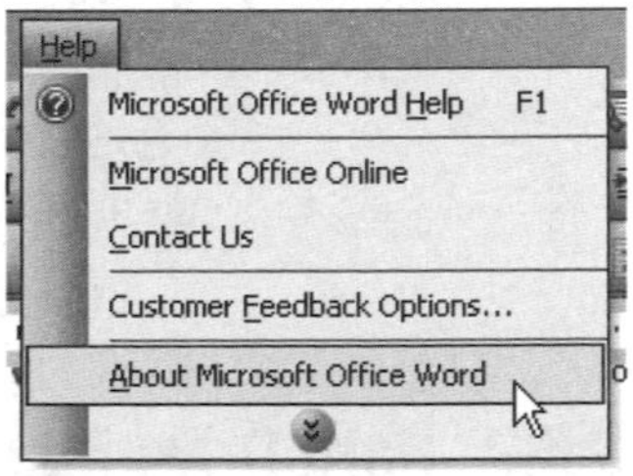

1 Click on the Help menu of the program you are using.

2 Click on the About [program name] option.

A box will open containing details of the program version you are using.

3.5.4 Finding Out Hardware Types

You can find a list of all the hardware running on your machine in the System Properties box.

1 Click on the Start menu.

2 Right click on the My Computer icon.

3 Click on Properties.

4 Click on the Hardware tab.

5 Click on the Device Manager button.

6 Click on the plus symbol next to any of the listed hardware types to see what hardware you are using for that task.

3.6 Cleaning Up Your PC

3.6.1 Checking for Viruses

If a virus sneaks its way onto your machine, you can be pretty sure it will cause a few errors to pop up. If lots of unexplained errors start appearing, try running a virus checker to see if you have any bugs, then follow the instructions to remove them.

For information on checking your system for viruses, take a look at Chapter 5 on security.

3.6.2 Hard Drive Space

It's good practice to keep plenty of free space on your hard disk drive. If you are using more than 75 per cent of the capacity of your hard drive, your computer may start running slowly.

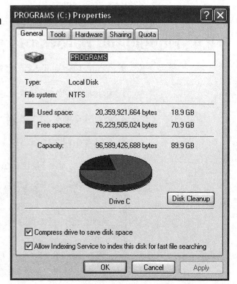

To check how much space you have:

1 Click on Start.

2 Click on My Computer.

3 Right click on the drive you want to check.

4 Click on Properties.

In the Properties box, you will see a pie chart showing you how much space you have remaining on your drive.

3.6.3 Creating More Space

Open up your drive in My Computer and take a look at what files are on there. Are they all necessary? You may have a folder of digital photos that is taking up a large amount of space. These can be saved onto a CD or DVD, enabling you to delete the files from your hard drive. Look for files that you can delete to give you more space – but be careful that you don't touch any files if you are unsure of what they do.

I can't see the files on my drive!

When you open the drive in My Computer, you may get a message telling you the files are hidden. To show the files, just click on the 'Show the contents of this folder' link. You can't cause any harm to your computer by doing this – just be careful that you don't delete any files unless you are certain of what they are.

3.6.4 Using Disk Cleanup

You can free up more space on your hard drive by using the Disk Cleanup utility.

1 Click on the Start menu.

2 Click on All Programs.

3 Click on Accessories.

4 Click on System Tools.

5 Click on Disk Cleanup.

6 Use the drop-down menu to choose the disk to clean up.

7 Click OK.

All the files with a tick next to them will be cleared out. If there are any files you want to keep, or are unsure about, make sure they are not ticked.

8 Click OK to clear out the selected files.

9 Click Yes.

3.7 Compatibility

3.7.1 About Compatibility

For your computer to work properly, all its components must be capable of working with each other. That means everything needs to be compatible.

Compatibility is about all the components of your computer speaking the same language. Imagine you went to Albania to work in telesales, but you could only speak English. You would find it pretty tricky to do your job.

In a similar way, if there is incompatible software, hardware or data on your computer, it will not be able to communicate with the rest of the system and will not work properly. You may notice programs crashing all the time, or find that some hardware does not work. You might not be able to open some files.

As compatibility is so important, computer manufacturers generally agree to build their kit to set standards. By making sure everyone is using the same type of technology, it makes it easier to ensure computers will work properly. It also means manufacturers can prosper without having to battle to establish a dominant technology.

Common compatibility clashes

- If you try to open a file that's been created with a newer version of a program than what you have installed on your computer (e.g. if you try to open a Word XP document with Word 95), the file may not open. Even if it does, you will probably find not all features are supported.

- If you buy software or hardware that is not supported by your operating system, you will not be able to install or use it. For example, many new software programs cannot be installed on Windows 98.

- If you try to open a file with a program other than the one used to create it, you will probably find the file will not open. For instance, you cannot open a spreadsheet using Microsoft Outlook.

Further compatibility issues

Compatibility isn't just about what's inside your computer. It affects the computing world as a whole. For instance, pages on the Internet are all written in the same type of computing code, so they can be viewed using any of the major web browsing packages.

3.8 Test Your Knowledge

The questions below will test what you know of the knowledge and understanding requirements of this unit. All the answers to these questions are contained or referred to within this chapter.

1 Which menu do you need to click on in Microsoft Word to find out the program's version details?

2 How would you find out the operating system being used on your PC?

3 What should you do first if a program appears to no longer be responding?

4 What is the phone number for your company's technical support department? If there is not one, how else could you find technical advice?

5 You are reading a Word document and try to move its file from your hard drive to a flash drive. Why would this result in an error message?

6 Your computer is not responding when you try to switch it on. List one thing you could try yourself to remedy this.

7 Why should you seek expert advice when unsure how to solve a technical problem?

8 Why should you try to keep plenty of free space on your hard disk drive?

9 Why is it important to ensure any software you buy is compatible with your computer's operating system?

10 What is the main reason why hardware manufacturers ensure their products are compatible with each other?

3.9 Evidence

The tasks you undertake as evidence for your ITQ should be work-related. Therefore, your supervisor at work should be able to give you guidance on the type of tasks you should take on. Below are some ideas of possible tasks for this unit. Consider how you can adapt these ideas to make them more relevant for your own workplace and to ensure you cover all the skills requirements.

- Create a spreadsheet to log any errors you come across during your working day. In the spreadsheet, list the error, what your initial thoughts were, whether you needed to seek additional help and how the problem was resolved.

- Use Microsoft's online service to get your version of Windows up to date. Take screenshots of the whole process.

- Create a document that explains how to restart a PC, why you would want to do so, and what precautions you should take when doing so.

- Update your virus checker and run a full virus check. Compile a document that explains how you did this, along with screenshots of the process.

CHAPTER 4

IT Maintenance for Users

4.1 About This Unit

4

What you need to know

To gain ITQ Level 2 in this unit, you should demonstrate the following competency:
Carry out appropriate routine and non-routine maintenance safely, so that hardware and software are kept in good condition and up to date.

To achieve this you should know:

1 What routine and non-routine maintenance can be done and how.

2 How to identify health and safety issues in using IT.

3 What is involved in upgrading hardware and software.

You should also be able to use the following skills and techniques:

1 Managing files appropriately.

2 Cleaning hardware.

3 Identifying and avoiding health and safety risks.

4 Maintaining hardware and software.

How to prove your skills

You need to carry out at least two work-based tasks which demonstrate the skills and knowledge listed above. In order to show your competency, it may well be necessary for you to complete more tasks than this.

Make sure you have plenty of evidence that shows how you completed each task, such as a copy of the file you worked on, or a document with screenshots of the processes you followed. You can back this up by producing a report which shows your knowledge of the subjects covered within the unit.

4.2 | Cleaning Your PC

4.2.1 Why your PC Needs Cleaning

With all the electricity flying around inside your PC, it's no surprise it's a dust magnet. Add to that people poking their fingers at the screen and eating their sandwiches over the keyboard and your computer can quickly get very mucky.

Of course, you'll want to keep it clean so it looks nice, but it's also important to keep things ship-shape so the computer runs well. For instance, if too much dust gets in the back of your computer, it can clog up the vents and fans and give you overheating problems. If your mouse gets too grubby, it can prevent your pointer from moving around the screen properly.

Switch everything off first!

Make sure everything is switched off and unplugged *before* you start cleaning. Otherwise you could damage the machine, or yourself!

4.2.2 Cleaning the Computer Case

- Use a damp cloth to wipe down the outside of your PC. Be careful to make sure it's not too soggy – water and computers aren't a great combination.

- Check the back of the case. If you haven't been round there for a while, you're certain to find stacks of dust clinging to the vents. Remove this so it doesn't get sucked into the machine, where it can cause overheating problems.

Assessor's tip

Sheena says:

There are plenty of cleaning fluids you can use on your PC. Before using any of these, make sure you read the instructions on the back so you know whether there are any precautions you need to take.

4.2.3 Cleaning the Screen

How you clean your display depends on what type of screen you have. The easiest to clean are CRT (cathode ray tube) displays. These are the big, old, heavy ones that take up half your desk. The screen on these displays is simply a sheet of glass, so you can clean it with a damp cloth or any glass-cleaning product.

If you have a TFT (flat-screen) monitor, you need to exercise more caution. These screens are delicate, and if you go anywhere near them with glass-cleaning products you can permanently damage them. To clean these screens, you are best off buying a specialist cleaning product from a computer store.

4.2.4 Cleaning Your Mouse

- **The outside**. Give this a wipe down with a damp cloth to remove any grubby marks.

- **The insides**. If your mouse is of the ball variety, it will require regular cleaning to keep it working properly. Drop the ball out of the mouse and give the rollers inside a quick clean (you will probably find lint wrapped around these rollers). Give the mouse ball a wipe with a dry cloth and replace it. Try not to touch the ball with your fingers as it will then be more likely to attract dust.

If your mouse doesn't have a ball (lots don't these days), you just need to give it a wipe over.

4.2.5 Cleaning Your Keyboard

You'll probably find dust, crumbs and all sorts of other debris in between the keys on your keyboard.

With your keyboard disconnected, turn it upside down and run your hands up and down the keys. This will loosen a lot of the bits and pieces. Now grab a can of compressed air (computer stores will sell this) and use it to blow the rest of the junk out. Alternatively, you can run the hose of your vacuum cleaner over the keys.

Once you've cleaned out all the rubble, wipe over the top of the keys with a damp cloth. If there's a lot of dust between the keys, you can use a cotton bud to remove that.

For extra thoroughness, you can take the keys off the keyboard before wiping it down, so you can clean each key individually. To do that, you need to ease them off with a flat-head screwdriver – but make sure you've taken note of where they go so you can put them all back!

4.2.6 Cleaning Disk Drives

To clean the insides of your floppy disk drive or CD-ROM/DVD drives, you will need specialist cleaning disks which can clean the lenses and drive heads. You can get these materials from any computer shop.

4.2.7 Cleaning Your Printer

Printers also need regular cleaning, but the only part you can clean by hand is the outer casing. Do this with a damp cloth. If the inner workings of your printer need a wash and brush up, you'll need to use the software that came supplied with the unit (or have your techies sort it if it's a networked printer).

To access this software:

1   Click on the Start menu.

2   Click on Printers and Faxes.

3   Double click on your printer.

4   Click on the Printer menu.

5   Click on Printing Preferences.

From here you will be able to access the maintenance options which will guide you through the process of cleaning your printer.

Assessor's tip

Rudy says:

For this unit you need to show that you understand the need to clean your computer often, and that you do so on a regular basis. Create a spreadsheet which you can use as a diary of when you cleaned your computer, what you cleaned and how you did it.

Practise this!

Go through the tips above and give your PC a thorough spring clean. Note down what you did and how you made sure you were keeping yourself and your computer safe while cleaning it.

4.3 Maintaining Hardware

4.3.1 Maintaining Your Printer

- **Adding more paper**. How you replenish your printer's paper supply depends on the type of printer you are using. Most home printers will have a paper holder at the back of the machine. To refill this, simply put a stack of paper into this holder.

  More expensive printers, such as those you will probably use at work, will use paper trays. When a paper tray is empty, you will see an error code appear on the printer's display. Pull out the printer tray, add more paper, then push the tray closed.

- **Changing the printer cartridges**. If you use an inkjet printer, you will find you regularly need to change the ink cartridges inside it. Your printer will let you know when the cartridges need changing by flashing up a warning screen when you are printing with low ink levels.

  To change the ink cartridges, open the software provided with your printer and follow the instructions that appear on screen. This software will do most of the work for you. All you need to do is take out the old cartridge and insert a new one.

Bagging bargain ink cartridges

The first time you buy replacement ink cartridges for your printer, you will be stunned by how expensive they are. Bizarrely, it can often work out cheaper to buy a new printer with cartridges included than it is to buy a set of replacements for your existing printer.

The solution is to buy non-branded replacement cartridges. Printer manufacturers don't recommend you do this as they say non-branded cartridges are of inferior quality. However, if you want to save some cash, this is the way to go. To find stores that sell non-branded cartridges, just run an Internet search for 'cheap printer cartridges'.

4.3.2 Dealing with a Paper Jam

Paper jams are an annoying fact of life when printing, but they are generally simple to rectify. First of all, try switching the printer off and then back on again. The jam may be cleared by the printer during its start-up process. If that brings no joy, take a look at the printer's display. Newer models will show instructions on how to clear the jam. If yours does not, turn off the printer. Then:

1 Take out any paper trays. Sometimes a sheet will not have cleared its way out of a tray properly. Remove any creased sheets of paper that may be causing an obstruction.

2 Open any doors that give you access to the printer's rollers.

3 Look for any jammed paper. When you find the paper, pull it gently with both hands, taking care not to tear it.

4 Close all doors and replace the paper trays.

5 Turn the printer back on.

4.3.3 Calling in the Professionals

You can't expect to solve all hardware problems yourself. If something goes wrong with your computer, your first port of call should be to check the manufacturer's instructions. Alternatively, you can open any software associated with the errant hardware and look for help files.

If you can't find useful assistance in this way, you should call your technical support department or a qualified repair company.

Check the obvious

If your printer doesn't seem to be working at all, make sure you check all the obvious options first. Is the printer plugged into the mains? Is it connected to your computer properly? If your computer accesses the printer via a network, is the network cable plugged into your PC properly? These simple issues will often be at the root of any printer problem.

4.4 Managing Files

4.4.1 Organising Your Files

Once you've been using your computer for even a short while, you will soon have bundles of files everywhere. You need to keep these organised, or it can become an absolute nightmare to wade through them all.

The solution is to keep your files in appropriate folders. For example, keep all your letters in one folder, all your files for that important project in another folder, and so on. By sticking to a defined folder structure, you'll be able to find any files you need quickly.

Take a look at Chapter 2, Operate a computer, for full instructions on managing your files.

4.4.2 Backing Up

If there is anything at all on your computer you don't want to lose, you must make a back-up. Everything may be OK right now, but there may come a day sometime soon when you go to turn on your computer and nothing happens. Your hard drive might get fried and with it all the data that was stored on there. Then what happens? How are you going to get back all those digital photos that were stored on there? Or that huge spreadsheet that's taken you six months to build? Or that important document that's got to be on the boss's desk tomorrow morning? It's all gone for ever!

Not if you make back-ups. Windows XP comes with a utility which you can use to make a back-up of your entire system.

If you just want to protect a few files, you can simply copy them to another storage location, such as a floppy disk, a flash drive, a CD or an external hard drive. By making an additional copy, you will still have the file even if you lose the original.

For step-by-step pointers on creating back-ups, see Section 5.2 in Chapter 5. For more on copying files, take a look at Section 2.14, Storing data, in Chapter 2.

4.4.3 Deleting Unnecessary Files

Sometimes, computers crash. When they do, it usually means they are switched off or restarted without going through the proper shutdown sequence. When this happens, temporary files are left scattered on the computer, files that would normally be deleted automatically. If this happens a lot they can clutter up the hard drive, so you should keep an eye out for them and delete them.

1 Click on the Start button.

2 Click on Search.

3 Click on All Files and Folders.

4 In the search box, type in *.tmp – this looks for all files that end in .tmp.

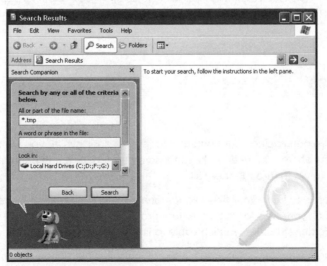

5 Click Search – Windows will search for the files, and show you a list on the right-hand side.

6 Select all the files Windows finds.

7 Press the Delete or Del key.

4.4.4 Disk Defragmenter

When you have been using your computer for a while, your hard drive can become 'fragmented'. This means files are split into several pieces and stored wherever there is space for them. Your hard drive then has to work harder to run them, fetching the bits from all over the place. That slows everything down.

It's a bit like storing lots of computers in a cupboard. To save space, you could dismantle the machines and stack everything efficiently – but then every time you wanted to use a machine, you'd have to put it back together again.

Defragmenting rearranges everything so that the files are stored in one piece. This helps your hard drive to run faster.

If you want to defragment your drive, it is best if you do it when you don't need to use the computer for a while, as it slows everything down.

Using Disk Defragmenter is an example of 'non-routine maintenance'. It's not something you need to do all the time – but it can be a useful way to perk up your computer's performance every now and again.

1 Click on the Start button.

2 Click on All Programs.

3 Click Accessories.

4 Click System Tools.

5 Click Disk Defragmenter.

6 Select the drive you want to defragment.

7 Click Analyze – this checks to see if you even need to defragment, without actually doing it, so if you don't need to, exit the program – otherwise, go to the next step.

8 Click Defragment, and wait until the program is finished – while the program is running, you will see the progress in the bottom part of the window.

9 Click Close when it is finished.

Practise this!

Check with your IT department whether you are allowed to run Disk Defragmenter on your computer. If so, have a go at defragmenting your C drive.

Assessor's tip

Lynne says:

An important skill for this unit is 'managing files'. The key skill you need to display here is that you are able to keep your files neat and tidy, and that you can keep your hard drive free of clutter. Take lots of screenshots of your day-to-day usage of files so you can show how you do this.

4.5 | Default File Locations in Office

4.5.1 File Locations

When you use Open or Save As in a Microsoft Office program, you are taken to the default file location. This is the place the program opens from or saves to automatically. You can change this default so files are automatically saved elsewhere on your computer.

4.5.2 Changing the Default File Location in Word

1 Click on the Tools menu.

2 Click Options.

3 Click on the File Locations tab.

4 Select the file type for which you wish to modify the location.

5 Click Modify.

6 Browse to the location you want to change it to.

7 Click OK.

4.5.3 Changing the Default File Location in PowerPoint

1 Click on the Tools menu.

2 Click Options.

3 Click on the Save tab.

4 In the Default file location box, type the full path of the folder you want to change it to.

5 Click OK.

4.5.4 Changing the Default File Location in Excel

1 Click on the Tools menu.

2 Click Options.

3 Click on the General tab.

4 In the Default file location box, type the full path of the folder you want to change it to.

5 Click OK.

4.5.5 Changing the Default File Location in Access

1 Click on the Tools menu.

2 Click Options.

3 Click on the General tab.

4 In the Default database folder box, type the full path of the folder you want to change it to.

5 Click OK.

4.6 Upgrading Your System

4.6.1 Why Should I Upgrade my Hardware?

The key benefits of upgrading hardware:

- *Improved performance*. Newer hardware will have improved technology and can therefore be installed to increase the performance of your computer.

- *Increased capacity*. Upgrading your hard drive to a larger model will enable you to store more data.

4.6.2 Why Should I Upgrade my Software?

The key benefits of upgrading software:

- *Fix bugs*. Newer versions of software will iron out many faults or 'bugs' that were present in previous versions.

- *Extra features*. Updated software versions will also include new features, which can make your work easier.

4.6.3 What Happens if I Don't Upgrade?

You don't need to constantly upgrade your computer's hardware to keep up with the latest technology. Doing so would be very costly. However, upgrades are required on a reasonably regular basis.

If your hardware has not been updated for a long time, you may find your computer unable to cope with newly released software. It may be very slow, or it may not work with new programs at all.

If your software is not upgraded, you will miss out on improved features present in newer versions. Additionally, older versions will cease to be supported by their manufacturers after a while.

4.6.4 Taking Care Before You Upgrade

- Back up *all* your files. All of them. The upgrade should be easy enough, but if you don't back up your files and your computer dies, you've lost everything.

- Keep a record of all shortcuts and custom settings you use – sometimes the upgrade needs to install a fresh copy of Windows, which wipes out all your custom settings.

- Talk to whoever is doing the upgrade for you, to find out what will happen and if there is anything you need to do.

4.6.5 Considering Compatibility

Before you upgrade to newer hardware or software, you should ensure your shiny new kit is compatible with your existing set-up. If you are running an older operating system, you may find lots of newer things aren't compatible and will not run on your PC. For further information on compatibility in computing, take a look at the relevant section in Chapter 3, IT troubleshooting for users.

4.7 Health and Safety

4.7.1 Keeping Your Workplace Safe

It is important to keep your working area safe so you do not put yourself, other people or your computer at risk.

Give your working area a once over to identify any possible health and safety issues. Things you should be looking out for include:

- Make sure your electrical connections are safe. It's a good idea to plug your computer into a power surge protector, as power surges can seriously damage your hardware. You should also ensure you do not overload power points with too many appliances.

- Check the arrangement of your workspace. Your desk should be clutter free, and you should be able to work there without stretching.

- Stay safe while working. Don't eat or drink near to your computer. Spillages are potentially disastrous to your data.

For a full rundown on health and safety considerations, take a look at Section 2.15, Working safely with computers, in Chapter 2.

4.8 Test Your Knowledge

The questions below will test what you know of the knowledge and understanding requirements of this unit. All the answers to these questions are contained or referred to within this chapter.

1 What is the file extension used for temporary files?

2 Why might you use the Disk Defragmenter utility?

3 Why is it important to clean your computer regularly?

4 What should you do if you are not confident with carrying out a maintenance task on your computer?

5 Name two things you can do to keep your working area safe.

6 List three responsibilities that your employer has to ensure your workplace is a safe place to work.

7 Give one reason why you might want to upgrade your software.

8 Give one reason why you might want to upgrade your hardware.

9 List one drawback to not upgrading.

10 Why should you check the compatibility of new software with your system before upgrading?

4.9 Evidence

The tasks you undertake as evidence for your ITQ should be work-related. Therefore, your supervisor at work should be able to give you guidance on the type of tasks you should take on. Below are some ideas of possible tasks for this unit. Consider how you can adapt these ideas to make them more relevant for your own workplace and to ensure you cover all the skills requirements.

- Copy some important work files from your hard drive to an external storage medium (such as a flash drive or CD-ROM). Take screenshots of how you did this and compile a document explaining the process.

- Create a checklist of the processes a colleague should follow when cleaning their computer. Include advice on staying safe while carrying out the cleaning process.

- Carry out a risk analysis of your workstation. Compile a document that lists all the areas of your workstation, showing which are safe and which (if any) are not. List possible changes that could make your workstation safer.

- Create a list of instructions that detail how to carry out basic maintenance to your printer, such as adding more paper and dealing with paper jams.

4

CHAPTER 5

IT Security for Users

5.1 About This Unit

What you need to know

To gain ITQ Level 2 in this unit, you should demonstrate the following competency:

Be able to select and use appropriate methods to keep common security risks to a minimum.

To achieve this you should know:

1 What common security risks there might be.

2 How to control access.

3 What laws and guidelines affect the use of IT and how they affect it.

You should also be able to use the following skills and techniques:

1 Protecting software and data in different ways.

How to prove your skills

You need to carry out at least two work-based tasks which demonstrate the skills and knowledge listed above. In order to show your competency, it may well be necessary for you to complete more tasks than this.

Make sure you have plenty of evidence that shows how you completed each task, such as a copy of the file you worked on, or a document with screenshots of the processes you followed. You can back this up by producing a report which shows your knowledge of the subjects covered within the unit.

5.2 Keeping Your Files Secure

5.2.1 Potential Threats

Your computer files are important to you, but there are myriad ways you can lose them.

■ **Theft**. One of the most likely ways to lose all your hard work is to make it too easy for someone to wander off with your stuff. Make sure unauthorised people are not allowed to stroll in and out of your office. Also ensure you are cautious when carrying portable equipment such as laptops. These are easily stolen if you are not being vigilant.

- **Viruses**. If your computer is infected with a virus, you could potentially lose data. Not all viruses are harmful, but many are and they will seek to damage data on your system. It is essential to run regularly updated anti-virus software to minimise your computer's risk of infection.

- **Unauthorised access**. Theft is no longer limited to someone physically taking something from you. Data can be stolen from your computer from halfway across the world if your PC does not have adequate security. Hackers can gain access to your computer using viruses or by simply hacking into your system. Firewall and anti-virus programs are essential in preventing this from happening.

- **Hardware/software failures**. Data loss can also happen when your computer fails. Malfunctioning software can make files corrupt, so they can no longer be opened. If your hard drive were to break down, it's very likely you would be unable to recover any of your files. An even more common way of losing data is when it is simply deleted by mistake.

Assessor's tip

Georgie says:

Think of any more threats there could be to your data – perhaps some that are specific to the place where you work. Make sure you mention these in the evidence you supply. It's important that you show you understand why it is necessary to have IT security.

5.2.2 Making Back-ups

Given all the above, it's a good idea to make sure your data is safe. The best way to do this is to make a back-up. If your data is lost, it can then be restored from the back-up.

Storing your back-ups

The whole point of creating a back-up is that you then store it in a safe place. If your computer explodes, spontaneously combusts or is swept away in a freak tornado, you want to still be able to access the back-up files. Consider storing the disk with your back-ups in another place from your computer – ideally a different building. Alternatively, there are many services that enable you to store your back-up online for a fee.

Stay the right side of the law

If the data is personal and covered by the Data Protection Act, you have a legal requirement to make sure it is adequately protected (i.e. not available for other people to access). You may also be required to destroy back-ups after a certain length of time. See the end of this chapter for more on the Data Protection Act.

5.2.3 Using Back-up Software

Windows XP comes with its own built-in back-up utility. You can use this software to quickly make a copy of selected data and store it on another hard drive or Zip disk. If you are running Windows XP Professional, this utility will be available to you straight away. If you are using Windows XP Home Edition, you first need to install it.

To install the back-up utility

1 Insert your Windows XP Home Edition installation disk.

2 Use My Computer or Windows Explorer to navigate to the folder D:\VALUEADD\MSFT\NTBACKUP (if your CD-ROM drive is assigned a letter other than D, that letter will be at the start of the file path).

3 Double click on the Ntbackup.msi file and follow the instructions for installation.

4 Click on the Finish button to complete installation.

To open Back-up:

1 Click Start.

2 Choose All Programs.

3 Choose Accessories.

4 Choose System Tools.

5 Click Backup.

The Backup or Restore Wizard is launched.

Using the Backup or Restore Wizard:

1 Click Next.

2 Click the circle next to Back up files and settings.

3 Click Next.

You now need to choose which items to back up.

Deciding what to back up

In the Backup or Restore Wizard, you can choose one of the default options, or select your own list of files to back up.

- **My documents and settings**: this stores all the contents of your My Documents folder, as well as other personal settings.

- **Everyone's documents and settings**: as above, but for all the profiles on your computer.

- **All information on this computer**: the whole caboodle. This makes a back-up of everything on your computer – so you'll need plenty of space for storage!

- **Let me choose what to back up**: this may be the most useful option depending on how you use your computer. If a lot of important files are stored outside your My Documents folder, you will need to choose this option and then select the files you want. If you go for this option, you need to click on the tick boxes next to each item you want to back up and then click Next.

Choose a place to save your backup:

NIKS DRIVE (H:)   Browse...

Type a name for this backup:

Backup

4 Click on the drop-down menu to choose where to save the back-up.

5 Type in a name for the back-up.

6 Click Next.

7 Click Finish to create your back-up.

8 Once the back-up is complete, click Close.

Backup.bkf

The completed back-up will be saved on your specified disk with the file extension bkf.

Alternative software

There are plenty of other packages you can use to make your system back-ups easy. Some are free, some you will have to shell out for.

Acronis True Image: www.acronis.com

Norton Ghost: www.symantec.com/ghost

Genie Backup Manager: www.genie-soft.com

NovaBACKUP: www.novastor.com/novabackup

Links to free back-up software: http://tinyurl.com/ujb3y

5.2.4 Controlling Access to Files

There's more to keeping your files safe than just making back-ups of them. You should also make sure other people can't get their mucky fingers on them. By controlling access to files, it prevents either people mistakenly deleting them or malicious users getting hold of them.

You can physically control access by preventing visitors to your office from wandering around at will. However, there are also plenty of controls you can set on your computer that will prevent people from getting hold of your work.

5.2.5 Passwords

You'll need passwords for all kinds of things. If your work computer is on a network, you'll need a password to log on in the morning. If you use online banking, you'll need a password to access your account. You even need a password to access your email. These passwords are an important barrier against people getting through to your personal data.

5.2.6 Choosing Good Passwords

Since passwords are so widely used, you might as well make yours good ones. Here are some tips for choosing a good password.

- **Make it a reasonable length**. Somewhere between 8 and 14 characters is ideal. Any longer than that and you'll probably have trouble remembering it.

- **Combine lots of different characters**. Use letters, numbers and symbols in your password. Mix up lower and upper case. The more different characters you use, the more difficult your password is to crack.

- **Don't make it easy to guess**. The name of your favourite football team, your pet dog or your company is not a good password. If you want to make it memorable, use one of the above but mix in some symbols and numbers to make the word tricky to guess.

- **Change it often**. Don't stick with the same password for too long. By changing your password regularly, you make it difficult for people to guess it.

An example of a good password

A good password should be memorable to you, but difficult for others to guess. Let's say the road you grew up in was called Acacia Avenue. That's going to be memorable to you, so let's use that as the basis of the password.

We'll make all the consonants upper case, so we get aCaCiaaVeNue. Too easy to guess at the moment, so let's add in some numbers. How about adding in your partner's birthdate, 19/04/66? Pop two numbers in after every four letters, so you get aCaC19iaaV04eNue66.

Excellent – that's a really strong password already, and the elements of it are very memorable to you.

To really ramp up the security, change some letters for symbols. We'll make every other 'a' an @ sign, and each 'e' a £ sign, giving aC@C19ia@V04£Nu£66. A high-strength password that will stick in your mind.

5.2.7 Logging On to Your PC

Even if you're not on a network, you can still set a password for logging onto your PC. By doing so, you ensure the software and data stored on there are kept safe.

To log onto your PC, just type in your password when prompted during start-up.

Creating a password

If your computer does not have a password set, you can set your own.

1   Click on the Start menu.

2   Click on Control Panel.

3   Open the User Accounts option.

4   Select the account on which you want to create a password.

5   Click on the Create a password button.

6   Type in the password and a hint (which will be given to you if you forget the password).

7   Click on Create Password.

8   Click on the appropriate button to choose whether to make your files private.

5.2.8 Changing Your Password

You can change your password whenever you like.

1   Click on the Start menu.

2   Click on Control Panel.

3   Open the User Accounts option.

4   Select the account on which you want to create a password.

5   Click on Change my password.

6   Type in the old and new passwords.

7   Click on Change Password.

If you are working on a network, you will find the process different.

1   Press the Ctrl, Alt, Del keys.

2   Click Change password.

3   Fill in the fields with your old password, then the new one.

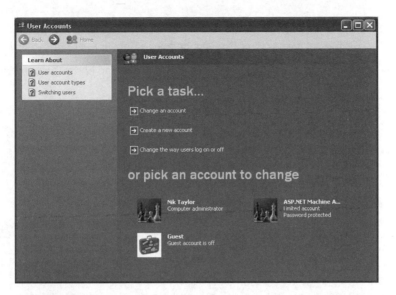

4 Click OK.

5 Click OK.

6 Click Cancel to return to your desktop.

Practise this!

Think up a strong password and set it as your new password.

5.2.9 Data Security

You can put passwords on your documents too. Only those who know the password will be able to open or modify the document.

For Word 2002 and PowerPoint 2002:

1 Click on the File menu.

2 Click on Save As.

3 Click on the Tools button.

4 Click on Security Options.

5 Choose the settings you require (see below).

For Excel 2002:

1 Click on the File menu.

2 Click on Save As.

3 Click on the Tools button.

4 Click on General Options.

5 Choose the settings you require (see below).

- Password to open – if you set this, only people who know the password can open the file.

- Password to modify – if you set this, only people who know the password can modify the file.

- Read-only recommended – the file will open as Read-Only, and if the user makes any changes, they will be forced to save it as a copy.

5.2.10 Making Files Read-only

If you don't mind other people opening particular files, but don't want them making changes, you can simply make the files 'read-only'. This means anyone who opens the file can only read the file. If they try to make any changes to it, they will see an error message.

To make a file read-only:

1 Locate the file in My Computer.

2 Right click on the file.

3 Click on Properties.

4 Click on the Read-Only check box, so it is checked.

5 Click on Apply.

6 Click on OK.

Practise this!

Try making an important file read-only.

5.2.11 Patches and Updates

Software takes ages to create, and can contains millions of lines of code. Although it is tested thoroughly, errors or 'bugs' will inevitably slip through. When several bugs have been discovered, the company usually releases an update (otherwise known as an upgrade, patch, bugfix, or service pack).

Sometimes, instead of bugs, people who create viruses find weaknesses and loopholes, and write programs to exploit these loopholes. In these cases, software companies release security updates or security patches.

When an update is released, you can go to the company's website, download it and install it.

5.2.12 Windows Update

Microsoft Windows has regular updates to fix bugs or seal security loopholes. When you go to the update site, it scans your machine to see what updates you need. To use Windows Update:

1 Click on the Start button.

2 Click on Programs or All Programs.

3 Click on Windows Update.

4 Click Express to scan for essential updates.

5 Follow the on-screen prompts to install any necessary updates.

Or

1 Open Internet Explorer.

2 Go to http://windowsupdate.microsoft.com.

3 Click Express to scan for essential updates.

4 Follow the on-screen prompts to install any necessary updates.

5.2.13 Office Update

Microsoft Office gets regular updates, too. To use it:

1 Open Internet Explorer.

2 Go to http://officeupdate.microsoft.com.

3 Click Check for Updates.

4 Follow the on-screen prompts to install any necessary updates.

5.3 Staying Safe from Threats

5.3.1 What is a Virus?

You've probably heard a lot of wild stories about viruses in the press. While they are not as ominous and disastrous as they sound, they can be extremely damaging. Viruses are programs designed to copy themselves and spread to other computers.

Some viruses do nothing else at all. Some simply display a message telling of the programmer's prowess, which are full of spelling mistakes, LOTS OF CAPITAL LETTERS and terrible grammar. Some will delete data from your hard disk, while others will burrow into your system and control it without your knowledge to send spam emails. The damage levels vary from virus to virus.

Your PC can become infected by opening an infected email attachment (a program sent within an email message), using an infected floppy disk, or downloading an infected file from the Internet.

To keep your PC safe from viruses:

- Make sure your PC has the latest virus software installed, for example AVG or McAfee VirusScan, and regularly update its data files so that it can recognise new viruses (roughly 500 new viruses appear every month).

- Always scan floppy disks for viruses before using any information on them.

- Never run an email attachment unless you are sure who it is from, and have scanned the attachment itself for viruses.

- Keep an emergency disk nearby just in case – your anti-virus software will create one for you. If your PC becomes infected, reboot with the emergency disk in the drive, and it will try to clean the infection for you.

5.3.2 Virus Hoaxes

This is a fairly recent problem, and a very annoying one: you get an email from a friend telling you about a scary new virus that has just come out. Apparently it has been reported by Microsoft or IBM or AOL or someone like that, is even worse than the last virus that came out, and has no cure. The message then tells you to forward the message on to all of your friends. You later find out the whole thing was made up.

This is a type of virus in itself. It is designed to create a panic, and get everyone sending the same message to all of their friends, who then send it to all of their friends, and so on and so on. It ties up your company mail PC with hundreds of emails going around, and wastes everyone's time. Sometimes the email traffic is so heavy, it can crash a company network.

The email text usually goes along these lines:

WARNING: If you receive an email with the subject line *InsertSubjectHere*, do not open the file. The file contains the *InsertVirusNameHere* virus. This information was announced yesterday morning at IBM/Microsoft/*InsertCompanyNameHere*. This is a very dangerous virus, much worse than 'Melissa', and there is NO remedy for it at this time. If you open/read/look at the email, it will completely delete your hard drive/do some other ridiculously frightening thing. This is a new, very malicious virus and not many people know about it. Pass this warning along to EVERYONE in your address book ASAP so that this threat may be stopped.

If you receive an email like this, do not send it to all of your friends – if you do, the hoaxer has won. Check with an online virus library, and find out if it is a hoax.

The Network Associates Virus Library:
http://vil.nai.com/vil/

F Secure Hoax Warnings:
http://www.f-secure.com/hoaxes/

Urban Legends – Virus Hoaxes Page:
http://urbanlegends.about.com/od/virushoaxes1/

The last site also contains information about other email hoaxes you will receive, for example the one about the businessman falling asleep in a hotel and waking up with his kidneys stolen, etc.

5.3.3 Virus Scanning Using AVG

AVG is available free for personal use, from http://free.grisoft.com. It comes with regular, free updates and is extremely effective. If you are using AVG version 7.5:

1 Click on Start.

2 Click on All Programs.

3 Click on AVG 7.5.

4 Click on AVG Test Center.

5 Click on the button next to Scan Computer – AVG will start scanning.

If it finds a virus, AVG will try to 'heal' it, and remove the virus. If the file cannot be healed (some viruses are particularly nasty), then it will move it to the Virus Vault. Click on Virus Vault from the main scanning window to see these files.

To delete the files, select the ones you want to delete, and press the Delete icon.

When AVG finishes scanning, it will show you the results. Click Close to exit the scan.

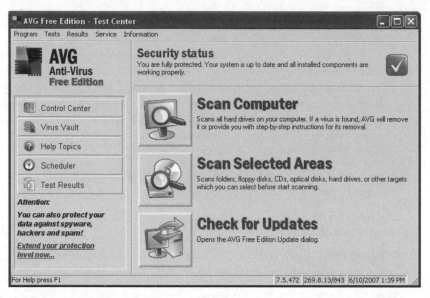

5.3.4 Updating Your Virus Scanner

In order to make sure you are keeping up to date with all the new viruses floating around out there, you need to regularly update your virus scanner. You need to be connected to the Internet for this to work. If you are using AVG:

1 Click on Start.

2 Click on All Programs.

3 Click on AVG 7.5.

4 Click on AVG Control Center.

5 Click Check for Updates.

6 Tick the box next to Do not ask for the update source next time – this ensures that AVG will do the same thing next time without asking you.

7 Click on Internet.

8 AVG will download the latest file.

9 Click OK to finish.

Practise this!

Now's a good time to ensure your anti-virus software is bang up to date.

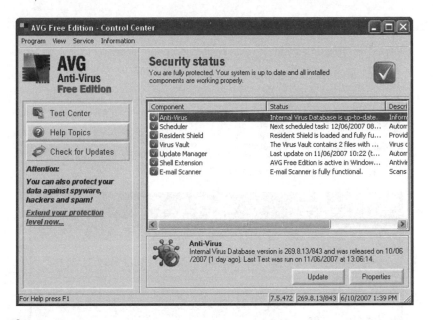

5.3.5 Protection

Most anti-virus programs will have a protection mode, where they run in the background, keeping an eye on what you do. Every time you open a file, they quickly check it, and if it contains a virus, it stops everything and tells you whether the file was fixed or removed. Click OK when this happens.

5.3.6 What is a Firewall?

A firewall is a security tool that protects a network or computer from unwanted traffic. They can stop any traffic that you haven't allowed permission for, and can make the network invisible to the outside world by hiding the IP addresses of the computers. If an outside hacker can see your IP address, they can scan your machine for open ports, which they can then use to get into your network.

There are two types of firewall, hardware and software.

- Hardware firewalls are usually installed between the Internet and the computers in your network.

- Software firewalls are usually installed on the computer that connects to the Internet, and sit between that machine and the Internet. Or you can install one on a single PC, like a home computer. Some common software firewalls are ZoneAlarm and Symantec Firewall.

A firewall does not stop:

- Harmful files that bypass the firewall, for example files that sneak in over a wireless network.

- Traffic that seems innocent.

- Viruses.

- People guessing weak passwords (birthdays, nicknames, etc.).

5.3.7 Windows XP Firewall

Windows XP comes with its own built-in software firewall. To switch it on:

1 Click on the Start button.

2 Click on Control Panel.

3 Click on Security Center.

4 Click on Windows Firewall.

5 Click inside the circle next to On.

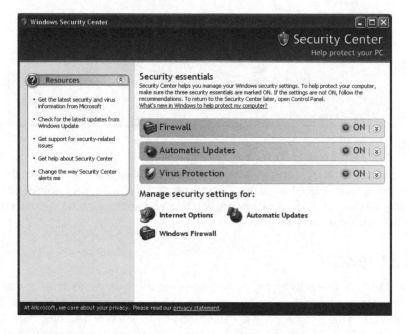

6 Click OK.

Practise this!

Go to the Windows XP firewall settings and make sure the firewall is switched on.

Assessor's tip

Sheena says:

It's likely that your security settings at work will be taken care of by your IT department. You may not have the authority to make changes to your anti-virus software and firewall – especially if you are on a network. If that is the case, just make sure you know what security settings there are in place, and find out what checks (if any) you are allowed to make yourself.

5.3.8 Internet Control Software

Companies will often utilise Internet control software to reduce the chances of users downloading viruses onto their computers.

Internet control software limits what you can do on the Internet. How heavily it affects what you can do depends on how strictly the controls are set.

Common settings include:

- Barred websites. Certain websites, normally those deemed to be inappropriate for work viewing, cannot be displayed.

- No downloads. Users are unable to download files from the Internet. This is generally intended to counter the spread of viruses from the Net onto the company's network.

- Networking software disabled. Chat programs such as MSN Messenger are often disabled.

5.3.9 What is Spam?

Sometimes you will get email from people you don't know. They'll offer you money for nothing, cheap pharmaceuticals, unlimited access to dubious websites and all sorts of other things you don't want. In other words, junk mail.

Remember when you would get piles of junk mail through your letterbox? Well now they can do it in an email, which means they don't have to spend money on printing or stamps. They can send out millions and millions of emails, within seconds.

Because of this, spam is a huge problem. It can overload the servers of your Internet service provider and sometimes even crash networks – all because there is so much of it.

The other problem with spam is the time wasted going through your emails, picking out the unwanted emails, and deleting them.

There are now laws designed to deal with the problem of spam. Check Section 5.4, Laws and guidelines, at the end of this chapter for more information.

5.3.10 Where Does it Come From, and How Do They Find You?

It's very difficult to find out where it comes from. They'll usually send it from a dummy account, which is closed after sending all the emails. A lot of the time they will forge the email headers to make it look like it came from somewhere else.

They don't always have your email address. Sometimes they guess email addresses, sometimes they get them from websites or newsgroup posts, sometimes they buy lists of customers. They also use 'robots', automated programs that search the Internet for any mention of email addresses.

5.3.11 The Unsubscribe Trick

Never, never, never reply to spam, and never click the 'Unsubscribe' link. All this does is tell the spammers that your address is real, and they will then deluge you with more. It's a clever trick because most genuine newsletters have an unsubscribe link that works.

5.3.12 How to Stop It

There are several ways to fight spam:

- Use two email addresses. Give your proper email address to people you trust – friends, work colleagues, etc. When buying things online, or filling in forms, use the second email address – you can get a free Google, Yahoo or Hotmail address quite easily. If – and when – the second address starts getting overloaded with spam, abandon it, and set up a different, second email address. You won't have to let anyone know, as all your friends and colleagues will have your proper, safe address.

- Some email software has special spam filters that let you automatically delete spam messages.

- Use a server-based spam blocker. If a company gets a lot of spam, this is the best strategy. The server-based software can filter out users who pass the test, and those who do not.

5.3.13 Spam Filters

There are several different types of spam filters:

- **User-defined filters**: most email packages contain these – they let you set up rules to move or delete emails based on the subject or contents. Many spam emails have similar contents, so, for example, you could safely set up a filter to automatically delete any emails that have Viagra in the subject line.

- **Header filters**: these filters check the email headers and see if any of them are forged – if they are, then the email may well be spam. Not all spam has forged headers though, so this won't stop all of it.

- **Language filters**: these filters check for any emails not written in your language.

- **Content filters**: these check the emails for certain words or phrases common in spam. They work quite well, but can sometimes eliminate genuine emails.

- **Permission filters**: these block any mail from unauthorised sources. When you email someone for the first time, their permission filter may email you back and send you to a website. You enter some information into the site, authorise your email address, and can then email the person.

Practise this!

Find out what provisions your company has to prevent spam and see if there is anything you can do to improve the security of your own email account.

5.4 Laws and Guidelines

5.4.1 Knowing the Law

This unit, along with several other ITQ units, requires you to have some knowledge of the laws relating to IT. Listed below are the key laws you should know about.

5.4.2 The Data Protection Act 1998

By using computers, companies can now store vast databases of names, phone numbers, addresses and other personal information. All that data can easily be shared with other companies and is, of course, extremely valuable for marketing purposes (i.e. junk mail and phone calls).

However, sharing data in this way is against the law. The purpose of the Data Protection Act is to ensure your permission is required before any company stores information about you.

The Data Protection Act came into force in March 2000, and has eight principles:

1 **Personal data must be processed fairly and lawfully**: the subject must give permission for information about them to be kept – unless it is to protect them, for example, medical records or legal obligations.

2 **Personal data shall be obtained only for one or more specified and lawful purposes**: the subject or the Data Protection Commissioner must be notified of the specific purpose for keeping the personal data.

3 **Personal data shall be adequate, relevant and not excessive in relation to the purpose for which it is processed**: organisations must state the purpose of the data processing, and cannot use it in any other way without further notification. For example, you agree to let a dating agency match you up with compatible people, but they are not allowed to send you adverts for other services, unless they notify you or the Commissioner.

4 **Personal data shall be accurate and, where necessary, kept up to date**: whoever is responsible for the data must ensure that the data is accurate, and carry out regular checks. The normal way of checking is to send the details to the subject, so they can confirm they are correct.

5 **Personal data processed for any purpose shall not be kept longer than is necessary for that purpose**: for example, you can collect data from job applicants, but once the interviews and job selection are over, the data must be destroyed.

6 **Personal data shall be processed in accordance with the rights of data subjects under the Act**: anyone can make a written request for their personal data. They will usually pay a fee, but must be given their data within 40 days. You must also tell them how it is processed, why it is kept, the people who will see it, and the company that will actually process it. If there is any incorrect information, they have the right to have it corrected or deleted. They can also stop you using it in a way that may cause damage or distress, or for junk mail, and can sue you for compensation if this condition is breached.

7 **Appropriate technical and organisational measures shall be taken against unauthorised or unlawful processing of personal data and against accidental loss or destruction of, or damage to, personal data**: you must keep the data private and secure, and regularly back it up, scan it for viruses, and make sure unauthorised people do not have access to it, for example, using passwords.

8 **Personal data shall not be transferred to a country or territory outside the European Economic Area, unless that country or territory ensures an adequate level of protection for the rights and freedoms of data subjects in relation to the processing of personal data**: the only exceptions to this are if the subject of the data has given permission for a transfer, or if the transfer is necessary for the public interest, or if it's in the data subject's interest, or is for legal reasons. (The European Economic Area is currently the EU countries, as well as Iceland, Liechtenstein and Norway.)

5.4.3 The Computer Misuse Act 1990

This Act was created to deal with hacking attacks on computer systems. All employees should be aware of the Act, and be given simple information about it.

It's fairly obvious that defrauding someone with a computer is wrong, but most people wouldn't know that changing some settings could also be classified as computer misuse. The three offences are:

1 **Unauthorised access to computer material**: if you find or guess someone's password, and use it to look at data you shouldn't have access to, then you have broken the law, even if you don't cause any damage or change/delete files. Just accessing it is illegal, and carries a maximum penalty of six months in prison and/or a fine.

2 **Unauthorised access with intent to commit or facilitate commission of further offences**: a combination of the unauthorised access of the previous offence, and using that access to copy or steal data or money. The maximum penalty is five years in prison, and/or a fine.

3 **Unauthorised modification of computer material**: deleting files, changing the settings, or putting a virus on a machine deliberately. This includes modifying things on a different computer from your own computer, even if you don't do anything else to your computer. The maximum penalty is five years in prison, and/or a fine.

5.4.4 Privacy and Electronic Communications Regulations 2003

This is designed to regulate how direct marketing is sent. The regulations are updated from the Telecommunications (Data Protection and Privacy) Regulations to include new rules on the sending of unsolicited emails and text messages. The main rules are:

- Do not send unsolicited marketing emails to anyone, unless they have given you permission to receive similar emails, or if they have given permission via a third party, or if they have been made aware that they may receive marketing emails (and they have not objected to receiving such emails – but there must be a clear and simple way to opt out).

- If someone has bought something from you, you may send marketing emails to them about similar products or services.

- Do not send any marketing emails (solicited or unsolicited) with a hidden or disguised identity, or without including a valid address to opt out from further emails. The recipient can opt out at any time, and must be told how to do this in every email you send.

5.4.5 Health and Safety at Work etc. Act 1974

This Act is the basis of the UK's health and safety law. The basic premise of the Act is that employers should 'ensure so far as is reasonably practicable the health, safety and welfare at work of all their employees'.

Employers must:

- Provide a safe working environment and place of employment.
- Provide a written safety policy/risk assessment.
- Provide and maintain safety equipment and safe systems of work.
- Ensure the proper storage, handling, usage and transportation of materials.
- Provide information, training, instruction and supervision for employees.
- Look after the health and safety of others, such as visitors.
- Talk to safety representatives.

Employees must:

- Take care of their health and safety and that of other persons. Employees may be liable.
- Co-operate with their employers.
- Not interfere with anything provided in the interest of health and safety.

5.4.6 Health and Safety (Display Screen Equipment) Regulations 1992

These regulations are more specific to IT users. They list the responsibilities of all employers to any employees who use computer screens as a regular part of their work. Below is a brief summary of these regulations.

The employer must:

- Carry out an analysis of each employee workstation to ensure it meets requirements.
- Ensure their employees' work is planned so they can take regular breaks.
- Pay for regular eyesight tests for any employees who regularly use a computer screen.
- Provide health and safety training for employees.

5.4.7 Copyright

The United Kingdom copyright law covers the rights of individuals to have their intellectual property protected. The current act is the Copyright, Designs and Patents Act 1988.

Copyright law gives the creators of literature, music, art and other creative works the right to control the ways in which the material is used. It is an automatic right and arises whenever an original work is created.

So what does that mean to you? Well, the rules of copyright are fairly complex, but there are two key points you should remember:

1 You should not use any creative work (such as images or artwork) without the prior permission of their author.

2 Copyright is automatic. Any original creative work is covered. Even if you can't see a copyright symbol on the image, you still can't use it as you wish.

No-one will stop you at the time of course, but if you publish work that includes a copyright image then you could be for the high-jump if the rights-holder finds out.

Copyright covers all kinds of images – regardless of artistic merit. For instance, there have been instances of people suddenly receiving invoices for the use of simple graphics they had added to their websites, which they had presumed to be free. The graphics were as basic as shopping trolley images and link buttons. However, they were protected by copyright and so could not be used without the consent of (and, in this case, payment to) their original author.

The golden rule is that if you are not sure whether something is covered by copyright, don't use it.

5.5 Test Your Knowledge

The questions below will test what you know of the knowledge and understanding requirements of this unit. All the answers to these questions are contained or referred to within this chapter.

1 List two ways in which you could lose your data.

2 What is a virus?

3 Why might a company choose to install Internet control software?

4 Why might it be dangerous to download a file from a website that is unfamiliar to you?

5 What process would you follow to set a password on a Word 2002 file?

6 What are the three offences covered by the Computer Misuse Act 1990?

7 It is an individual's responsibility to ensure information stored about them by a company is up to date. True or false?

8 What process would you follow to make a file read-only?

9 What is spam?

10 How would you open Windows XP's Backup utility?

5.6 Evidence

The tasks you undertake as evidence for your ITQ should be work-related. Therefore, your supervisor at work should be able to give you guidance on the type of tasks you should take on. Below are some ideas of possible tasks for this unit. Consider how you can adapt these ideas to make them more relevant for your own workplace and to ensure you cover all the skills requirements.

■ Download the latest update for Windows from the Internet. Create a document that shows the process you followed, along with screenshots of what you did.

■ Create a document that describes how you reduce the chances of a virus infecting your computer. Take screenshots of the process of updating your anti-virus software and running a virus check with it.

■ Devise a strong password to use as your Windows log-in. Change your existing password for this new one, taking screenshots of the whole process.

■ Find out your company's policy on making back-ups (i.e. whose responsibility it is, what software is used to do this). Make a back-up of your system if you are authorised to do so, and create a document that explains the process you followed.

CHAPTER 6

Internet and Intranets

6.1 About This Unit

What you need to know

To gain ITQ Level 2 in this unit, you should demonstrate the following competency:

Use computer and other hardware efficiently to access, retrieve and exchange relevant information of different types.

To achieve this you should know:

1 The benefits and drawbacks of own connection methods.

2 More advanced browser facilities.

3 What information and other opportunities are available and ways to access them.

4 Ways to avoid Internet security risks.

5 How laws and guidelines affect the use of IT.

You should also be able to use the following skills and techniques:

1 Searching for relevant information efficiently.

2 Finding and evaluating information using appropriate methods.

3 Exchanging information by using appropriate methods.

4 Customising browser software.

How to prove your skills

You need to carry out at least two work-based tasks which demonstrate the skills and knowledge listed above. In order to show your competency, it may well be necessary for you to complete more tasks than this.

Make sure you have plenty of evidence that shows how you completed each task, such as a copy of the file you worked on, or a document with screenshots of the processes you followed. You can back this up by producing a report which shows your knowledge of the subjects covered within the unit.

6.2 | Introduction to the Internet

6.2.1 What is the Internet?

- The Internet is a global network of computers connected to each other.

- It is not intangible, but a physical structure that connects computers together.

6.2.2 The Main Parts of the Internet

The Internet has two main parts:

- The World Wide Web (WWW).

- Email.

6.2.3 What is the World Wide Web?

Here are just some of the things you can do over the World Wide Web:

- **Read pages of information**. People throughout the world have produced web pages on their computers. Other people can then read that information if they are also connected to the Internet.

- **E-commerce**. You can shop for goods over the World Wide Web. Anything you can think of is up for sale, from books to last-minute flights to houses.

- **Download software**. You can download files from the Web onto your computer. All sorts of stuff is available, including music and movie files, free software, photographs and more. Once they are downloaded, they can be used on your computer.

- **Chat**. Some web pages enable you to chat with other people who are connected to the Internet at the same time as you. You can type messages to each other which appear on the screen immediately.

- **Create your own material**. Anyone is free to create their own part of the Web. You can make your own websites using site-building software, or you can use specialised sites like MySpace which do all the hard work for you.

6.2.4 Web Browsers

A web browser is a program that displays web pages. Some commonly used browsers are Internet Explorer, Netscape, Firefox and Opera.

6.2.5 Web Terms

The Internet is full of information and it's also full of barely penetrable jargon. Here are some of the more important Net terms.

- *http* hypertext transfer protocol. This is one of the languages used on the Internet to help computers to communicate.

- *ftp* file transfer protocol. Another computer language, this one is used for transferring files.

- *URL* uniform resource locator – the address of a website. For example, the URL of the BBC's website is www.bbc.co.uk.

- *Hyperlink* how people get around on the Web. When you click on a hyperlink, you are taken to another web page.

- *ISP* Internet Service Provider – the company that connects you to the Internet. To go online you must pay a fee to an ISP. It's a bit like having a telephone – you can buy a phone, but you need to pay the telephone company to let you connect to the telephone lines.

If you come across Internet terms you're not familiar with, the best place to look is…the Internet. Use a search engine to look for more information on the term. There are loads of sites which list common definitions – such as www.bbc.co.uk/webwise/course/jargon/a.shtml from the BBC.

6.3 Connecting to the Internet

6.3.1 Internet Connections

Below is a list of the most common Internet connections. At work, your company is most likely to use an ADSL, SDSL or leased line connection, which will then be supplied to all staff via the network.

Connection type	Description	Typical speed	Advantages	Disadvantages
Dial-up	The Internet is accessed via a modem which is connected to a standard telephone line	56kbps	Cheap to use and requires little in the way of additional equipment	You can't use the phone while using the Internet – or vice versa. You have to make a new connection each time you use the Internet. Very slow compared to other connections
ISDN	Uses standard telephone lines to transmit data digitally	64–128kbps	Faster than dial-up. Quick to connect. Can be used in areas not serviced by faster technologies	Requires conversion of your existing telephone line and additional equipment. Superseded by faster options
Cable	Uses available bandwidth on TV cable network to transmit data	2–20Mbps	'Always-on' connection. Cable connection enables very high speeds	Only available in cabled areas. Set-up costs can be expensive
ADSL (asymmetric digital subscriber line)	Uses high-frequencies to enable fast data transmission over standard telephone lines	512 kbps–8Mbps	Widely available. Enables use of telephone and Internet simultaneously	Not available in all areas. Set-up costs can be expensive

Connection type	Description	Typical speed	Advantages	Disadvantages
SDSL (symmetric digital subscriber line)	Very similar to ADSL, except it also offers high upload speeds	512 kbps–8Mbps	Enables users to upload data at very high speeds	Requires an additional line for phone calls to be made
Leased line	A dedicated Internet connection leased to a single business	Up to 1Gbps	Extremely high speeds. Very reliable	Very high cost – only practical for larger companies

The speed of your Internet connection affects how quickly you can access pages and files on the Internet. Below you can see how the connection speed affects how quickly you can download data.

Connection type	Time to load BBC News homepage	Time to download a three-minute mp3 track	Time to download a 60 Mb software file
Dial-up (56k connection)	13 seconds	11 minutes	2 hours 30 minutes
ADSL (1.5Mb connection)	<1 second	24 seconds	5 minutes 30 seconds
Leased line (10Mb connection)	<1 second	3 seconds	50 seconds

As you can see, there is a huge difference in what you can achieve online depending on the speed of your connection. Bear in mind also that your connection is unlikely to regularly reach its full speed. Your connection isn't used only by you – it's shared by other people in your area, and that will affect the speeds you can expect to achieve.

There are some exceptions to that, the most common of which is a leased line. This is a direct connection that is not shared with anyone else, guaranteeing reliably high speeds.

Practise this!

Find out what type of Internet connection your company uses.

Assessor's tip

Rudy says:

Think about the difference between your Internet connection at work and at home. Which is quicker? What more can you achieve using the faster connection? Make sure you give plenty of evidence that you understand the difference between connection types.

6.3.2 Connecting to the Internet

Connecting to the Internet requires several things. First, you need a contract with an ISP. This company provides you with access to its network, which in turn grants you access to the Internet.

Second, you need the necessary hardware. Most important is a modem. This piece of kit is what translates the information from your Internet connection into something your computer can understand. The modem will normally be supplied by your ISP.

Third, you will need a web browser. The most common web browser is Microsoft's Internet Explorer, although Mozilla's Firefox software is gaining in popularity. The first time you open this software, it will take you through the set-up process to access your Internet connection.

At work, your technical department will manage your Internet connection for you. The physical connection to the Internet will be situated elsewhere in the building – you will just need to ensure your PC is connected to the network, which will enable you to connect to the Internet.

Connecting to the Internet

While you're sitting at your desk, you will probably connect to the Internet using your computer. However, there are other types of hardware that can connect to the Internet:

- *Mobile phone*: as mobile phones become more advanced, they are becoming increasingly popular for connecting to the Internet. WAP phones can display a text-based version of the Internet, but newer 3G (third generation) phones can provide a full version of the Internet.
- *PDA/Laptop*: using a mobile phone connection, you can access the Internet from your PDA or laptop.
- *Games console*: the current generation of games consoles is capable of connecting to the Internet. This makes it easy to surf the Web via your TV.

6.3.3 What is an Intranet?

Many larger companies have their own intranets. An intranet works in basically the same way as the Internet, but the content will be limited to anything relevant to your company. Think of it as your company's own personalised version of the Internet.

If your company has its own intranet, you will probably access it via a website. The important thing to remember is that you can only connect to your company's intranet if you are an employee. It is not accessible to the general public via the Internet and you will probably need a username and password to log onto it.

6.4 Using an Internet Browser

6.4.1 Starting Internet Explorer

1 Click the Start button.

2 Click on All Programs.

3 Click on Internet Explorer.

Internet Explorer

Or

Double click on the desktop shortcut.

6.4.2 Closing Internet Explorer

To close it, just click on the big X at the top right of the Internet Explorer window.

6.4.3 The Screen

Title bar

Menu bar

Standard buttons toolbar

Address bar

Web page

Status bar

Links bar

Scroll bars

Screenshot provided courtesy of Happy (www.happy.co.uk)

Part of the screen	What does it do?
Title bar	Tells you the title of the web page you are looking at.
Menu bar	Gives you access to the commands available in Internet Explorer. All commands are grouped under one of the menus.
Standard buttons toolbar	The icons on the Standard toolbar provide a quick way of carrying out standard commands.
Links toolbar	The icons on the Links toolbar provide a quick way of accessing web pages you frequently visit.
Scroll bars	Use the vertical scroll bar to move down through a long web page and the horizontal scroll bar to move across a wide web page.
Address bar	Use this to enter the address of a website you want to visit. It will also display the address of a website you are currently viewing.
Status bar	Displays messages, such as the progress on connecting to a website. The right-hand side will indicate the security settings for the web page you are looking at.

6.4.4 Switching Toolbars On and Off

1 Click on the View menu.

2 Click on Toolbars – a list will appear.

3 Click on the toolbar you would like to turn on or off – a tick appears before toolbars that are switched on.

6.4.5 The Standard Buttons Toolbar

This toolbar gives you quick access to some of the standard commands available from the menus.

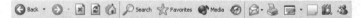

Going from left to right in the illustration above, here is what each icon does:

- Goes back to the previous page.

- Goes forward to the next page (you cannot use this unless you have gone back at least one page).

- Stops the page loading.

- Refreshes the page, or loads it again.

- Goes to the homepage.

- Uses Microsoft's search facility.

- Displays the Favorites list (a list of sites you have bookmarked).

- Displays the Media options.

- Displays the History list (sites you have recently visited).

- Lets you read or send email.

- Prints the current page.

- Lets you edit the page with another piece of software.

- Lets you link up to a discussion server.

- Displays the Research tool.

- Runs Microsoft Messenger.

6.4.6 The Address Bar

This toolbar is used to enter the address of websites you want to visit. When you are viewing a web page, its address will be displayed in this bar.

Address http://www.google.co.uk/ Go

6.4.7 Typing in the URL

If you know the URL (the website address) of a web page, it is easy to get to:

1 Click into the Address bar – the existing URL will go blue.

Address http://www.google.co.uk/ Go

2 Delete any existing address.

3 Type the address you require, e.g. www.bbc.co.uk.

4 Press Enter or click Go – Internet Explorer will load the page.

How much longer do I have to wait?

If you check the status bar at the bottom left of the screen, you will often see an indicator of how much has been downloaded already.

Opening page http://www.microsoft.com

When it is finished it will say *Done*.

Done

Practise this!

Start up your web browser software and go to the BBC home page (www.bbc.co.uk).

6.4.8 What if I Don't Know the Address?

If you don't know the address, you can use a search engine to find it.

6.4.9 Matches in the Address Bar

If you have typed in an address before, a list will probably appear as you begin to type. Just click on the site you want to visit to save time.

6.4.10 Accessing a Web Address You Have Already Visited

To return to an address you have typed in recently:

1 Click the drop-down arrow at the end of the Address bar.

2 Click on the address you require.

6.4.11 Clearing the History

Your web browser automatically keeps a list of the websites you have visited. This is called the History. To clear out this list:

1 Click on the Tools menu.

2 Click on Internet Options (may just be called Options depending on your browser version).

3 Click Clear History.

4 Click Yes.

5 Click OK.

6.4.12 The Homepage

- When you first connect to a site you will see its homepage.

- This is like the front cover of a magazine which welcomes you in and gives you an idea of what you can expect to find inside.

- The homepage will usually contain links to other pages in the site.

Links are usually underlined text (frequently blue), or pictures – the mouse pointer will turn into a pointing hand when you hover it over a link. Use the scroll bar to see more of the page if necessary.

6.4.13 How Can I Tell Where the Links Are?

Clicking on a link (hyperlink) takes you to another web page, or another part of the page you are on. When you pass your mouse over a link it will look like a pointing hand. Links can be either text or graphics.

6.4.14 Using Links

1 Position the mouse over the hyperlink you require.

2 Click when the mouse looks like a hand – the linked page will open.

6.4.15 Opening Pages in a New Window

| Open |
| Open in New Window |
| Save Target As... |
| Print Target |
| Cut |
| Copy |
| Copy Shortcut |
| Paste |
| Add to Favorites... |
| Properties |

1 Right click on the link.

2 Click on Open in New Window.

Shortcut

To quickly open a page in a new window, just hold down the Shift key when you click on the link.

6.4.16 Downloading from a Link

1 Right click on the link.

2 Click on Save Target As.

3 Choose a save location.

4 Click Save.

6.4.17 Downloading an Image

1 Hold the mouse pointer over the image.

2 Click on the save icon on the toolbar that appears.

3 Choose a save location.

4 Click Save.

No toolbar?

If you are using an older version of Internet Explorer, you may not see the toolbar appear when you hold the mouse pointer over the image. If not, right click on the image and then choose the Save Picture As option.

6.4.18 Completing a Web Form

Web forms let you type in information, to log in, or buy things, or sign up for newsletters, and so on. There are several types of items in forms:

What they are	What they look like	What to do
Text boxes		Click inside the box with the mouse, and type something
Buttons	Click Me!	Click on the button
Radio buttons	⦿ Option 1 ◯ Option 2	Click inside the circle – only one can be selected at a time
Check boxes	☑ Option 1 ☑ Option 2	Click inside the box – many can be selected at a time

6.4.19 The Back Button

To revisit the last page you viewed, click on the Back button.

6.4.20 Going Back a Long Way

1 Click the drop-down arrow next to the Back button.

```
Back  ▾
Welcome to Happy Computers - Award winn
Google
Microsoft Windows Server System: Home
Microsoft Corporation
BBC - bbc.co.uk homepage - Home of the
Google
Welcome to Happy Computers - Award winn
Pearson Plc
Pearson Education

History  Ctrl+H
```

2 Click on the site you require.

6.4.21 The Forward Button

To go forward again, once you have been back, click on the Forward button.

6.4.22 Going Forward a Long Way

1 Click the drop-down arrow next to the Forward button.

2 Click on the site you require.

6.4.23 The Home Button

Clicking on the Home button takes you to your default homepage. You can set this to be any web page you want.

6.4.24 The Stop Button

The Stop button stops a page downloading. Click on it if:

- A page is taking a long time to appear on the screen.

- You think you might have typed in the wrong address.

- Internet Explorer is going somewhere you don't want it to!

6.4.25 The Refresh Button

The Refresh button tells Internet Explorer to download the web page you are looking at from the server. Click on it if:

- Internet Explorer hasn't finished downloading the page and seems to have stopped doing anything.

- You think the page may have changed since you downloaded it the first time.

6.4.26 Sending a Web Page by Email

If you come to a page on the Internet that you know a friend would like to read, it's easy to email the whole page:

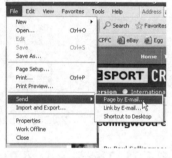

1 Click on the File menu.

2 Click on Send.

3 Click on Page by E-mail.

A new email will be opened in your mail program, with the web page included in the main body of the message. All you have to do is address the email and hit the Send button.

Assessor's tip

Lynne says:

Spend some time searching for useful sites on the Web – particularly any that would be work-related. Look for regularly updated sites, such as news pages for your industry, and for interactive sites that you can get involved in. You want to show that you're able to contribute to the Internet as well as simply using it.

6.5 Customising Your Browser

6.5.1 Changing Your Homepage

If you find a site that you really like or find particularly useful, you may want to set it as your homepage. This is the page that Internet Explorer will open with.

1 Click on the Tools menu.

2 Click on Internet Options.

3 Click on the General tab.

4 Click in the Address box in the Home page area.

5 Type the address of the page you wish to set as your homepage.

6 Click OK.

6.5.2 Creating a Favourite

When you find a useful site, you will want to return to it regularly. If you make it a favourite, then going back is easy.

1 Go to the page which you would like to make a favourite.

2 Click on the Favorites menu.

3 Click on Add to Favorites.

4 Give your favourite page a name if required – type it into the Name box.

5 Click OK.

6.5.3 Adding a Favourite to a Folder

1 Go the page which you would like to make a favourite.

2 Click on the Favorites menu.

3 Click on Add to Favorites.

4 Give your favourite page a name if required.

5 Click on Create in.

6 Double click on the folder you wish to add the page to.

Or

Click on New Folder to create a new folder to put your page in.

Type in the name of the folder.

Click OK.

The dialog box shows:

Add Favorite

Internet Explorer will add this page to your Favorites list.

☐ Make available offline — Customize...

Name: Welcome to Happy Computers - Award winning I.T. T

Create in: Favorites
- Dell
- Links
- Media

Buttons: OK, Cancel, Create in <<, New Folder...

7 Click OK.

6.5.4 Accessing One of Your Favourites

1 Click on the Favorites button – a list of favourites appears on the left.

2 If necessary, click on the folder you wish to open.

3 Click on the page you wish to go to.

4 Click on the Favorites button again to remove the list.

6.5.5 Deleting Favourites

1 Click on the Favorites button.

2 Right click on the site you wish to delete – a new menu will appear.

3 Click on Delete.

4 Click Yes to delete the page.

6.5.6 Creating Folders in Favourites

By creating folders, you can store favourite sites of similar types. For instance, all your favourite news sites can go in a 'news' folder, all your shopping sites in a 'shopping' folder, and so on.

1 Click on the Favorites menu.

2 Click on Organize Favorites.

3 Click on Create Folder.

4 Type in a name for your folder.

5 Press Enter.

6 Click Close.

6.5.7 Moving a Favourite to a Folder

1 Click on the Favorites menu.

2 Click on Organize Favorites.

3 Click on the favourite you want to move from the list on the right.

4 Click on the Move to Folder button.

5 Click on the folder you want to move the favourite to.

6 Click on OK.

7 Click Close.

6.5.8 Renaming Folders or Favourites

1 Click on the Favorites menu.

2 Click on Organise Favorites.

3 Click on the folder or page you wish to rename.

4 Click on Rename.

5 Type in a new name.

6 Press Enter.

7 Click Close.

Practise this!

Open your web browser and go to the ITQ home page (http://itq.e-skills.com). Save this as a favourite in a new folder called ITQ. Now change your home page to Google UK (www.google.co.uk).

Assessor's tip

Georgie says:

By setting up a long list of favourite websites, you can make your browsing time much easier. Instead of typing in a web address every time, you just need to click on the Favorites menu. Doing this is a good way to show you know how to customise your browser.

6.5.9 Deleting Temporary Internet Files

Temporary Internet files are downloaded onto your computer whenever you load a web page in your browser. When you return to that site, your computer will load the stored sections of the page from its memory, rather than downloading them all over again from the Web. The result is that the page appears on your screen more quickly.

Over time you can end up with stacks of temporary Internet files taking up space on your hard drive. If hard drive space is a bit thin on the ground, you can delete these files to free up some more room.

1 Close down Internet Explorer and Outlook.

2 Click on the Start button.

3 Click on Control Panel.

4 Choose Internet Options.

5 Click on the General tab.

6 Click on the Delete files button.

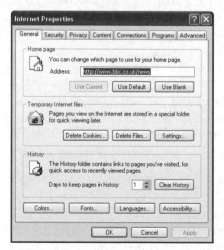

7 In the Delete Files dialog box that appears, click on the Delete all offline content box so it is ticked.

8 Click on the OK button.

9 Click OK again.

6.5.10 Dealing with Cookies

Websites use cookies so they can remember who you are. The next time you visit that website, it finds its cookie on your system which tells it something about you. They're used for lots of different purposes, such as:

- Remembering your username and/or password, so you don't have to type them in again.

- Remembering the way you like the website to be displayed, so you don't have to change it again.

- Remembering previous orders you've made from the website, so you can quickly track those orders.

They can also be used to do other things, such as keeping a list of products you've looked at on a website so that you can be shown more relevant adverts.

Some people consider cookies to be an invasion of privacy, but they can also be very useful. If you don't like them, you can delete them. Here's how:

1 Close down Internet Explorer and Outlook.

2 Click on the Start button.

3 Click on Control Panel.

4 Choose Internet Options.

5 Click on the General tab.

6 Click on the Delete Cookies button.

7 Click on OK.

8 Click OK again.

Dealing with individual cookies

Some cookies can be useful, so you may not want to delete all of them. To go through your cookies individually…

1 Click on the Start button on the desktop.

2 Click on Search.

3 Click on Files and folders.

4 Type in 'cookie'.

5 Click Search.

All the folders containing cookies on your system will appear in the search window. You can now open the folders and delete the cookies one by one. The file name of each cookie will tell you which website it belongs to.

6.6 Images

6.6.1 Hiding Images

Images take up more data than text. If you're downloading a web page that has many images, it will take longer to download than one comprised only of text.

If you've got a nippy connection, this won't really matter to you and will probably be barely noticeable. However, if your connection is a bit clunkier, or you want to really supercharge your surfing speeds, you can prevent images from appearing.

1 Click on the Tools menu.

2 Click on Internet Options.

3 Click on the Advanced tab.

4 Scroll down until you see the Multimedia options.

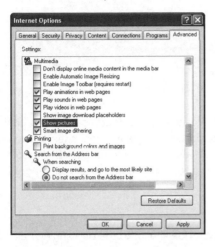

5 Remove the tick next to Show pictures.

6 Click OK.

Images will now appear as icons on any new sites you go to

Any pages that you have previously visited may still show pictures, as they are still stored in your computer's memory.

6.6.2 Seeing Images Temporarily

If a web page is not making sense without its images, you can turn them back on temporarily.

1 Right click on the picture you would like to see.

2 Click on Show Picture.

6.6.3 Switching Images Back On

1 Click on the Tools menu.

2 Click on Internet Options.

3 Click on the Advanced tab.

4 Scroll down to the Multimedia Options.

5 Click in the box next to Show pictures so that it is ticked.

6 Click OK.

Practise this!

Turn off images for web browsing and visit a few sites to see how it looks. Now turn the images back on.

6.7 Searching for Information

6.7.1 What are Search Engines?

Search engines are ordinary websites with huge databases hidden behind them. The databases contain information about web pages and websites on the WWW. If you wanted to find pages about monkeys, or cheese, you could use a search engine to find them, instead of trying to guess some bizarre, complicated address.

6.7.2 Using Search Engines

- All search engines have a search box similar to the one shown below.

	Search

- To find information, you click into the search box and type in keywords to describe what you are looking for. So, if you wanted to find information on Shakespeare's tragedies you might type something like this:

shakespeare tragedy	Search

- The search engine will then search its database looking for all the web pages which contain those two words.

- Any sites which have both of the words, or have a high occurrence of either of the words, will be listed near the top of your results. However, you may also get sites that have got the word 'tragedy' in them, but have nothing to do with Shakespeare, and nothing to do with drama either!

Saving search results

You can save any useful search results you find by simply storing the results page in your Favorites list.

6.7.3 How Many Search Engines are on the Web?

- There are hundreds of search engines on the Web, and they all have different sites in their database.

- Because they are all different, it is sometimes worth using more than one to find the information you are after. Alternatively, you can try using a meta-search engine. These run your search on several search engines at once, so you can get all your results from one site.

6.7.4 Some Common Search Engines

You can just type in the URL of a search engine to use it.

Often you will find that search engines give you predominantly American sites, so there is often a UK version which will let you search for UK sites.

Search engine name	Global version	UK version
Google	www.google.com	www.google.co.uk
Yahoo	www.yahoo.com	www.yahoo.co.uk
Excite	www.excite.com	www.excite.co.uk
Alta Vista	www.altavista.com	uk.altavista.com

6.7.5 Getting to a Search Engine

1 Click into the Address bar.

2 Type in the address of the search engine, e.g. www.google.co.uk.

3 Press Enter.

Or

Click on the Go button.

6.7.6 Searching for Words or Phrases

1 Go to the search engine page.

2 Type the words you want to search for into the Search box.

3 Click on the Search button to show a list of possible sites.

By kind permission of Google (www.google.co.uk)

4 Click on the website that you require.

Use phrases

To search for an exact phrase, put quotation marks around it. For example, if you wanted to find the phrase fish and chips, you would type in 'fish and chips'.

6.7.7 Advanced Searching

Most search engines allow you to use additional techniques to make your searches more specific. Different engines allow different techniques, but below are some of the most common.

- *Boolean searching*. This uses words (known as 'operators') to fine-tune your search.

  AND. Use this to connect two or more words, so they are all included in your search. For example, a search for 'punks AND daisies' will find sites that mention both. Using this operator is usually unnecessary as most search engines do this by default.

  OR. Use this to find sites that mention one or the other of your search terms. A search for 'football OR soccer' would find sites that include either of these words.

  NOT. Use this to eliminate words from a search. e.g. A search for 'camera NOT aztec' would find sites on photographic equipment, but ignore any that reference obscure 1980s' bands.

- *Using symbols*. You can get the same results by using symbols. Putting the plus symbol (+) before a word (with no gap) has the same effect as using AND. Using a minus symbol (–) instead has the same effect as using NOT.

- *Wildcard searches*. An asterisk (*) can be used on many search engines to represent additional characters. For example, searching for flower* will find words such as flowery and flowers, as well as the main search term flower.

  On Google, the asterisk is used in a different way, to represent missing words in a search term. For example, a search for 'famous * players' will find matches for phrases such as 'famous football players' and 'famous shove ha'penny players'.

Assessor's tip

Lynne says:

Everyone has their favourite search engine, so make sure you get to know yours really well. Look for a link on the search engine's home page that says 'advanced' or something like that. Click on there and you will find all the advanced features for that search engine, which you can then experiment with.

6.7.8 Working with the Results You Get

Once you've run a search, the search engine will display all the results it has found. The idea is that the top result is the most relevant – though things might not always work out that way.

Each result will be listed as a hyperlink, so you can click on it to go straight to the associated page. Underneath the hyperlink will be a brief explanation of the page, so you can decide whether it contains the information you are looking for.

If the results you've found don't seem particularly relevant, you might want to change the words you've included in your search, or you might want to try using the search engine's advanced features. Either way, you should be able to narrow down the type of results you are getting.

Practise this!

Use a search engine to find a website that has news on your company's industry.

6.8 Exchanging Information Online

6.8.1 Interactive Websites

The Internet isn't just about finding information. Most sites also offer some element of interactivity, such as shopping, adding your own content, downloading files, and so on. One of the most popular uses of the Internet is communication. Below we look at some common methods of communicating via your web browser.

6.8.2 Sending Webmail

You may already have an email account set up on your work computer, but you can also send email directly from your web browser.

There are many web-based email sites around and learning to use one is useful as evidence for proving you are competent at exchanging information online.

The example we are using here is Google Mail – a free webmail site set up by the popular search engine. You will find others work in a similar way.

6.8.3 Signing up for Google Mail

1 Open the Google Mail site (www.google.co.uk/mail) in your browser.

2 Click on the Sign Up for Google Mail link.

By kind permission of Google (www.google.co.uk)

3 Fill in the form with your details.

4 Click on the I accept. Create my account button.

5 Click on the I'm ready – show me my account link to get started.

6.8.4 Checking Your Google Mail Inbox

New emails that arrive in your account will be highlighted in bold. To read the message, simply click on the sender name or subject header.

6.8.5 Sending Email from Google Mail

By kind permission of Google (www.google.co.uk)

1 Click on the Compose Mail link at the top left of the screen.

2 Type the email addresses of the people you want to email into the To box.

3 Type a subject for the email into the Subject box.

4 Type the email text into the main box.

5 Click on the Send button.

Automatic address book

Google Mail automatically remembers the addresses of all the people you email. Next time you write an email, you just need to start typing their name and their email address will pop up on screen. Click on the address to use it, or carry on typing if you want to type a different address.

6.8.6　Viewing a Message Board

Message boards are a hugely popular method of communicating online. Any member of the message board can publish a message about a relevant subject on the board. Other users can then add their own replies. The result is a conversation that anyone can read and respond to. Below we look at the BBC's busy message boards.

1 Open the BBC message boards (www.bbc.co.uk/messageboards) site in your browser.

2 Click on the button for the type of message board you want to view.

3 Click on the message board name you're interested in.

4 Click on the title of the discussion you want to read (you can see how many replies each discussion has in the column next to its title).

Screenshot from BBC (www.bbc.co.uk)

Screenshot from BBC (www.bbc.co.uk)

6.8.7 Joining a Message Board

1 Open the BBC message boards (www.bbc.co.uk/messageboards) site in your browser.

2 Click on the type of message board you want to view.

3 Click on the message board name you're interested in.

4 Click on the Create your membership link.

5 Follow the step-by-step process to join up.

Screenshot from BBC (www.bbc.co.uk)

6.8.8 Posting on a Message Board

1 Open the BBC message boards (www.bbc.co.uk/messageboards) site in your browser.

2 Click on the type of message board you want to view.

3 Click on the message board name you're interested in.

4 Click on the Sign in button.

5 Type in your member name and password.

6 Click on the Sign In button.

7 Click on the Take me to the message board link.

8 You may now need to click on the message board link again, depending on which one you are viewing.

9 Click on the topic you would like to reply to.

10 Click on the Reply to this message button for the message you would like to respond to.

11 Type in your message, then click on the Post Message button.

Screenshot from BBC (www.bbc.co.uk)

Screenshot from BBC (www.bbc.co.uk)

Screenshot from BBC (www.bbc.co.uk)

Netiquette

When chatting online, many users try to be polite by sticking to some Net etiquette standards (netiquette). Check out Chapter 7 for a full explanation of netiquette.

6.9 Internet Security

6.9.1 Downloading Files

When downloading files and software from the Internet it is always a good idea to exercise a little caution. One of the most common ways of infecting your computer with a virus is by downloading a contaminated file. Such occurrences are fairly uncommon, but you can easily reduce your risk to practically nil by simply following a few guidelines.

■ Never download files from a site you are unsure of. If the site seems dodgy, or what it's offering is too good to be true, or if there's any other reason for you to feel a bit wary about it, you should forget it and look to download the file from a more reputable site.

■ Run a virus scan on any files you download before you open them. Even if you download an infected file, it can do nothing to your computer unless it is opened. Use anti-virus software to check over files to make sure they are clean.

■ Install security software. If you are connected to a broadband connection, a firewall is essential. Operating your computer without one is like leaving the keys in the ignition of your shiny, unlocked Mercedes. Someone is going to take advantage. Also make sure you have an up-to-date anti-virus program installed.

For more information on viruses, anti-virus software, firewalls and more, take a look at Chapter 5, IT Security for Users. In that chapter, you should also read the information on downloading software patches.

6.9.2 Supplying Details

You should also think twice when you are asked for information about yourself on the Internet. Con artists have a field day online as there are many people who are new to the Web who are unsure of how things work.

If you get an email from someone you don't know asking for your details, delete it. (Check Chapter 5, IT Security for Users, for more on dealing with spam emails.)

If you are shopping online, make sure the site you are using is secure before you supply your card details. This is easy to check. First, make sure the URL in the address bar starts with the letters https (rather than just http). The s at the end tells you the site is secure. Also look for a padlock in the status bar at the bottom of your browser screen.

Don't get phished!

Phishing is a fairly recent con trick which aims to get people to willingly hand over sensitive information, such as the log-in details for their online bank account. Criminals get hold of email addresses and then send authentic-looking messages that typically appear to have come from your bank or credit card company. The email will ask you to click on a link to a (fake) website, where you are asked for your log-in details. If you supply the details in this way, they are sent to the con artists who can then access your account.

The tricky part about phishing scams is that all the emails and fake websites look very authentic. What you need to remember is that reputable companies such as your bank will *never* ask you to supply your details in this way. If you are in any doubt, contact the company by telephone to double check.

The law online

There are a number of laws which apply to the use of the Internet and which you need to understand for this unit. For information on these, see the Laws and guidelines section of Chapter 5.

6.9.3 Browser Security Features

Your Internet browser also comes with a host of built-in security features that you can use to make your web surfing safer.

To access the security features on Internet Explorer:

1 Click on the Tools menu.

2 Click on Internet Options.

3 Click on the Security tab.

4 Click on the Internet icon.

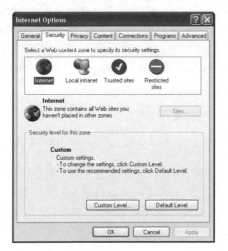

To make changes to your browser's security levels, click on the Custom Level button. The Security Settings dialog box now opens. Change the security settings by clicking on the relevant check boxes, then click OK twice to save the changes.

Security settings

There are lots of options you can change in the Security Settings box. What you need to change will depend on your own situation. Here are some you may find particularly useful.

- Automatic prompting for file downloads. Make sure this is set to enable so your browser will always check with you before it downloads a file. This ensures websites cannot load files onto your system without your knowledge.

- File download. This option can be disabled if you wish, making it impossible for anyone to download a file onto the computer from the Internet. This can be useful if you want to protect a computer that has multiple users.

- Installation of desktop items. This can be disabled, or you can ensure the browser always checks before installing an item on the desktop. Doing so ensures items cannot be loaded onto your desktop without your knowledge.

Resetting your security levels

If you find you have made mistakes when changing your security settings, you can quickly reset them to their default level. Open the Security tab of the Internet Options box as detailed above, then click on the Internet icon. Now click on the Default Level button, then click on Apply, then on OK.

6.10 Test Your Knowledge

The questions below will test what you know of the knowledge and understanding requirements of this unit. All the answers to these questions are contained or referred to within this chapter.

1 Why might you want to delete your browser's temporary Internet files?

2 How would you download an image from the Internet?

3 What would you use a search engine for?

4 Why should you be careful when downloading a file from the Internet?

5 What is phishing?

6 What is a firewall?

7 Which connection is likely to be the quickest: dial-up, ISDN or ADSL?

8 What is a cookie used for?

9 It is possible to set your browser so it does not display website images. True or false?

10 What is an intranet?

6.11 Evidence

The tasks you undertake as evidence for your ITQ should be work-related. Therefore, your supervisor at work should be able to give you guidance on the type of tasks you should take on. Below are some ideas of possible tasks for this unit. Consider how you can adapt these ideas to make them more relevant for your own workplace and to ensure you cover all the skills requirements.

- Create a document that describes a time when you had to search the Internet for information for a work project. Describe the information you had to find, how you decided where to look, what information you discovered and how you narrowed it down to what you needed. Make sure you use advanced search techniques such as phrase searching and Boolean searching. Include screenshots of the whole search process.

- Find a message board site that deals with a subject relevant to your work. Start a new topic on the site asking for help with some aspect of your job. Create a document that explains what you did, including screenshots of the whole process. Make sure you follow netiquette guidelines in your message board post.

- Set up your Favorites list so it includes a selection of sites useful to you at work. Create a document that explains how you did this, including screenshots showing how you did it.

- Customise your browser so it no longer displays images and the homepage is www.google.co.uk. Delete your temporary Internet files and any cookies that you don't want on your system. Create a document with screenshots of everything you did.

CHAPTER 7

Email

7.1 About This Unit

What you need to know

To gain ITQ Level 2 in this unit, you should demonstrate the following competency:
Use more advanced facilities to send and receive messages.
To achieve this you should know and understand:

1 More advanced email facilities.

2 Common problems with email and how to sort them out.

3 What laws and guidelines affect the use of IT and how they affect it.

You should also be able to display the following skills and techniques:

1 Sending and receiving emails using more advanced facilities.

2 Exchanging information by using appropriate methods.

3 Using address books and other facilities available.

4 Formatting emails in different modes.

How to prove your skills

You need to carry out at least two work-based tasks which demonstrate the skills and knowledge listed above. In order to show your competency, it may well be necessary for you to complete more tasks than this.

Make sure you have plenty of evidence that shows how you completed each task, such as a copy of the file you worked on, or a document with screenshots of the processes you followed. You can back this up by producing a report which shows your knowledge of the subjects covered within the unit.

7.2 Understanding Email

7.2.1 What is Email?

As well as using the Internet to look at websites and web pages, you can send and receive text messages called email. This is short for electronic mail.

Just like the Internet, you need a modem and an Internet Service Provider to use email. You either need email software (like Outlook, Outlook Express, Eudora, Thunderbird) or an Internet-based email account (like Google Mail, Yahoo or Hotmail), which lets you read and send mail through your Internet browser.

7.2.2 Advantages of Email

You're not limited to text messages in email – it is possible to attach files (like documents or pictures, for example) to send things to other people.

Email is fast, cheap, and if you use a web-based account you can read your email from any PC in the world.

7.2.3 Email Addresses

Email addresses are usually made up of four parts. Let's use fredbloggs@johnsons.co.uk as an example.

- The first part is usually the username, or full name of the user.
- The second part (johnsons) is either the company name, or the name of the ISP.
- Like internet addresses, the last two parts refer to the organisation type and country (co meaning commercial business, uk meaning United Kingdom). Also like Internet addresses, these can vary enormously.

7.2.4 What are Folders?

Folders are used to organise the messages you receive, send and save, and give you access to other components of Outlook. You can also create your own folders to store your messages.

7.2.5 Email Etiquette

- Emails are not letters, so keep things fairly short and to the point.
- Try not to type everything IN CAPITAL LETTERS, AS IT IS CONSIDERED SHOUTING! KEEP YOUR VOICE DOWN!
- Make sure you ask permission before sending someone an attachment, unless you know them well – they may not want it.
- Every email should have a subject line so that the person receiving it knows what it is about – and don't just put 'urgent' or 'important'. The subject line should relate to the content of the email.
- Spell check your emails before sending them.
- Never send an email in anger – it is far too easy to send off a quick reply when you're angry, and you could regret it later. Wait a day, and see how you feel then.

- Last, but not least – please, please, please write properly. You don't have to have perfect English, but saying things like 'plz snd files kthxbye' can be irritating to the other person. If you can't even be bothered to type the full word, why should they bother replying? On a similar note, putting thousands of exclamation marks after every sentence is really annoying!!!!!!!!!!!!!!!!!!!!!!! See???!!! And it makes your email look like Spam (see the next section).

7.3 Email Security

7.3.1 Spam

Sometimes you will get email from people you don't know. They'll offer you amazing deals, or free things. There will also be lots of capital letters and way, way too many exclamation marks, LIKE THIS!!!! FREE!!!!!!!! Usually, they'll be about extremely naughty things, and will involve naked people.

This is called spam (the email, not the naked people).

They don't always have your email address. Sometimes they guess email addresses, sometimes they get them from websites and sometimes they buy lists of customers.

Spam is any unsolicited email. Do not – ever! – reply to spam, or click the 'Unsubscribe' link. This will just tell the spammers that your address is real, and they will then deluge you with more.

It's called spam after the Monty Python sketch, where everything on the menu is served with SPAM (the luncheon meat made by Hormel Foods), and a song about the meat eventually drowns out all conversation.

One way of avoiding spam

If you want to avoid email spam you have several options:

- Have an alternative email address that you use to sign up to websites or request brochures etc.
- If your email address is listed on a website include something like: CatherineNOSPAM@hoppy.co.uk. Human people will know to ignore the 'No spam' but computer programmes looking for email addresses won't.
- Always tick the box that says 'No, I don't want to receive carefully selected promotions that may be of interest to me' when signing up to anything.
- Only give your email address to people and companies that you trust, otherwise think about using an alternative email address (such as Hotmail, Yahoo, Google Mail etc.) for these purposes.

Practise this!

Write a description of spam and what you should and shouldn't do about it.

7.3.2 Viruses

A virus is a nasty program written to waste your time or damage your PC. It may come in the form of a file attached to an email – never run or open any files that you are not expecting, even if they're from a friend. Check that the friend really sent them – they may be suffering from a virus too.

7.3.3 Virus Hoaxes

If someone emails you telling you to email everyone you know about a new, scary virus, or to delete a file from your PC, don't. Check a virus library first – never forward these hoaxes, that's what the hoaxer wants. Hoax virus alerts waste time and fill up mailboxes.

Assessor's tip

Sheena says:

To check out which viruses are genuine go to http://www.viruslibrary.com.

More on viruses

For more on viruses and how to avoid them, take a look at Section 5.3, Staying safe from threats, in Chapter 5.

7.3.4 Digital Signatures

A digital signature is a way of letting people know an email from you is really from you.

You can set them up in your email software, so that if anyone receives an email supposedly from you, they'll know that only the digitally signed ones are real.

7.4 Opening Outlook

7.4.1 Starting Outlook

1 Click on the Start button.

2 Click on All Programs.

3 Click on Microsoft Outlook.

Microsoft
Outlook

Or

From the desktop, double click on the Microsoft Outlook icon.

7.4.2 Closing Outlook

1 Click on the File menu.

2 Choose Exit.

Or

Click on the X on the top right of the title bar.

7.5 | Outlook Screen

7.5.1 The Outlook Screen

The Outlook screen looks different depending on which component you are in. The picture below shows the Inbox screen.

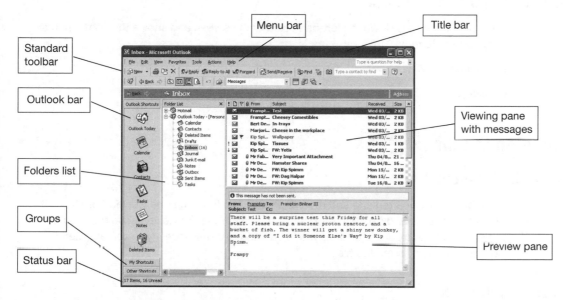

7.5.2 What are the Components of Outlook?

Outlook has several different components. Each component allows you to perform a different kind of task. This list below names the components and gives a brief description of what each one is for.

Outlook Today	This is an introductory screen to Outlook. It shows you any appointments or events booked in your calendar for the coming week. It also shows you any tasks you have set for yourself, and whether you have email messages waiting for you in your inbox.
Inbox	The Inbox stores the emails you receive.

Calendar	The Calendar allows you to book out times for appointments, or meetings, just like a normal diary. You can also use the calendar to schedule meetings with other people.
Contacts	This is just like an address book. It holds information about all the people you are in contact with.
Tasks	A bit like a to-do list. Use it to keep track of all the things you need to do.
Notes	Just like Post-It notes. You can stick them to your computer screen as a reminder.
Deleted Items	The same as the Recycle Bin in Windows. Use it to throw away any unwanted information.
Journal	This keeps track of all the programs and files you have opened in a day.

7.5.3 Displaying the Outlook Bar

The Outlook bar runs down the left-hand side of the screen and shows the components listed above. To turn it on or off:

1 Click on the View menu.

2 Click Outlook Bar.

7.6 Opening the Inbox

7.6.1 What is the Inbox?

The Inbox allows you to send and receive emails. The Inbox can be viewed from the Outlook Shortcut bar or the My Shortcuts bar. A list of the emails you have received is shown here. Outlook does not limit you to sending text messages, you can also send pictures and other formatted files.

7.6.2 Opening the Inbox

Inbox (15)

Click on the Inbox icon on the Outlook bar.

Or

Inbox (15) *Click on the Inbox in the folder list.*

7.7 Using Help in Outlook

Outlook comes with a Help feature which you can use to find answers to simple queries – see Section 3.3.1 of the Troubleshooting chapter for more details.

7.8 Creating a Message

7.8.1 Creating an Email

New ▾

1 Go to the Inbox (if you are not already there).

2 Click New.

3 Type in the address you wish to send the email to in the box next to To, e.g.
   fredbloggs@fishface.com.

7

4 If required, type in the address(es) you wish to send a copy to in the box next to Cc
   (**C**arbon **c**opy).

5 Type the subject in the box next to Subject.

6 Type your message in the white space underneath.

7.8.2 Blind Copy

If you want to send a copy of your email to someone, but don't want everybody else to know that they have been sent it, you can send a blind carbon copy (bcc).

1 Create a new message.

2 Click on the View menu.

3 Click Bcc Field – a new box will appear under the Cc box.

| Bcc... | |

4 Type in the address(es) next to the Bcc.

The Bcc field remains

You will still see the Bcc box for your future messages. To turn it off, click on the View menu and then click on Bcc Field.

7.8.3 Sending an Email

Send

Click Send.

The message goes to the Outbox if you *are not* connected to a network or the Internet. It is sent immediately if you *are* connected to a network or the Internet. Unless you are connected to a network or the Internet, your message will go to the Outbox and will sit there until you do connect. To send your message from the Outbox:

Send/Receive

Click on the Send/Receive icon.

7.8.4 Saving a Message

If you start to type a message, and then don't send it, you can save it in your Drafts folder.

Click on the Save icon – the message is saved in the Drafts folder.

To get back to your message:

1 Click on the View menu.

2 Click Folder List.

3 Click Drafts.

4 Double click on the message you require.

7.8.5 Flagging Mail Messages

You can indicate how urgent an email is by flagging it. A symbol will appear next to the message in the recipient's inbox, so they can prioritise their mail.

1 Create your message as normal.

2 Click on the Flag icon.

3 Click the drop-down arrow next to Flag to and choose the subject for the flag.

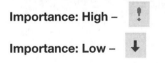

4 Click the drop-down arrow next to Due by and choose the response date for the email.

Or

Click Clear Flag to remove the flag.

5 Click OK – a flag message will appear above the email.

7.8.6 Making your Message Important

You can let people know that your message is important – it will be marked with a red exclamation mark in the Outlook inbox. Similarly, you can mark the message as not important, so that if they are busy they can safely leave it for a while.

1 Create the message as normal.

2 Click the Importance: High icon or the Importance: Low icon – the icon will appear 'pushed in' when you have clicked on it.

Importance: High –

Importance: Low –

They didn't read my important message!

Just because you have flagged a message as important, it doesn't mean that Outlook will force the other person to read it. Shockingly, many people will sometimes still ignore emails, no matter how many flags or red things you stick on them. If it's really, really important, it might be better to phone them or, better yet, meet them.

Emails and the law

Various laws cover the use of email, and you should understand these laws for this unit. For information on email and the law, take a look at the Laws and guidelines section of Chapter 5, IT security for users.

7.9 Formatting a Message

7.9.1 Changing the Format of your Email

Your email can be nice and simple: just text, no fuss. Or you can jazz it up with fonts and colours galore. There are three types of format in which you can send a message.

- Plain text – this is just as it sounds. This type of message can be read by anybody.
- Rich Text Format (RTF). This type of message can be formatted but can only be read by people with certain email software.
- HTML. This type of message can be formatted and read by most people.

To format your email you must set it to RTF or HTML.

7.9.2 Changing the Font

1 Position the cursor where you want to type.

   Or

   Select the text you wish to change.

2 Click the drop-down arrow on the Font box.

3 Click on the font you require.

7.9.3 Changing the Font Size

1 Position the cursor where you want to type.

   Or

   Select the text you wish to change.

2 Click the drop-down arrow on the Font Size box.

3 Click on the font size you require.

7.9.4 Changing the Font Colour

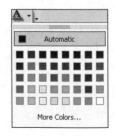

1 Position the cursor where you want to type.

   Or

   Select the text you wish to change.

2 Click the drop-down arrow on the Font Color box.

3 Click on the font colour you require.

7.9.5 Changing the Alignment of Text

Alignment determines whereabouts your text will line up on the page. There are four ways you can align your text:

- Align Left.
- Center.
- Align Right.
- Justify (fully justified text has straight edges at both sides).

1 Click into the paragraph you wish to change.

Or

Select several paragraphs.

2 Click on the icon you require.

You can change the alignment at any time!

For example, if you have made a piece of text justified, you can left align it by following the instructions above again!

7.9.6 Adding Bullets and Numbering

A bulleted list looks like this:

- A.
- Bulleted.
- List.

The following instructions are in a numbered list. To create a bulleted or numbered list:

1 Position your cursor where you would like to start the list.

Or

Select the text you would like to change.

2 Click Bullets or Numbers icon.

3 Type your first point.

4 Press Hard Return or the Enter key whenever you require a new number or bullet.

7.9.7 Spell Checking Messages

You can spell check any messages that you compose. Outlook comes with a spell checker which works in exactly the same way as the one in Word. See the Spelling and grammar section in Chapter 8, Word-processing software, for more details.

Note: To start the spell checker in Outlook, you must be in the message part of an email – the big white box at the bottom of the email. Then click on the Tools menu, and click on Spelling. If you are not in the message part, then the Spelling option will be greyed out.

7.10 Receiving Email

7.10.1 Receiving an Email

If you are connected to a network or the Internet, you do not have to do anything!

Your messages will just appear in your Inbox when they have arrived. As they are arriving, you should see a message at the bottom of the screen saying something like 'Receiving message 1 of 3'.

If you are not connected to the network or Internet, just click on the Send and Receive icon. When you click it, a box will appear:

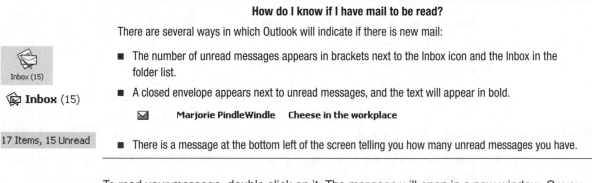

When this box disappears, Outlook has finished sending and receiving. If you don't have any new mail, then nobody has sent you any. Don't worry, I'm sure you'll get some soon.

7.10.2 Reading Mail

How do I know if I have mail to be read?

There are several ways in which Outlook will indicate if there is new mail:

Inbox (15)

Inbox (15)

17 Items, 15 Unread

- The number of unread messages appears in brackets next to the Inbox icon and the Inbox in the folder list.
- A closed envelope appears next to unread messages, and the text will appear in bold.

  ✉ **Marjorie PindleWindle   Cheese in the workplace**

- There is a message at the bottom left of the screen telling you how many unread messages you have.

To read your message, double click on it. The message will open in a new window. Or you can click once on the message, and it will appear in the preview pane.

Once a message has been read, the envelope will look as if it has been opened, and the text will no longer be in bold.

✉   Marjorie PindleWindle   Cheese in the workplace

7.10.3 Marking a Message as Unread

Once you have read a message you can make it look as though it still hasn't been read to draw your attention to it.

1 Click on the message in the Inbox, or select the messages you want to change (use the Shift or Control key to select multiple emails).

2 Click on the Edit menu.

3 Click on Mark as Unread.

Or

Click on Mark as Read to make it look as though you have read the email, without having to open it.

7.10.4 Closing an Email Message

1 Click the X on the title bar of the email message (not the one on the Outlook bar!).

Or

1 Click on the File menu of the email message (not the one in the main Outlook window).

2 Click on Close.

7.11 Forwarding and Replying to Email

7.11.1 Forwarding a Message

Sometimes you might want to send a message on to someone else – this is called forwarding.

1 Go to the Inbox.

2 Select the message you wish to forward.

🔄 Forward

3 Click Forward – a new message window will appear.

4 Enter the email address of the person you wish to forward the message to in the box next to To.

5 Enter any text in the message area.

6 Send the message as normal.

7.11.2 Replying to an Email

1 Select the message you want to reply to.

Reply

2 Click Reply – a new message window will appear.

3 The address will already be filled in, and the original text of the message will appear.

4 Type in your message.

5 Send the message as normal.

The sender gets their message again!

When you reply to a message, your reply will include the text from the original message. See the section after the next one to learn how to delete this text.

7.11.3 Replying to all the Recipients

If the message you are replying to was sent to more than one person originally, you can reply to all of them.

1 Select the message you want to reply to.

Reply to All

2 Click Reply to All – a new message window will appear.

3 The addresses will be filled in, and the original text of the message will appear.

4 Type in your new message.

5 Send the message as normal.

Assessor's tip

Georgie says:

Before using Reply All, make sure you really, really need all the recipients to see your email. Does everyone on the list need a copy of your reply if it just says something like 'me too', or 'haha!'? Make absolutely sure you know who you are replying to! Careers have been damaged and lost by careless use of the Reply and Reply All buttons.

7.11.4 Deleting Text

You may want to delete some text when you are forwarding or replying, if you do not want the whole of the original message to be included – particularly if the email has been replied to or forwarded several times.

1 Select the text you wish to delete.

2 Press the Delete or Del key on the keyboard.

7.11.5 Not Including the Original Message

It's often useful to include the original message, so that the person you are replying to knows what they said to you in the first place. However, you can turn this feature off.

1 Click on the Tools menu.

2 Click Options.

3 Click on the Preferences tab.

4 Click E-mail Options.

5 Click the drop-down arrow next to When replying to a message.

6 Click Do not include original message.

7 Click OK.

7.12 Sending and Receiving Attachments

An attachment is a file that you send with an email. The attachment can be any sort of file – a Word document, an Excel spreadsheet, a film, a picture, etc. It is an easy way of sending someone a file. Always check with them first, so they know it is coming, and don't send anything too large – 500K is usually the maximum.

7.12.1 Sending a Message with an Attachment

1 Create a new email as normal.

2 Click on the Insert menu.

3 Click on File.

4 Change the Look in box to the folder where the file you require is saved.

5 Click on the file you require.

6 Click Insert – the file will appear in an Attach box.

7 Click Send.

Someone isn't receiving my attachment!

Some companies may block attachments for security reasons. You can either resend the email to an Internet-based email account or get the recipient to check with their techies.

7.12.2 Receiving an Attachment

If your message has an attachment, you will see a paper clip symbol next to it in the Inbox.

    ** Mr Fabulous**   **Very Important Attachment**

To open the attachment:

1 Double click the email you wish to open.

2 Right click the attachment icon in the message.

3 To open the file, click Open.

or

Click Save As if you wish to save the file onto your computer before you open it.

Or

1 Ensure the preview pane is displayed.

2 Click on the email that contains the attachment you wish to open.

3 Right click on the file at the top of the preview pane.

4 To open the file, click Open.

Or

Click Save As if you wish to save the file onto your computer before you open it.

I can't find my attachment!

Try to remember where you saved your attachment; maybe have a folder called *attachments* for this. If you really can't remember where it is, try searching your computer's files and folders. And promise not to do it again.

I can't open my attachment!

If the attachment was created in a program which you do not have on your machine, you may not be able to open it. For example, if someone sends you a Word XP document and you have Word 6, you will not be able to open it. You must obtain the software, or ask the person who sent it to you to send it in a format which you can open.

Beware – Viruses!

Be careful with attachments! If you are not sure that your attachment is completely virus free, check for viruses before opening the attachment. Most virus checkers will allow you to right click the attachment and scan it with the virus-checking software. Do this even if it is from someone you trust – they could be infected without realising!

7.12.3 Deleting an Attachment from an Email before Sending

If you attach the wrong file, it is easy to delete it.

1 Click on the attachment icon in the email – it will become highlighted.

Attach... | Attached.doc (19 KB)

2 Press the Delete or Del key on the keyboard.

7.12.4 Deleting an Attachment from an Email in a Folder

You may want to delete an attachment from an email in your Inbox or another folder. For instance, this might be to save space if you no longer need the attachment, but want to keep the message. Or, you may have already saved the attachment somewhere on your computer.

1 Open the email with the attachment.

2 Right click on the attachment icon in the email.

3 Click Remove.

4 Click on the File menu.

5 Click Save.

6 Close the message.

7.12.5 Why Compress Your Attachments?

When you send a file of reasonable size, it's good practice to compress it. File compression is a way of squishing large files so that they take up less room. It's good for files which need to travel across the internet.

7.12.6 Compressing Your File Attachments

You will need a program such as WinZip to be able to do this.

1 Open My Computer or Windows Explorer.

2 Find the file you want to compress.

3 Right click on the file. The name of your compression software should appear in the menu.

4 Click on the name of your compression software, e.g. WinZip.

5 Click on Add to (your filename). Your compressed file will be added to the folder you are currently in.

7.12.7 Extracting Compressed File Attachments

When you receive a compressed attachment, you may be itching to read it but be patient, a little work is needed first.

1 Go to the email with the attachment.

2 Click once on the email to open it.

3 Click once on the link to the attachment.

4 Click Open.

What you see now will depend on whether you have a program called WinZip installed on your computer. If you do, carry on reading. If you don't, look at the bit called 'Non WinZip Users'.

7.12.7.1 WinZip users

1 Click once on the file.

2 Click Extract.

3 Choose a location to save the file.

4 Click Extract.

7.12.7.2 Non WinZip Users

1 Click once on the file.

2 Click Extract all files on the left-hand side. A wizard will open.

3 Click Next.

4 Click Browse.

5 Choose a location to save the file to.

6 Click OK.

7 Click Next.

8 Click Finish.

7.13 Using Instant Messaging

Instant messaging is like email, but you can chat to people in real time. You and the person you are chatting to need to be online at the same time. When you log on you will be able to see which contacts are online or offline. Below are instructions on using the popular Windows Live Messenger program.

7.13.1 Opening Windows Live Messenger

1 Double click on the Windows Live Messenger icon.

2 Enter your email address and password.

3 Click Sign in. A window with your list of contacts will appear.

7.13.2 Sending Instant Messages

1 Right click on the contact you want to chat to.

2 Select Send an instant message.

3 Write your message in the space at the bottom.

4 Click Send.

I can't send an instant message!

Check that the other person is online. If they are not online you may need to leave a message for them or send an email.

7.13.3 Receiving Instant Messages

If your chat partner replies, their message will appear in the window above. Each reply will keep appearing there until the world ends, or you stop chatting. Whichever happens sooner.

7.13.4 Sending Attachments with Instant Messaging

1 Click the Share Files icon.

2 Click Send a file or photo.

3 Double click the file you want to attach.

7.13.5 Receiving Attachments with Instant Messaging

You will see when a contact has sent you a file.

1 Double click the file to start the transfer.

2 Click OK only if you know that it is virus free, otherwise you will need to scan it.

3 The location of the file will appear in the window.

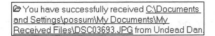

7.13.6 Closing Windows Live Messenger

To close the window and keep the program running 'behind the scenes', click on the X in the top right-hand corner.

To sign out of Windows Live Messenger completely:

1 Click the drop-down arrow next to your username.

2 Click Sign out.

3 Click the X in the top right-hand corner to close.

7.14 Organising Your Emails

The more emails you get, the more you will need to organise them. Delete old emails, and create folders to store emails of a similar type or from the same person.

7.14.1 Email Folders

Email is stored in several different folders within Outlook. The table below gives a brief description of what these folders do:

Inbox	Contains messages you have received
Drafts	Contains messages which you have written, but not yet sent
Outbox	Contains messages waiting to be sent over your network, or the Internet
Sent Items	Contains messages which you have sent

7.14.2 Displaying the Folder List

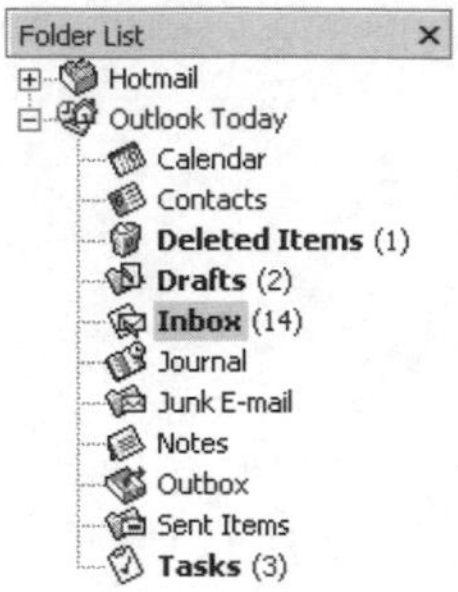

1 Click on the View menu.

2 Click Folder List.

Any folders shown in bold contain new messages.

7.14.3 Closing the Folder List

1 Click on the View menu.

2 Click Folder List.

Or

Click the X at the top right of the folder list.

7.14.4 Switching Between Folders

Click on the folder you require from the list – the contents are displayed on the right.

7.14.5 Creating Your Own Folders

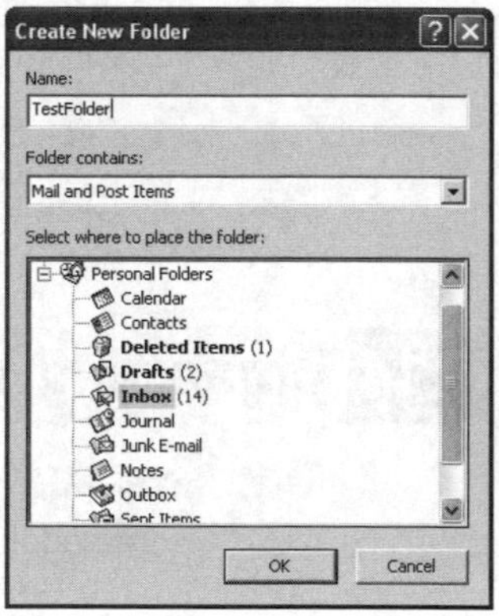

1 Click on the File menu.

2 Click New.

3 Click Folder.

4 Type a name for your folder into the Name box.

5 Click on the drop-down arrow underneath Folder contains, and choose what the folder will be used for – usually you can leave it set at Mail and Post Items.

6 Click on the folder which will hold the folder you are creating, e.g. Inbox.

7 Click OK.

8 You may be asked if you want to create a shortcut – click Yes if you wish a shortcut to appear on the Outlook Bar.

Practise this!

Create a new folder called Pending. Create a shortcut for this folder on the Outlook Bar.

7.14.6 Moving Emails to a Folder

1 Click on the email you wish to move.

2 Click on the Edit menu.

3   Click Move to Folder.

4   Click on the folder you want to move the email to.

5   Click OK.

Practise this!

Move an email that you have not already replied to, to your new Pending folder (see above). Move it back again.

Shortcut

If you want to select more than one message you don't need to move each one separately, you have two options:

1   To select multiple messages that are not next to each other hold down Ctrl as you click each one.

2   To select multiple messages that are next to each other, click on the first email, hold down the Shift key and then click on the last email. This way every message in between will also be selected.

7.14.7 Copying Emails to a Folder

1   Click on the email you want to copy.

2   Click on the Edit menu.

3   Click Copy to Folder.

4   Click on the folder you want to copy the email to.

5   Click OK.

7.14.8 Deleting Folders

1   Click on the folder you want to delete.

2   Click on the Edit menu.

3   Click on Delete.

4   Click Yes.

7.14.9 Sorting Emails

1   Go to the folder you wish to sort.

2   Click on the grey message headers (From, Subject, etc.) to sort the emails.

3   Click on them again to sort the emails the other way around.

From	Subject	Received	Size

7.15 Deleting Email

7.15.1 Deleting Emails

You can delete email from any of your folders.

1 Click on the email you wish to delete.

2 Press the Delete or Del key – the email is sent to the Deleted Items folder.

7.15.2 Deleted Items Folder

🗑 **Deleted Items** (1)   The Deleted Items folder stores all the messages that you have deleted. The number in brackets next to it indicates how many messages it contains.

7.16 Finding Messages

7.16.1 Finding Messages in your Inbox

🔍 Find

1 Go to the Inbox.

2 Click on the Find icon – a new pane will appear at the top of the Outlook screen.

| Look for: | ▾ | Search In ▾ | Inbox | Find Now Clear | Options ▾ ✕ |

3 Type in words to search for in the box next to Look for.

4 Click Find Now – any found messages are displayed.

5 Double click on a message to open it.

To start a new search, or to display all your messages again:

Click Clear.

Clear

To close the Find pane:

Click on the X at the top right of the Find box.

7.16.2 Advanced Searching

1 Click on the Tools menu.

2 Click on Advanced Find.

3 Click on the Messages tab.

4 Enter the words you wish to find in the box next to Search for the word(s).

5 Click the drop-down arrow next to In, and choose the area you wish to find the words in (subject, message body, etc.).

6 If required, click From to look for messages from particular people – double click their name, then click OK to come back to the Advanced Find box.

7 If required, click Sent By to look for messages sent by particular people – double click their name, then click OK to come back to the Advanced Find box.

8 Click Find Now – any found messages appear at the bottom.

9 Double click a message to open it.

Practise this!

Run a search in your inbox for all messages sent from your line manager.

7.16.3 Finding Messages Based on Time

1 Click on Inbox from the Outlook Bar.

2 Click on the Tools menu.

3 Click Advanced Find.

4 Click on the Messages tab.

5 Click the drop-down arrow next to the Time box.

6 Click the time you wish to search, e.g. received, sent, etc.

7 Click the drop-down arrow next to anytime.

8 Click on the specific time you wish to find, e.g. yesterday, today, etc.

9 Click Find Now – any found messages appear at the bottom.

10 Double click the message to open it.

7.16.4 Closing the Advanced Find Box

Click the X at the top right of the box.

Archiving your emails is a way of keeping old emails safe by moving them to another location, usually on your hard drive. It also helps spring clean your inbox, keeping just recent messages in there.

7.17.1 Archiving Email Folders

1 Click File.

2 Click Archive.

3 Click on the folder you wish to archive.

4 Click the down arrow next to 'Archive items older than'.

5 Click on the date you require.

6 Check the address underneath 'Archive File'. This is where your archived emails will be stored.

7 Click OK.

7.17.2 AutoArchiving Emails

If you would like Outlook to archive emails automatically, you can set up AutoArchive.

1 Click Tools.

2 Click Options.

3 Click Other tab.

4 Click AutoArchive.

5 Tick the boxes next to the options you require.

6 If required, click Browse to change the archive file.

7 Click OK.

7.18 Creating Contacts

7.18.1 What are Contacts?

Contacts contain information about the people and businesses you are in touch with. You can store all sorts of information about a person, such as

- Email address.
- Postal address.
- Phone number.
- Job title.

7.18.2 Getting to the Contacts

Click Contacts on the Outlook Bar.

Or

Contacts

Click Contacts in the folder list.

7.18.3 The Contacts Screen

- Contacts are shown in the big white area in the middle.
- Click a letter tab on the right-hand side of the screen to move to the contacts that start with that letter.

7.18.4 Creating a Contact

1 Go to the Contacts.

2 Click New.

3 Click on the General tab.

4 Fill in the information you require – make sure you add their email address, or the contact won't be much use in Outlook!

5 Click Save and Close.

Practise this!

Create a contact for John Higgle-Piggle. His email address is higglepjohn@pigglefarm.co.uk.

7.18.5 Creating a New Contact from an Email

When you receive an email, you can add the person who sent it to you as a new contact.

1 Open the email from the sender.

2 Right click on their email address with the right mouse button – a menu will appear.

3 Click Add to Contacts.

4 Enter any more details that you wish.

5 Click Save and Close.

7.18.6 Using the Contacts for Email

You can use the contacts to add the address quickly.

1 Create a new email.

2 Click the To button.

3 If necessary, click the drop-down arrow next to Show Names from the, and choose the address book you wish to use.

4 Click on the name you wish to use from the left-hand side.

5 Click To, Cc or Bcc – the name will appear on the right, in the relevant box.

6 Click OK.

7 Send the email as normal.

7.19 Editing and Deleting Contacts

7.19.1 Editing a Contact

1 Go to the Contacts.

2 Double click on the contact you wish to change.

3 Make any changes you require.

4 Click Save and Close.

7.19.2 Deleting a Contact

1 Go to the Contacts.

2 Click on the contact you wish to delete – it will go blue.

3 Press Delete.

Practise this!

Delete the contact for John Higgle-Piggle (see above).

7.20 Using Personal Distribution Lists

7.20.1 What is a Distribution List?

A distribution list allows you to group a set of email addresses together (e.g. all the people in the personnel department). When you want to write to everyone in that group, you can use the distribution list instead of typing out all the individual addresses.

7.20.2 Creating a Personal Distribution List with New Contacts

If you want to create a distribution list, but haven't already created the contacts:

1 Click on the File menu.

2 Click New.

3 Click Distribution List.

4 Type a name for your list into the Name box.

5 Click the Select Members button.

6 Select a contact to add.

7 Click Members.

8 Click OK.

9 Repeat steps 5 to 9 for everyone else you wish to add.

10 Click Save and Close.

7.20.3 Sending an Email using a Personal Distribution List

1 Create a new, blank email.

2 Click the To button.

3 Click on the distribution list you wish to use.

4 Click To or Cc.

5 Click OK.

All the addresses in the distribution list will be visible to the recipient

When a recipient receives a message using a distribution list, every name on the list appears in their message window. So the members of your distribution list cannot be kept secret from other members. Make sure they are happy with this.

7.20.4 Editing a Personal Distribution List

1 Go to the Contacts.

2 Double click the Distribution List you want to edit.

3 Select the person you want to remove.

4 Click Remove.

Or

Click Select Members to add a new member from your contacts.

5 Click Save and Close.

7.20.5 Deleting a Personal Distribution List

1 Go to the Contacts.

2 Select the Distribution List you want to delete.

3 Press the Delete or Del key.

7.21 Working with the Calendar

7.21.1 Introduction to Calendar

The Calendar allows you to book out times for appointments, or meetings, just like a normal diary. You can also use the calendar to schedule meetings with other people.

Click the Calendar icon on the Outlook Bar.

7.21.2 Changing the View

There are four main views to Calendar:

- **One day**: shows one day at a time on the screen.
- **Working Week**: shows five days at a time on the screen.
- **Week**: shows a week at a time on the screen.
- **Month**: shows a month at a time on the screen.

Click the view you require.

`[1] Day  [5] Work Week  [7] Week  [31] Month`

7.21.3 What are Appointments?

- **Appointments** are set for a specific time on a specific day, e.g. an interview, a lunch etc.

7.21.4 Scheduling Appointments

1 Click File.

2 Click New.

3 Click Appointment.

Subject:	
Location:	
Start time:	Tue 10/04/2007 ▼ 08:00 ▼ ☐ All day event
End time:	Tue 10/04/2007 ▼ 08:30 ▼

4 Type in the subject for the appointment next to 'Subject'.

5 Type in the location for the appointment next to 'Location'.

6 Enter the start date and time (see above).

Save and Close

7 Enter the end date and time (see above).

8 Click Save and Close.

7.22 Working with Tasks

7.22.1 What are Tasks?

Tasks are like a 'to-do' list which you can keep in Outlook. You can keep track of which tasks have been done, and you can also assign tasks to other people!

7.22.2 Creating Tasks

1 Click File.

2 Click New.

3 Click Task.

4 Type in a subject for the task, e.g. book train tickets.

5 Click the down arrow next to Due date, and click on the date the task must be completed by.

Save and Close

6 Click the down arrow next to Start date, and click on the date the task must be started.

7.23 Test Your Knowledge

The questions below will test what you know of the knowledge and understanding requirements of this unit. All the answers to these questions are contained or referred to within this chapter.

1 Name three ways you can avoid or reduce the amount of spam you receive in your inbox.

2 How could you send the same email to more than one person?

3 What does it mean to forward a message?

4 What is a virus?

5 What can you do to protect your computer against viruses?

6 Why would you compress an attachment?

7 Where could you seek advice if you didn't know what to do?

8 What extra facilities are provided with email software?

9 How would you schedule an appointment in a calendar?

10 Why can't some people receive attachments?

7.24 Evidence

The tasks you undertake as evidence for your ITQ should be work-related. Therefore, your supervisor at work should be able to give you guidance on the type of tasks you should take on. Below are some ideas of possible tasks for this unit. Consider how you can adapt these ideas to make them more relevant for your own workplace and to ensure you cover all the skills requirements.

- Send an email to your line manager with an attached document. Ensure that this attachment is compressed before sending.

- Using a distribution list that you have either created or that exists at your workplace, send an appropriate email to your colleagues. Adjust the message to high priority, if necessary, and make any formatting changes that need to be done.

- Carry out an archiving of your emails. Take a screenshot of your inbox before and after.

- Write a short report on how you would deal with spam and viruses when using email or instant messaging. Detail what you could do to avoid these things and how to deal with them when they arrive in your inbox.

CHAPTER 8

Word-processing Software

8.1 About This Unit

What you need to know

To gain ITQ Level 2 in this unit, you should display the following competency:

Use word-processing software effectively to produce professional-looking documents that communicate clearly and accurately.

To achieve this you should know:

1   How to produce information that is clear and appropriate.

2   How to produce professional-looking word-processing documents.

You should also be able to display the following skills and techniques:

1   Handling files appropriately.

2   Combining information of different types.

3   Editing text.

4   Formatting text.

5   Laying out and checking text to make documents look professional.

6   Improving efficiency through the use of shortcuts.

How to prove your skills

You need to carry out at least two work-based tasks which demonstrate the skills and knowledge listed above. In order to show your competency, it may well be necessary for you to complete more tasks than this.

Make sure you have plenty of evidence that shows how you completed each task, such as a copy of the file you worked on, or a document with screenshots of the processes you followed. You can back this up by producing a report which shows your knowledge of the subjects covered within the unit.

8.2 What is Word?

Word is a word processor. You can use it to type letters, write stories, pretty much anything you could do on a normal typewriter. The great thing about a word processor is that, unlike a typewriter, you can edit your words as you go along, copy sections, rearrange bits, and do all sorts of fancy things with the text. It is also much, much quieter than a typewriter.

Why am I creating this document?

With great power comes responsibility. When working on a document, make sure you know who you are writing it for and that the style and content are appropriate. Otherwise it will just look really silly.

Thinking about your work

Imagine your boss has asked you to make a list of tasks that needs to be completed this week. Below are the kinds of questions to ask to make sure you are creating the right kind of information:

1 Who will see the document?

2 How formal does it need to be?

3 Does it need to have colour or images?

4 Is there an existing structure or template that your boss would like you to use?

5 Will it be printed, emailed or viewed online?

6 Will anyone with any visual impairment need to use the information?

7 How much detail is necessary – just the key points?

8 When is the information needed?

8.3 Entering and Deleting Text

8.3.1 Typing Text

- When you start Word a blank document appears ready for you to start typing.

- A blinking vertical bar called the Insertion Point (or cursor) indicates where text will come out when you type.

- Unlike using a typewriter, you do not have to press the carriage return when you get to the end of the line. Word will automatically wrap the text onto the next line. If you want to finish a line and go to the next one, just press Enter or Return.

- You can delete text to the left or the right of the cursor.

- To type text, position your cursor where you would like to begin and just start typing!

8.3.2 Insert or Overtype?

- Normally when you type you will be in Insert mode. This means that if your cursor is in the middle of an existing sentence and you start typing, nothing will be deleted. The text that is already there will shuffle along to make way for the new text.

- If you are in Overtype mode, then any text you type will go over the top of existing text.

To change modes:

Press the Insert key on the keyboard.

Or

Double click the OVR mark on the status bar at the bottom of the screen.

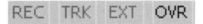

8.3.3 Creating a Space

Press the Space Bar at the bottom of the keyboard – it is the long, blank key between the Alt keys.

8.3.4 Creating a New Paragraph

1 Make sure your cursor is flashing where you would like a new line.

2 Press the Enter or Hard Return key (found on the right of the keyboard).

8.3.5 Adding Extra Text to What You Have Typed

1 Position your cursor where you would like to start typing.

2 Start typing!

My document is disappearing as I type!

Make sure you are in Insert mode. The rest of the text will shuffle along to make way for your new text.

8.3.6 Delete and Backspace

To get rid of text, use the Delete and Backspace keys.

1 Position your cursor next to the text you would like to get rid of.

2 Press Delete (or Del) if the text is to the right of the cursor.

Or

Press Backspace if the text is to the left of the cursor.

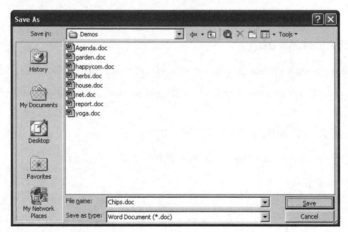

8.4 Saving, Closing, Opening and New

Saving a document creates a copy inside the computer that you can use again at a later date.

8.4.1 Saving a Document

1 Click on the File menu.

2 Click Save.

Or just click on the Save icon.

3 Type in your filename.

- You do not need to click into the Filename box if the name is highlighted in blue.

- You can have up to 255 letters.

- Ensure that your filename is relevant to the document.

4 Click the drop-down arrow in the Save in box.

5 Click the drive/folder you wish to save into.

6 Click on Save.

Or

Press Enter.

How do I know the document has been saved?

You should be able to see the filename you have given the document on the blue title bar at the top of the screen.

Word adds the extension .doc to the end of your filename

This is to distinguish the file as a Word document.

How do I change the filename?

Click into the Filename box and the existing filename should go blue. If you press Delete while it is blue, the filename will disappear, and you can type a new one.

If you cannot get the filename to go blue, just use Delete and Backspace to get rid of the existing filename.

8.4.2 Saving a Document Again After Changes

After you have saved the document for the first time, you must continue to save any changes you make to it. Word does not save your changes automatically.

1 Click on the File menu.

2 Click Save.

Or

Click on the Save icon – the changes will be saved.

Shortcut

Press Ctrl (Control) + S on the keyboard to save.

You will not be asked to enter a filename or specify the folder you wish to save in

You specified these things when you first saved the document, so Word will just save the document in the same place and with the same filename. If you want to change these things, you must use the Save As command from the File menu.

Save regularly!

As you are working on a document, get into the habit of clicking the Save icon every few minutes. This will update the document and protects it if your PC crashes.

8.4.3 Creating a Copy of a Document Using Save As

If you want to create a copy of your document with a different name or in a different folder, you can use Save As. Your original document will remain intact.

Save As is often used to create a copy onto a floppy disk. Floppy disks are very beneficial as a back-up because they can be stored separately from your main computer. They also allow you to take your work to a different computer, if you need to.

1 Click on the File menu.

2 Click Save As.

3 If required, type in a name for the document next to Filename.

4 Click on the drop-down arrow next to the Save in box.

5 Choose a location to save into.

6 Click on Save.

Or

Press Enter.

Word uses the last folder you saved into

When you first use Save As, the Save in box will show you the last folder you saved into. You may need to navigate to another folder, if necessary.

If I make changes, where will they be saved?

When you use Save As and type a different filename, you are creating a copy. If you make any changes, and then click on Save, only the version you are working on will change.

8.4.4 Closing Documents

Closing a document takes it off the screen and files it away inside the computer if it is to be saved, or gets rid of it if it is not to be saved.

1 Click on the File menu.

2 Click Close.

Or

Click on the lower X at the top right-hand side of the screen – the grey and black one, *not* the red and white one!

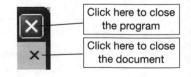

Click here to close the program

Click here to close the document

The screen has gone grey and I can't use the menus or toolbars

This means that you have closed all documents, which is a bit like having an empty desk. You can't use menus and toolbars because there is no piece of paper for the commands to be carried out on. Start a new document, or open one that you have already created.

Did you remember to save?

If you have made changes to a document and forgotten to save them, Word will prompt you and ask if you would like to save when you close. If you do not want to save, just click No.

8.4.5 Opening Documents

You can only open documents which you have saved previously.

1 Click on the File menu.

2 Click Open.

Or

Click on the Open icon.

If required, click the drop-down arrow next to the Look in box to change the folder Word is looking in.

Double click name of the file to be opened.

Or

Click name of the file to be opened.

Click Open.

8.4.6 Creating New Documents

1 Click on the File menu.

2 Click New.

3 Click Blank Document from the Task Pane on the right.

New

☐ Blank Document

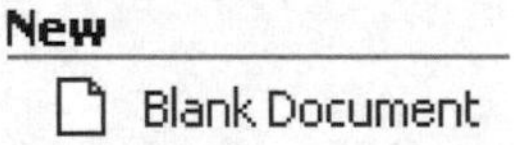

Or

Click on the New Document icon. ☐

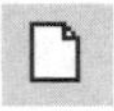

8.4.7 Creating New Documents Based on a Template

Templates give you a head start in creating documents. When you create a new document based on a template, some of the text will already be there and you just have to fill in the rest.

1 Click on the File menu.

2 Click New.

3 Click General Templates in the Task Pane on the right.

New from template

🗔 General Templates…

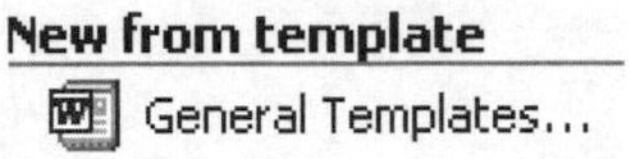

> **Templates**
>
> | Publications | Reports | Web Pages | Script Smart |
> | General | Legal Pleadings | Letters & Faxes | Mail Merge | Memos | Other Documents |
>
> Blank Document   Web Page
>
> **Preview**
>
> Preview not available.
>
> **Create New**
> ⊙ Document ○ Template
>
> OK   Cancel

4 Click on the tab you require, e.g. Letters & Faxes, General, etc.

5 Click on the template you wish to use, e.g. Blank Document.

6 Click OK.

8.5 Printing

To print a document once, just click on the Print icon. Yes, it's that simple.

Assessor's tip

Georgie says:

Be careful not to click the Print icon more than once!

Sometimes it can take a while for your document to reach the printer. If you click on the Print icon again you will get two copies. Some people get impatient and think it hasn't worked, so they click a million times – then they end up with a million copies.

8.5.1 Printing More Than One Copy

1 Click on the File menu.

2 Click on Print.

3 Change the number of copies to the number you require – click on the up or down arrows in the box next to Number of copies, or just click inside the box and type a new number.

> **Copies**
>
> Number of copies: [1]
>
> ☑ Collate

4 Click OK.

Shortcut!

Press Ctrl (Control) + P on the keyboard.

8.5.2 Printing the Current Page

1 Click on the File menu.

2 Click on Print.

3 Click in the circle next to Current Page.

4 Click OK.

> **Page range**
> ○ All
> ● Current page   ○ Selection
> ○ Pages: [   ]
>
> Enter page numbers and/or page ranges separated by commas. For example, 1,3,5–12

Current page means the page your cursor is on!

You must check that your cursor is on the page you wish to print out. If you have used the scroll bar to move somewhere else, what you see on the screen may not be the page the cursor is on!

8.5.3 Printing Certain Pages

1 Click on the File menu.

2 Click on Print.

3 Type in the pages you require into the Pages box (see below).

> **Page range**
> ○ All
> ○ Current page   ○ Selection
> ● Pages: [1,2,5-10]
>
> Enter page numbers and/or page ranges separated by commas. For example, 1,3,5–12

4 Click OK.

Individual pages can be separated by a comma, e.g. 1,2. If you are printing a range of pages, you can use a hyphen – for example, typing in 5-10 will print pages 5, 6, 7, 8, 9 and 10.

8.6 Changing the Look of Text

Changing the look of text is known as formatting. Formatting makes your documents look more professional and allows you to give emphasis to the important parts.

8.6.1 Applying Bold, Italic and Underline

1 Select the text to change.

2 Click on the icon you require (shown below).

If you want to remove bold, italics or underline, just select the text and click the relevant icon. If you want to remove the bold, just click on the Bold icon and so on.

Shortcut!

Press Ctrl + B, I or U on the keyboard for either **B**old, *I*talic or Underline.

8.6.2 What is a Font?

A font is the style of the letters in your document.

This font is Arial and has a size of 10 points.

This font is Arial, 16 points.

This font is Times New Roman, 10 points.

This font is Times New Roman, 16 points.

`This font is Courier New, 12 points.`

`This font is Courier New, 18 points.`

8.6.3 Which Font am I Using?

1 Position the cursor inside the text you wish to check.

2 Check the Font boxes on the Formatting toolbar.

In the picture below, the font face is Arial and the size is 10.

Arial   ▼   10   ▼

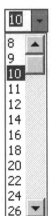

8.6.4 Changing the Font size

1 Select the text you wish to change.

2 Click on the drop-down arrow next to the Font Size box.

3 Click on the size you require – the bigger the number, the bigger the text.

8.6.5 Changing the Font

1 Select the text you wish to change.

2 Click on the drop-down arrow next to the Font box.

3 Click on the font you require.

Assessor's tip

Sheena says:

The font names are displayed in the actual font so that you can see what the font looks like before you apply it. If you want to switch this off (or switch it back on):

1 *Click on the Tools menu.*

2 *Click Customise.*

3 *Click the Options tab.*

4 *Add or remove a tick next to List font names in their font.*

5 *Click Close.*

8.7 Aligning Text

8.7.1 What is Alignment?

■ Alignment decides how your text will line up on the page.

> This is left aligned for normal text
>
> This is centre aligned for headings
>
> This is right aligned for dates
>
> and this piece of fully justified text that has straight edges at both sides. It looks very neat and tidy, doesn't it?

■ Alignment will change the whole paragraph that your cursor is in. Word thinks that paragraphs are where you have pressed Return, even if it is only a blank line.

8.7.2 Using the Icons

1 Click into the paragraph you wish to change.

Or

Select several paragraphs.

2 Click on the icon you require (shown below).

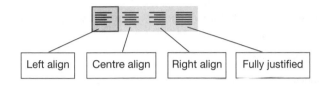

| Left align | Centre align | Right align | Fully justified |

You can change the alignment at any time!

For example, if you have made a piece of text justified, you can left align it by following the instructions above again!

8.8 Inserting Special Characters and Symbols

8.8.1 Inserting Symbols

Symbols can be particularly useful for foreign words and names containing accented letters that don't exist in English.

1 Position the cursor where you require the symbol.

2 Click on the Insert menu.

3 Click on Symbol.

4 Click on the Symbols tab.

5 Choose the font to use from the drop-down list next to Font.

6 Click on the symbol you want to insert.

7 Click on Insert.

8 Click on Close.

8.8.2 Inserting Special Characters

As well as providing special characters such as © or ™, this is also useful for different types of spaces between words.

1 Click on the Insert menu.

2 Click on Symbol.

3 Click on the Special Characters tab.

4 Choose the special character you require.

5 Click Insert.

6 Click Close.

8.9 Bullets and Numbering

8.9.1 Bulleted and Numbered Lists

Bulleted and numbered lists are basically just lists. Bulleted lists have little symbols or 'bullets' at the start of the lines, and numbered ones have – can you guess, boys and girls? – numbers.

■ This is.

■ A bulleted.

■ List.

1 And this is.

2 A numbered.

3 List.

Word will create these lists automatically for you.

8.9.2 Creating a Simple Bulleted or Numbered List

1 Position your cursor where you would like to start the list.

2 Click the Bullets or Numbers icon.

3 Type your first point.

4 Press Return whenever you require a new number or bullet.

8.9.3 Turning Bullets or Numbers Off

Press Return twice.

Or

1 Position your cursor in the paragraph where you do not require a bullet or number.

2 Click the Bullets or Numbers icon again.

8.9.4 Applying Bullets or Numbers to Existing Text

Word will put a number or a bullet wherever there is a paragraph.

1 Select the text to change.

2 Click the Bullets or Numbers icon.

Assessor's tip

Lynne says:

To add extra points in the middle of a numbered list:

1 *Place your cursor at the end of the point where you require the new point.*

2 *Press Return – Word will automatically renumber!*

8.9.5 Removing Bullets or Numbers

1 Select the text you wish to remove bullets or numbers from.

2 Click the Bullets or Numbers icon.

8.10 Customising Bullets

8.10.1 Changing the Style of Bullets

1 Select the text you want to change.

2 Click on the Format menu.

3 Click Bullets and Numbering.

4 Click on the Bulleted tab if you are not there already.

5 Click on the bullet style you require.

6 Click OK.

8.11 Customising Numbers

8.11.1 Changing the Number Style

1 Select the text you want to change.

2 Click on the Format menu.

3 Click Bullets and Numbering.

4 Click on the Numbered tab if you are not there already.

5 Click on the number style you require.

6 Click OK.

8.11.2 Continue and Restart Numbering

If your numbering does not work correctly and you find that you are getting the wrong number, you can choose to restart it again at 1 or continue a list that you were doing previously.

1 Click the cursor into the paragraph where you would like to restart or continue numbers.

2 Click on the Format menu.

3 Click Bullets and Numbering.

4 Click on the Numbered tab.

5 Click in the circle next to Restart numbering.

Or

Click in the circle next to Continue previous list.

8.12 Indenting Text

8.12.1 What are Indents?

This is a normal paragraph with no sort of indentation whatsoever. It is just straightforward and normal and not a single thing is special about it. Sad, really, isn't it?

> This is an indented paragraph. When I type, the text is indented from the left-hand margin, and when I get to the next line it remains indented.
>
> This paragraph is different again because it is indented from the left and also from the right.
>
> This paragraph has a first line indent. The first line is indented from the left and the rest of the paragraph has no indent.
>
> And finally here is a hanging indent, which we often use for numbers because the first line is normal, but the rest of the paragraph is indented slightly from the left-hand side. This means that if you had a numbered list, it would line up nicely. The moral of this story? It's good to be different.

You would use indents to give emphasis to a paragraph, for quotes or for creating numbered or bulleted lists manually.

8.12.2 Indents Affect Paragraphs

Word does not see paragraphs in quite the same way as you would expect. To Word, a paragraph is wherever you have pressed the Return key, so even blank lines are paragraphs.

8.12.3 Indenting a Paragraph from the Left

Position your cursor in the paragraph you want to change.

Or

Select the paragraphs you wish to change.

Click on the Increase Indent icon.

You can indent more than once

Every time you click the Increase Indent icon, the text is indented by half an inch more.

8.12.4 Removing the Left Indent from a Paragraph

1 Position your cursor in the paragraph you want to change.

Or

Select the paragraphs you wish to change.

2 Click on the Decrease Indent icon.

Look closely at the icons

They look very similar, so make sure you are clicking on the right one. You would expect the Increase Indent icon to be the first one, but it isn't – it's the second one. If you click the wrong one, just click Undo, or the other indent icon.

8.12.5 Understanding the Indent Markers

On the ruler you will see several grey triangles – an upper and lower one on the left, and a lower one on the right. These represent different indents.

- The top triangle lines up to the first line of the paragraph you are in.

- The bottom triangle lines up to the rest of the paragraph which you are in, i.e. anything but the first line.

- If the paragraph you are in is indented from the right-hand side as well as the left, the bottom triangle will be dragged in from the right-hand margin.

Assessor's tip

Sheena says:

Indent markers will change depending on which paragraph your cursor is in.
If your document has paragraphs with different indents, you must click into the paragraph you require to see the indents it contains.

8.12.6 Indent Markers in Action

So I says to Mabel, I says, Mabel – what do you think you're doing, putting the chips on the bean shelf? So she says to me, she says, Bernie, she says, there's no room on the chip shelf, I've got to put the chips on the bean shelf.

Of course, once she'd pointed out the space difficulties on the chip shelf, I was forced to agree with her. Mabel, I says to her, your powers of observation and bean/chip shelf management are beyond reproach.

But it was too late. The damage was done. Mabel never spoke to me of beans, or chips, ever again. The days stretched out into winter, and our conversations, while enjoyable, were never quite as sparkling as they were during the halcyon chip and bean days.

Look at the example above. The cursor is positioned in the middle paragraph, so it is the indents for that paragraph that show on the ruler.

8.12.7 Changing Indents with the Ruler

1 Position your cursor in the paragraph to change.

Or

Select the paragraphs to change.

2 Click and drag the indent marker you require (see below).

- Drag the top left triangle to move the first line of the paragraph.

- Drag the bottom left triangle to move the rest of the paragraph.

- Drag the square to move the rest of the paragraph and the first line together.

- Drag the bottom right indent marker to indent the right-hand side of the paragraph.

Set the indents *after* the paragraphs are typed!

Otherwise the indents you set will affect everything you type afterwards and you will have to change them back again.

8.13 Borders and Shading

Sometimes you might want to add a bit of colour to a paragraph or maybe a nice border, and there's absolutely nothing wrong with that, in this enlightened day and age. Let's have a look at how to do it.

8.13.1 Adding Shading to Paragraphs

1 Select the text you want to change.

2 Click on the Format menu.

3 Click Borders and Shading.

4 Click on the Shading tab.

5 Click on the colour you require.

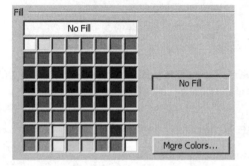

6 Click OK.

If the colour you require is not available

1 Click on the More Colors button.

More Colors...

2 Click on the Standard tab.

3 Click on the colour you require.

4 Click OK.

5 Click OK.

What is the shading being applied to?

Check the Apply to box:

Apply to:

Paragraph

This whole paragraph is shaded.

Isn't it?

Only this text is shaded, but not the paragraph.

8.13.2 Removing Shading

1 Select the text you wish to remove shading from.

2 Click on the Format menu.

3 Click Borders and Shading.

4 Click on the Shading tab.

5 Click No Fill.

6 Click OK.

8.13.3 Applying Borders to Paragraphs

1 Select text to apply borders to.

2 Click on the Format menu.

3 Click Borders and Shading.

4 Click on the Borders tab.

- The Box, Shadow and 3D settings give you a border all the way around your selection.

- With the Custom setting, you do not have to have a border all the way around – for example, you can choose just to have a top and bottom border.

- The Preview box shows you what your borders will look like.

- Click on the border buttons (in and around the Preview box) to specify which borders you require.

5 Choose the setting you require from the left-hand side (under Setting).

6 If required, choose a different style from the list underneath Style.

7 If required, click on the down arrow underneath Color and choose a different colour for your border.

8 If required, click on the down arrow underneath Width and change the width of your border.

9 If you have chosen Custom settings, click the Borders buttons (in and around the Preview box) to add selected borders.

10 Click OK.

My styles aren't working

- If you can't change the width of the border, you have probably chosen a style which has only one width.

- You can't apply a 3D or Shadow setting unless your border goes all the way around the selection.

- Some styles will not allow you to have a 3D or Shadow setting.

8.13.4 Removing Borders

1 Select the text you wish to remove the borders from.

2 Click on the Format menu.

3 Click Borders and Shading.

4 Click on the Borders tab.

5 In the Setting area, click on the None box.

6 Click OK.

8.14 Styles

A style is a collection of formats which you can apply to your text. For example all your main headings could be in Arial, Bold, 16 point and centred. Taken together these formats would be your Heading 1 Style.

8.14.1 Why use Styles?

Styles make working with Word a lot easier. Once you have mastered them you can:

- Format your documents quickly and consistently.

- Change the formatting in your documents quickly and consistently.

- Use the styles you create in other documents and templates.

- Create a Table of Contents.

- Use Outline View to work with long documents.

8.14.2 Which Style is My Text in?

1 Position your cursor in the text you wish to check.

2 Look at the Style box on the formatting toolbar – in the example shown below, the selected text is in the Normal style.

Normal ▾

8.14.3 The Styles and Formatting Task Pane

You can use the Styles and Formatting Task Pane to create and use styles more easily. It will show you what styles you have, which are applied, and you can rename or apply them quickly. To display the Styles and Formatting Task Pane:

1 Click on the Format menu.

2 Click on Styles and Formatting.

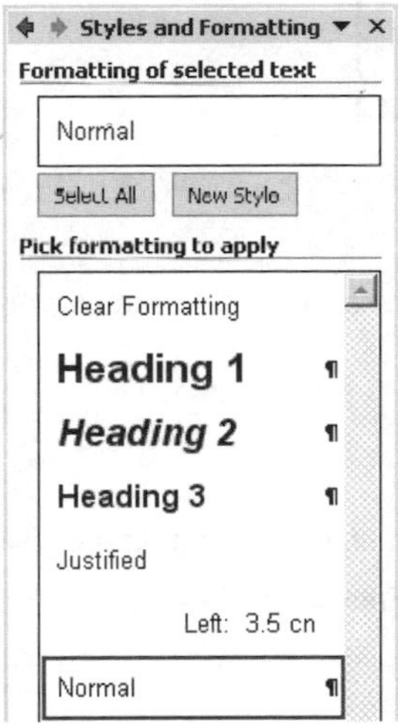

8.14.4 Applying an Existing Style

1 Position your cursor in the paragraph you wish to change.

Or

Select the text you wish to change.

2 Click on the drop-down arrow next to the Style box.

3 Click on the style you require.

Or

1 Select the text you wish to change.

2 Display the Styles and Formatting Task Pane.

3 Click on the style you require.

8.15 Page Numbering

Page numbers are a good thing. They tell you what page you are on, and might prevent athlete's foot (though it's not likely). What page are you on now? See? If this book didn't have page numbers, you'd have been completely stumped.

8.15.1 Page Numbering with the Menu

1 Click on the Insert menu.

2 Click Page Numbers.

3 Click the drop-down arrow under Position and choose where you would like to put your page numbers.

4 Click the down arrow underneath Alignment and choose the alignment for your page numbers.

5 Click OK.

You can only see your page numbers in Print Layout view

So don't panic if you can't see them! To change to Print Layout View:

1 Click the View menu.
2 Click Print Layout.

8.15.2 Deleting Page Numbering

1 Double click on any page number – you will be taken into the Header and Footer view.

2 Click on top of the number – diagonal lines should appear.

3 Click on top of the diagonal lines – black boxes should appear.

4 Press the Delete key on the keyboard.

Once you have deleted one page number, all the others will be deleted as well!

8.16 Improving Efficiency

Improving efficiency is great!

It means you can get your work done in half the time and spend the rest of the day with your feet up.

8.16.1 Common Shortcuts

There are a few shortcuts already set up for you. They cover those well-loved tasks that you frequently use such as open, close, save.

- Ctrl + O   Open
- Ctrl + S   Save
- Ctrl + W   Close
- Ctrl + B   Bold
- Ctrl + I   Italic
- Ctrl + U   Underline
- Ctrl + X   Cut
- Ctrl + C   Copy
- Ctrl + V   Paste

8.16.2 Setting up Shortcuts

If there's something that you find yourself doing a lot of, it can get pretty frustrating going through the menus each time. The solution? Set up your own shortcuts: whatever action you like, whichever key combination you like plus your favourite topping.

1 Click the Tools Menu.

2 Click Customize.

3 Click Keyboard.

Keyboard...

Customize Keyboard dialog box will appear.

4 Click on a Category from the list on the left.

5 Click on a Command from the list on the right.

Any existing shortcuts will appear in the Current keys box.

Customize Keyboard

Specify a command

Categories:
- File
- Edit
- View
- Insert
- Format
- Tools
- Table

Commands:
- AnnotationEdit
- AutoText
- BrowseNext
- BrowsePrev
- ClearFormField
- ContinueNumbering
- CopyFormat

Specify keyboard sequence

Current keys:
Ctrl+Shift+C

Press new shortcut key:
Ctrl+J

Currently assigned to: JustifyPara

Save changes in: Normal.dot

Description

Copies the formatting of the selection to a specified location

Assign   Remove   Reset All...   Close

To set up a new shortcut:

1 Click in the Press new shortcut key box.

2 Press your new shortcut, e.g. Ctrl + J.

Your new shortcut will appear in the box.

3 Click on Assign.

4 Click Close.

Assessor's tip

Georgie says:

Try not to assign commonly used shortcuts. It will avoid great hair pulling and exasperation in the future when you try to print and can't work out why your document keeps closing! Be inventive: you can use Ctrl + key, Alt + Key or Ctrl + Alt + Key (for those with long fingers).

8.17 Moving and Copying Text

Sometimes you might want to move a piece of text somewhere else or copy another piece of text to save yourself from having to type it out again. Word uses the Windows Clipboard to help you do this, which is a special area where copied and cut text goes to. Let's have a look at what this means.

8.17.1 Moving Text

1 Select the text you would like to move.

2 Click on the Cut icon – the text is moved to the Windows Clipboard.

3 Position the cursor in the place you would like to move the text to.

4 Click on the Paste icon.

8.17.2 Copying Text

1 Select the text you would like to copy.

2 Click on Copy icon – the text is copied to the Windows Clipboard.

3 Position the cursor in the place you would like to copy the text to.

4 Click on the Paste icon.

The cut or copied text remains on the clipboard

If you click Paste more than once, whatever was last cut or copied will appear again.

8.17.3 Switching Between Documents

1 Click on the Window menu to display a list of open documents.

2 Click on the document you require.

Or

Press Ctrl and F6 to cycle through the open documents.

Or

Click on the button for that document on the Taskbar.

8.17.4 Copying Text Between Documents

1 Open the document you are copying from.

2 Open the document you are copying to – they will appear as icons on the taskbar.

3 Select the text you would like to copy.

4 Click on Copy.

5 Click on the document you would like to copy to on the taskbar.

6 Position the cursor where you would like to copy to.

7 Click on Paste.

8.17.5 Copying and Moving Objects

You can copy and move objects – pictures, drawings, charts, and so on – in the same way as you do with text. The Office Clipboard can be used in the same way.

8.18 Page Breaks

A page break forces Word to end the current page and start a new one. This is useful if you need to start a new page without filling up the page you are on. Sometimes people press Return lots of times to create blank lines to get onto the next page, but this is A Very Bad Thing. If you add text to the page later on, it will push all those blank lines further down, and the next page will have a big gap at the top. The document will look bad, and everyone will laugh at you.

8.18.1 Creating a Page Break

1 Position the cursor where you would like a page break.

2 Press Ctrl and Enter.

Or

1 Click on the Insert menu.

2 Click Break.

3 Click the circle next to Page Break.

4 Click OK.

8.18.2 Deleting a Page Break

1 Make sure you are in Normal view.

2 Position your cursor on the page break.

··Page Break··

3 Press the Delete or Del key.

8.19.1 Margins

Margins are the gaps between your text and the edge of the page. There are four margins on your page: top, bottom, left and right. Word usually determines their size automatically, but you may want to change them. Here are some of the reasons why.

- If you increase the size of the margins you create more white space on the page. This makes your document more legible and also provides room for people to make notes.

- You may have a document which has only one or two lines on the last page. If you decrease the size of the margins, you create more space for text in the document, and the lines may fit back onto the previous page.

8.19.2 Changing the Margins with the Menu

1 Click on the File menu.

2 Click Page Setup.

3 Change the margins as required.

8

- In the box next to Top, Bottom, Left or Right, use the up or down arrows or type in the size of your new margin.

- If necessary, change the Gutter margin to make room for binding – if you are not sure about this, just ignore it.

- Tick Mirror margins if you are printing on both sides of the paper – again, if you are not sure if you need this, just leave it unticked.

- A preview of your margins is shown on the right-hand side of the box.

- Under the preview, look at the box marked Apply to – you can change the margins for the whole document, just the section you are currently in or from that point forward.

4 Click OK.

8.19.3 Changing the Paper Size

1 Click on the File menu.

2 Click Page Setup.

3 Click on the Paper tab.

4 Click on the drop-down arrow underneath Paper size.

5 Click on the paper size you require, e.g. A4.

6 Click OK.

8.20 Line Spacing

Line spacing refers to the spacing between lines, funnily enough. Normally, single line spacing is fine, but sometimes you might want to space text out a bit to make it easier to read.

This is single (1) line spacing	This is 1.5 line spacing	This is double line spacing

8.20.1 Changing the Line Spacing

1 Position your cursor in the paragraph you wish to change.

Or

Select several paragraphs.

Or

Press Ctrl and A to select the whole document.

2 Click on the Format menu.

3 Click Paragraph.

4 Click on the Line spacing drop-down arrow to choose the spacing you require.

Line spacing: At:
Single

5 Click OK.

Or

Click on the drop-down arrow by the Line Spacing icon and choose one of the spacing options.

8.20.2 Changing the Spacing Around Paragraphs

1 Position your cursor in the paragraph you wish to change.

Or

Select several paragraphs.

Or

Press Ctrl and A to select the whole document.

2 Click Format.

3 Click Paragraph.

4 Change the options as required in the Spacing section.

Spacing
Before: 0 pt
After: 0 pt

- In the Before box, use the up and down arrows or click inside the box and type the amount of space you require before the paragraph.

- In the After box, use the up and down arrows or click inside the box and type the amount of space you require after the paragraph.

5 Click OK.

8.21 Headers and Footers

Headers and footers appear at the top and bottom of every page. They are usually used to display information such as page numbers, the title of the document, the date, the filename and path, the author's name, etc. If you have something that you want to appear on every page, then the header or footer is the place to put it.

8.21.1 Going into the Header and Footer Area

1 Click on the View menu.

2 Click on Header and Footer.

3 Position your cursor in the dotted area.

4 Start typing! What you type will appear on every page of the document.

Or, if you are getting back to Headers and Footers which you have already created,

Double click on the header or footer area on any page.

When you are in the Header or Footer, the Header and Footer Toolbar will appear.

8.21.2 Using Headers and Footers

If you want to move to the middle of the header/footer, press the Tab key. Press it again to move to the right-hand side. If you are on the header and want to go to the footer (or vice versa), click on the imaginatively named Switch Between Header and Footer icon, which is on the Header and Footer toolbar.

8.21.3 Inserting Items

Position your cursor where you want to insert something.

- If you want to insert the date or time, click on the Insert Date icon or the Insert Time icon.

- If you want to insert the page number, click on the Insert Page Number icon.

- To insert the number of pages, click on the Insert Number of Pages icon.

- To add the author, page number and date all in one go, place your cursor at the left of the header or footer, click on the Insert AutoText icon on the Header and Footer toolbar, then click on Author, Page #, Date.

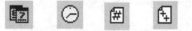

8.21.4 Closing the Header and Footer View

Click Close on the Header and Footer toolbar.

Choose the correct view

You will only see your headers and footers if you are in Print Layout view.

Have you ever tried to line up text using the space bar? It may look nice and neat on the screen, but when you print, you'll find that it doesn't line up at all. Instead you should use tabs. There are invisible markers across the page called tab stops. When you press the tab key, your cursor jumps to the next available tab stop. You can then line up text to these tab stops.

You would use tabs:

- For lining up text on the page.

- For creating neat columns of text or numbers.

If you want to see tabs, have a look on the ruler – tabs are indicated by small black symbols:

Left	Centre	Right	Decimal
Text	Text	Text	Text
Words	Words	Words	Words
100.5	100.5	100.5	100.5
12.50	12.50	12.50	12.50
£1,343.54	£1,343.54	£1,343.54	£1,343.54

8.22.1 Types of Tabs

 Left tab (the start of the text will line up to the tab stop).

Centre tab (text will line up around the centre of the tab stop).

Right Tab (the end of the text will line up to the tab stop).

Decimal tab (the decimal point in figures will line up to the tab stop).

8.22.2 Lining Up Text with Tabs

Press the Tab key, and the cursor will jump to the next tab stop.

8.22.3 Moving Tabs with the Ruler

1 Select all the paragraphs that are affected by this tab.

2 Position your mouse on the tab mark at the bottom of the ruler.

3 Click and drag it to the new position.

8.22.4 Removing Tabs with the Ruler

1 Select all the paragraphs you wish to remove this tab from.

2 Click on the tab mark at the bottom of the ruler.

3 Drag down off the ruler.

8.22.5 Removing Tabs using the Menu

1 Click on the Format menu.

2 Click Tabs.

3 Click on the tab position to be deleted.

4 Click Clear.

5 Click OK.

8.23 Spelling and Grammar

Nobody's perfect – even the best of us makes the odd spelling mistake now and again. Luckily, we can get Word to check the spelling of our documents for us.

1 Click on the Spell Check icon.

- A word highlighted in red inside the white box at the top indicates a misspelling – just above this, Word says what it thinks is wrong (e.g. Not in Dictionary).

- A word or sentence highlighted in green at the top indicates a grammatical error.

- In the Suggestions box, Word offers you some words to choose from that might be correct.

- On the right-hand side, there are buttons that let you change the spelling, ignore the word, and so on – see the next page for more on these.

2 Click on the appropriate icon on the right-hand side.

3 Click Cancel to finish the spell check early.

Or

Click OK once the spell check is complete.

Word is not perfect!

Don't just casually let Word change whatever it likes – keep an eye on it, otherwise it will try to change someone's name, use American spellings, or mess up all your grammar.

Don't skip this bit!

No matter how confident you are in your typing abilities, checking your work is a must. Otherwise your readers could end up reading gobbledygook.

8.23.1 How to Correct Your Mistakes with the Spell Check Buttons

8.23.1.1 Spelling corrections

If the word is spelt correctly	*Click on Ignore Once*
If the word is spelt correctly and occurs several times in the document	*Click on Ignore All*
If the word is spelt correctly and is a word that you use very commonly, e.g. your name	*Click on Add to Dictionary* *This will add the word to the dictionary so that it is never seen as a misspelling again*
If the correct spelling is listed in the Suggestions box	*1 Click on the correct suggestion* *2 Click on Change*

If the correct spelling is listed in the Suggestions box and the mis-spelling occurs commonly in the document	1 *Click on the correct suggestion* 2 *Click on Change All*
If the word is spelt incorrectly and the correct suggestion is not listed	1 *Click into the white box containing the text* 2 *Make the correction manually* 3 *Click on Change*

8.23.1.2 Grammar corrections

If there is no grammatical error	*Click on Ignore Once*
If there is no grammatical error and similar sentences appear in the rest of your document	*Click on Ignore Rule*
If the correct grammar appears in the Suggestions box	1 *Highlight the correct suggestion* 2 *Click on Change*
If the grammar is incorrect, but the correct suggestion does not appear	1 *Click into the white box containing the text* 2 *Make the correction manually* 3 *Click on Change*

Quick spelling and grammar check

When you are typing the document, sometimes you will see that Word has put red or green squiggly lines under some of the words. Right click any of these words and a shortcut menu of suggested corrections will appear.

If you have the American dictionary

Try clicking on Tools, Language, Set Language, English (UK), OK.

8.24 Go To, Find and Replace

It's fairly easy to work out what these three tools do, but I'm going to explain them anyway. Go To lets you go to a page or section. Find lets you find text. Replace lets you replace text. It's as simple as that, really.

8.24.1 Going to a Page

1 Press Ctrl and G to make the Go To box appear.

2 Type in the page number you require in the box underneath Enter page number.

3 Click the Go To button – Word will move to the top of the page you typed in.

4 Click Close.

Closing the Go To box

The Go To box does not disappear once it has gone to the correct page. You must close it by clicking on the Close button.

8.24.2 Finding Text

1 Click on the Edit menu.

2 Click on Find.

3 Type in the word you require in the box next to Find what.

4 Click on the Find Next button – Word will highlight the first occurrence of the word in the background.

5 Click on Find Next again – Word will highlight the second occurrence in the background etc.

When Word has found all occurrences it will display the message 'Word has finished searching the document'.

Microsoft Word

Word has finished searching the document.

OK

6 Click OK.

7 Click on Cancel to close the dialog box.

8.24.3 Replacing Text

1 Click on the Edit menu.

2 Click on Replace.

Find and Replace

Find | Replace | Go To

Find what: dog

Replace with: cat

More ∓ | Replace | Replace All | Find Next | Cancel

3 Type the word you wish to replace in the box next to Find what.

4 Type the word you wish to replace it with in the box next to Replace with.

5 Click on Replace All to replace all occurrences at once.

or

Click on Replace to replace the first occurrence.

Click on Replace again to replace the second occurrence etc.

When Word has finished it will display a message saying that it has completed its search, and tells you how many replacements it has made.

6 Click OK.

7 Click Cancel to close the dialog box.

8.25 Proofing

8.25.1 Proofing Your Document

Before you print your document, or even show it to anyone, it is a good idea to check over it. Make sure it is readable, laid out correctly and will print properly. Some things to look out for are:

- Fonts – are the fonts a reasonable size? Is one line much bigger than the next one? Are any lines too small to read easily?

- Margins – margins should be about 2.5 cm (1 inch) on each side. Too much, and you won't fit much text in; too little, and it might not all get printed properly.

- Spelling and grammar – make sure there are no spelling or grammar mistakes.

Make it look good!

A final check is crucial to make sure that your document looks good, reads well and communicates effectively. If you do this, your boss will love you and you will become rich and famous. Really.

Assessor's tip

Rudy says:

Try reading aloud when you check your document, you'll be surprised how often what is actually written is not quite the same as what you think has been written! You can also try reading through your document backwards – although it sounds strange, it's a really good way to spot errors.

Practise this!

Look at the following text and see how many errors you can spot, using the above techniques:

I work for Great Hairstyling ltd,it is a Conpany that has over 35 people working there. I have worked here for about five years and my role is creative styleist.

We are try to increase our number of of customer's this year by avertising to local buisnesses. This is proving be quite successful and I will be invoved in analysing, the data to plan for the next year.

8.26 Creating and Editing Tables

Tables are little boxes divided up into smaller boxes that help you to arrange text in a certain way. They look something like this:

Tables	Let	You
Line	Up	Things

8.26.1 Creating a Table with the Icon

1 Position the cursor where you would like the table to be.

2 Click on the Table icon, and hold down the mouse button – a set of boxes will appear just under the icon.

3 Still holding the mouse button down, click and drag over the number of columns and rows you require.

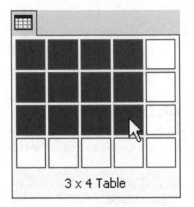

3 x 4 Table

4 Once you have the size you require, release the mouse button.

8.26.2 Creating a Table with the Menu

This is useful if you require a large table.

1 Position cursor where you require a table.

2 Click on the Table menu.

3 Click on the Insert submenu.

4 Click Table.

5   Type in the number of columns you require (or use the up and down arrows).

6   Type in the number of rows you require (or use the up and down arrows).

7   Change the AutoFit options as required.

8   If required, click AutoFormat to choose a preset format for your table.

9   Click OK.

8.26.3 The Parts of a Table

A table has three parts – cells, rows and columns:

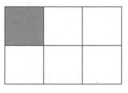   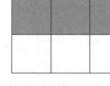   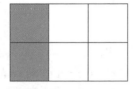

This is a cell   **This is a row**   **This is a column**

8.26.4 The Tables and Borders Toolbar

The Tables and Borders toolbar allows you to do common table tasks quickly. To display the toolbar, click on the Tables and Borders icon. The Tables and Borders toolbar will appear on the screen with the Draw Table icon switched on, but you can click on it to switch it off if you don't need it. Click on the Tables and Borders icon again to hide the toolbar.

Display the Tables and Borders toolbar

It is easiest to insert rows and columns using the Tables and Borders toolbar.

8.26.5 Adding Text to a Table

To add text, position the cursor inside the cell you wish to add text to, and type the text.

Pressing return will increase the height of a row

You cannot use Return to get onto the next row of a table, it will just increase the height of the row you are in.

You can move around with the keyboard using these keys:

TAB	Moves to the next cell
SHIFT AND TAB	Takes you to the previous cell
↗	Up a row
↙	Down a row
←	Left a cell
→	Right a cell

If you want to move around with the mouse, just click into the cell you require. The mouse must look like the I bar just before you click. ⌶

8.27 Selecting Parts of a Table

In order to work with tables, you must know how to select the different parts. Selection will allow you to:

- Format parts of the table.
- Delete parts of the table.
- Add extra rows and columns.

8.27.1 Selecting Cells

1 Click at the bottom left corner of the cell – the mouse changes to a black arrow.

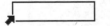

2 Click and drag to select more cells.

Or

1 Position the cursor at the start of the text inside the first cell.

2 Hold down the Shift key.

3 Press End.

4 Press End again to select the cell to the right.

Or

Press arrow keys to select adjoining cells.

8.27.2 Selecting Rows

1 Position the mouse outside the table to the left of the row – it will change to a white arrow.

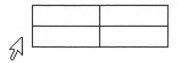

2 Click the left mouse button.

or

Click and drag to select several rows.

Or

1 Click anywhere in the row you want to select.

2 Click on the Table menu.

3 Click on Select.

4 Click Row.

8.27.3 Selecting Columns

1 Position the mouse above the table. It will change to a black down arrow.

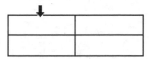

2 Click the left mouse button.

Or

Click and drag to select several columns.

Or

1 Click anywhere in the column to select.

2 Click on the Table menu.

3 Click on Select.

4 Click Column.

8.27.4 Selecting the Whole Table

1 Click inside the table.

2 Click on the Table menu.

3 Click Select.

4 Click Table.

Or

1 Hold down the Alt key.

2 Double click inside the table when the mouse looks like an I bar.

Or

1 Hover the mouse pointer over the table.

2 Click on the small box that appears over the top left of the table.

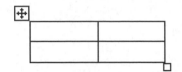

8.28 Inserting and Deleting Rows and Columns

Display the Tables and Borders toolbar before you do this

It is easier to insert rows with the Insert icon on the Tables and Borders toolbar. This icon changes

shape depending on your last action. It will look like this to start with:

8.28.1 Inserting Rows

To insert a row at the bottom of the table:

1 Position your cursor in the last cell.

2 Press the Tab key.

To insert a row somewhere else in the table:

1 Position the cursor in the row above or below where you require a new one.

2 Click the down arrow next to Insert icon.

3 Click Insert Rows Above.

Or

Click Insert Rows Below

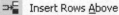
Insert Rows Above
Insert Rows Below

8.28.2 Inserting Several New Rows

For example, inserting six new rows:

1 Select six rows above or below where you require six new ones.

2 Click down arrow next to the Insert icon.

3 Click Insert Rows Above.

Or

Click Insert Rows Below – six new rows will be inserted.

Adjust the number from six to the number of rows you require.

8.28.3 Inserting a New Column

1 Click inside the column next to where you require a new one.

2 Click the down arrow next to Insert icon.

3 Click Insert Columns to the Left.

Or

Click Insert Columns to the Right.

 Insert Columns to the Left

Insert Columns to the Right

8.28.4 Inserting Several New Columns

For example, inserting six new columns:

1 Select six columns next to where you require six new ones.

2 Click down arrow next to Insert icon.

3 Click Insert Columns to the Left.

Or

Click Insert Columns to the Right.

Adjust the number from six to the number of columns you require.

8.28.5 Deleting Rows and Columns

1 Click inside the row/column to delete.

Or

Select several rows/columns to delete.

2 Click on the Table menu.

3 Click Delete.

4 Click Rows.

Or

Click Columns.

8.29 Resizing Rows

8.29.1 Changing Row Height with the Mouse

If your rows are too big or small, just resize them. Here's how:

1 Make sure you are in Print Layout view.

2 Position the mouse at the bottom border of the row you wish to resize, until the mouse pointer changes to a double-headed arrow. ⯭

3 Click and drag to the right or left to make the row bigger or smaller.

Or

1 Make sure you are in Print Layout view.

2 Click inside the table.

3 Position your mouse over a row marker on the vertical ruler to the left.

4 Click and drag it up and down to make the row bigger or smaller.

8.30 Resizing Columns

8.30.1 Changing Column Widths with the Mouse

1 Position the mouse between the border of two columns until the mouse pointer changes to a double-headed arrow. ↔

2 Click and drag to the right or left to make the column bigger or smaller.

Or

1 Click inside the table.

2 Position your mouse over a column marker on the horizontal ruler at the top.

3 Click and drag to make the column bigger or smaller.

Be careful not to select any cells!

If you have any cells selected whilst you click and drag you will only resize that cell rather than the whole column.

If you are resizing the far right-hand column, you may accidentally select the end of the row marker (see below), which can lead to the same problem!

8.31 | Moving and Resizing Tables

8.31.1 Moving the Table

1 Position the mouse pointer in the middle of the table until a cross appears at the top left (a white box will also appear at the bottom right).

2 Move the mouse pointer towards the cross at the top left – you must not take the mouse outside the table or you will lose the cross!

3 Position the mouse pointer over the cross – it will change to a four-headed arrow.

4 Click and drag the table to a new position.

8.31.2 Resizing the Whole Table

1 Position the mouse pointer in the middle of the table until a cross appears at the top left (a white box will also appear at the bottom right).

2 Move the mouse pointer towards the box at the bottom right – you must not take the mouse outside the table, or you will lose the box!

3 Position your mouse pointer over the box – it will change to a double-headed arrow.

4 Click and drag to resize the table.

8.32 | Borders

8.32.1 Creating Borders Using the Menu

1 Select the part of the table you wish to add borders to.

2 Click on the Format menu.

3 Click Borders and Shading.

- ■ The None setting removes all borders.

- ■ The Box setting gives you a border all the way around your selection.

- ■ The All setting applies inside and outside borders to your selection.

- ■ The Grid setting gives a thick outside border, and thin inside borders.

- ■ With the Custom setting, you do not have to have a border all the way around – for example, you can choose just to have a top and bottom border.

- ■ The Preview box shows you what your borders will look like.

- ■ Click on the border buttons (in and around the Preview box) to specify which borders you require.

4 Choose the setting you require from left hand-side (see above).

5 If required, click on a different style from the list.

6 If required, click on the down arrow underneath Color and click a different colour for your border.

7 If required, click the down arrow underneath Width and click on a different width for your border.

8 If you have chosen the Custom setting, click the borders buttons to add selected borders (see above).

9 Click OK.

8.32.2 Using the Table Toolbar

1 Select the part of the table you want to change.

2 If it is not displayed already, click on the Tables and Borders icon to display the toolbar.

3 Make sure the Pencil icon (the first icon on the left) is turned off.

4 Click the down arrow next to Line Style icon (third icon from the left) and click the style you prefer.

5 Click down arrow next to Line Width icon (fourth icon from the left) and click width you prefer.

6 Click Border Color icon (fifth icon from the left) and choose the colour you prefer.

7 Click down arrow next to Borders icon (last icon on the right) and click the borders you would like to set (see below).

Applies a border around the outside of your selection.

All borders – applies inside and outside borders.

Top border.

Left border.

Inside horizontal border.

Inside borders.

No borders.

Bottom border.

Right border.

Inside vertical borders.

Apply diagonal borders top left to bottom right through the cells in your selection.

Apply diagonal borders top right to bottom left through the cells in your selection.

Inserts a grey decorative border wherever your cursor is.

8.33 Shading

Tables, like paragraphs, can have coloured shading applied to them as well as borders. If you have a complex table, you can make it easier to read by shading parts of it.

8.33.1 Shading Using the Menu

1 Select the part of the table you wish to colour in.

2 Click on the Format menu.

3 Click Borders and Shading.

4 Click the Shading tab.

5 Click on the colour you require from the grid.

Or

Click More Colors if the colour you require is not found.

Or

Click No Fill to remove the shading.

6 Click OK.

8.33.2 Using the Toolbar

1 Select part of the table you wish to colour in.

2 If it's not displayed already, click the Tables and Borders icon to display the Tables and Borders toolbar.

3 Make sure the Pencil icon is turned off.

4 Click the drop-down arrow next to the Shading icon.

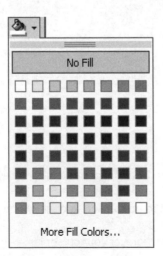

5 Click on the colour you require.

Or

Click More Fill Colors if the colour you require is not found.

Or

Click on No Fill to remove the shading.

8.34 Table AutoFormat

AutoFormat is a quick way of making your table look good. You can choose from a list of fancy table styles, and Word will do all the hard work for you.

8.34.1 Autoformatting a Table

1 Click inside the table you want to AutoFormat.

2 Click the AutoFormat icon on the Tables and Borders toolbar.

Or

Click on the Table menu.

Click Table AutoFormat.

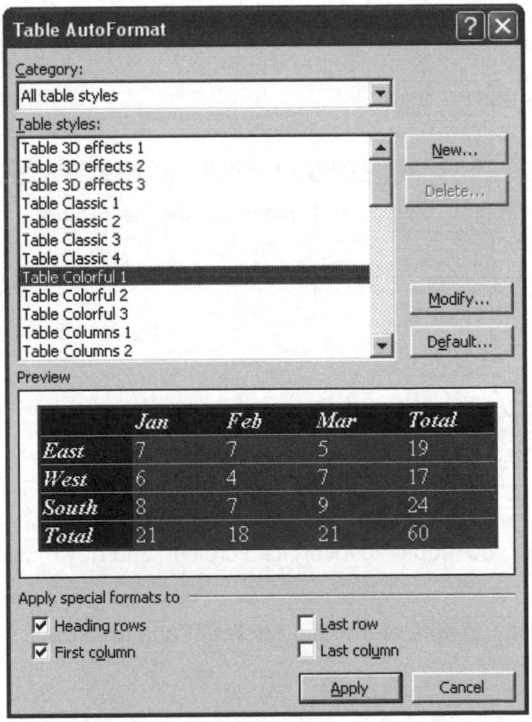

3 Click on the format you like in the list at the top left.

4 Click OK.

8.35 Adding Graphics

8.35.1 Inserting Pictures

1 Position the cursor where you would like to insert the picture.

2 Click the Clip Art icon on the Drawing toolbar.

Or

Click on the Insert menu.

Click on the Picture submenu.

Click Clip Art – the Clip Art Task Pane will appear.

3 Type the sort of picture you are looking for into the Search box, e.g. monkey.

4 Click Search – some pictures will be displayed in the Task Pane.

5 Click on the picture you require to insert it – scroll up and down using the scroll bar if necessary.

6 Click on the X at the top right of the Clip Art Task Pane to close it.

8.35.2 Deleting Pictures

Click on the picture you want to delete, and press the Delete key.

8.35.3 Inserting Pictures From Your Computer

1 Click on the Insert menu.

2 Click on the Picture submenu.

3 Click on From File.

4 Change the Look in box to the folder where your picture is saved.

5 Select the picture file you want to insert.

6 Click Insert.

8.36 Selecting, Moving and Resizing Pictures

8.36.1 Selecting

8

Select the picture as you would select anything else – click once on the picture. When a picture is selected, handles will appear around the edge (black handles for in line pictures, white handles for pictures that are floating over the text). To deselect the picture, just click away from it.

8.36.2 Moving

A picture which is in line with the text can only be moved in the same way as text. It cannot go anywhere on the page. To move it, click into the middle of the picture, then click and drag to a new location. A fuzzy grey cursor will show you where you are going. To move a picture that is floating over the top of text, click into the middle of it, and drag it to a new location. The mouse pointer should look like a four-headed arrow when you are moving it.

8.36.3 Resizing

1 Select the picture you want to resize.

2 Position the mouse over a handle – the mouse pointer will change to a double-headed arrow.

3 Click and drag outwards to make the picture bigger.

Or

Click and drag inwards to make the picture smaller.

8.36.4 Deleting a Picture

Select the picture you want to delete, and press the Delete key.

8.37 Charts

8.37.1 Adding a Chart

1 Place the cursor where you want the chart to appear.

2 Click on the Insert menu.

3 Click on Object.

4 Click on the Create New tab.

5 Select Microsoft Graph Chart (or Microsoft Graph 2000 Chart, depending on your installation).

Object type:

| Microsoft Excel Worksheet |
| Microsoft Graph 2000 Chart |
| Microsoft Map |
| Microsoft Photo Editor 3.0 Photo |
| Microsoft Photo Editor 3.0 Scan |
| Microsoft PowerPoint Presentation |
| Microsoft PowerPoint Slide |
| Microsoft Word Document |

6 Click OK.

7 Click anywhere on the page to deselect the chart.

8.37.2 Editing a Chart

1 Double click on the chart.

2 Change the figures in the mini spreadsheet.

3 Click anywhere on the page to deselect the chart.

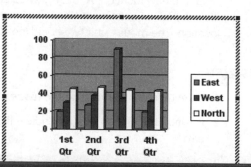

C:\LearnFishStuff\IdiotGui... - Datasheet

		A	B	C	D	E
		1st Qtr	2nd Qtr	3rd Qtr	4th Qtr	
1	East	20.4	27.4	90	20.4	
2	West	30.6	38.6	34.6	31.6	
3	North	45.9	46.9	45	43.9	
4						

8.37.3 Moving, Resizing and Deleting a Chart

Charts are moved, resized and deleted in the same way as pictures – see the previous section on moving, resizing and deleting pictures on page 229.

8.38 Excel Worksheets in Word

8.38.1 What is an Excel worksheet?

An Excel worksheet lets you perform spreadsheet functions in Word without having to open Excel separately.

8.38.2 Creating Worksheets

1 Click on the Insert Microsoft Excel Worksheet button.

2 Click and drag over the number of cells you require.

3 Insert your data into the spreadsheet.

4 Click away from your spreadsheet, inside your Word document.

8.38.3 Editing a Worksheet

1 Double click on your Excel Worksheet.

2 Click in the cell to edit and make your changes.

3 Press Enter (Return).

4 Click away from your spreadsheet, inside your Word document.

8.38.4 Importing Excel Worksheets

1 Click on the Insert menu.

2 Click on Object.

3 Click on Create from File.

4 Click on Browse.

5 Locate the file you wish to insert and double click on it.

To create a Linked object:

6 Click on Link to File.

Linked object: when the original (source) file is changed, the object will update automatically.

To create an Embedded object:

7 Do not click on Link to File.

Embedded: not linked, exists as a separate mini spreadsheet in its own right.

8 Click OK.

8.38.5 Deleting a Worksheet

1 Click outside of the worksheet, and then select it.

White boxes will appear around the edge.

2 Press the Delete key.

8.39 Excel Charts in Word

8.39.1 Importing Charts from Excel into Word

1 Open the Excel spreadsheet containing the chart you wish to import.

2 Select the chart. Black squares will appear around the whole chart border.

3 Click Edit.

4 Click Copy.

5 Click on Word document on the taskbar.

6 Place the cursor where you want the chart to appear.

7 Click on Edit.

8 Click on Paste Special.

9 Click on Microsoft Excel Chart Object.

10 Click in circle next to Paste link.

11 Click OK.

Any changes made to the original Excel spreadsheet will also change the chart in Word.

8.39.2 Creating an Embedded Excel Chart

1 Click on Insert.

2 Click on Object.

3 Click on Create New tab.

4 Click on Microsoft Excel Chart.

5 Click OK.

6 Click outside the chart to deselect it.

8.39.3 Editing a Chart

1 Select the chart by double clicking on it.

2 To switch between the chart and the worksheet, click on the Chart1 and Sheet1 tabs.

3 Type the data into the worksheet.

4 When you have finished entering your data, click outside the chart.

8.40 Advanced Saving

8.40.1 Creating a Copy of a Document Using Save As

If you need to quickly make a copy of a file you are working on, use the Save As tool. You might need to make a copy if you are testing something and want to make sure that your original document is safe in case anything goes wrong.

1 Click on the File menu.

2 Click on Save As.

3 If required, type a new name for the document.

4 If required, change the folder to save the document into.

5 Click on Save.

8.40.2 Creating Folders

1 Click on File.

2 Click on Save As.

3 Change the Save in box to the folder or drive you wish to be the parent of the new folder, e.g. if you click on (C:) the new folder will be created on the (C:) drive.

Save in:	⬬ Local Disk (C:)	▼

4 Click on New Folder icon.

5 Type in a name for your folder.

6 Press Enter (Return).

8.40.3 Saving as a Different Format

Word documents can be saved in various different formats. Which one you choose depends on what you want to do with the file:

- **RTF** (Rich text format) will allow the file to be opened in programs other than Word.

- **Web page** (i.e. HTML, Hypertext mark-up language) will allow the file to be seen on the World Wide Web (see below).

- **Word 97 – 2000 and 6.0/95** and **Word 6.0/95** will allow the file to be opened in previous versions of Word.

1 Click on the File menu.

2 Click Save As.

3 Click the drop-down arrow to the right of the Save as type box.

4 Click on the file type you require.

5 Click Save.

8.40.4 Saving a Document as a Web Page

This will save your file in HTML format, suitable for viewing on the Web.

1 Open the document you wish to save as a web page.

2 Click on the File menu.

3 Click on Save as Web Page.

4 Type in the filename you require.

5 Change the folder to save into as required.

6 Click on Save.

8.41 Mail Merge

Mail merge is used to send the same letter to lots of different people. Suppose you had 100 people you wanted to send your letter to – you could create the standard letter, and insert a special mail merge code for their name and address. Using a separate file containing all the names and addresses, Word can merge the letter with each name and address, printing out each one.

A mail merge always involves three steps.

1 Creating the Data Document – which contains all the personal information that will change from letter to letter.

2 Creating the Main Document – which is the letter you are sending.

3 Merging the data document and the main document together into individual letters.

Word XP combines the second and third steps into one, using a wizard to make it easier. Once you have created the main document, you have almost finished doing the mail merge.

8.41.1 The Data Document

- The data document is laid out in a table.

- In the columns of the table are fields, or the types of information that will change from letter to letter. The field names are held in the first row.

- In the subsequent rows are the records, or the information that will show on each of the letters.

Name	Address	Salutation	Previous Course	Date Attended
Mr Frederick Bloggs	13, Cheese Lane Onion Street London	Mr Bloggs	Word Essentials	12/6/2005
Mrs Bianca Watford	27, Salt Avenue Vinegar Road London	Mrs Watford	Excel Advanced	5/2/2005
Mr Arthur Mitchell	57, Smokey Street Bacon Road London	Mr Mitchell	Access Intermediate	3/1/2005

Field names are held in first row

Records are held in subsequent rows

8.41.2 The Main Document

- The main document contains all the standard text which will not change between letters.

- At the point where information will change, a merge field has been inserted, to indicate to Word that it must find the required information in the data document.

«Name»
««AddressBlock»»

Dear «Salutation»

We hope you enjoyed the «Previous_Course» course which you attended with us on «Date_Attended». We are writing to offer you a special discount on any future courses which you book with us, and a barrel of monkeys for luck.

Yours sincerely

Malcolm Geezer

8.42 Creating your Data Document

1 Create a new, blank document.

2 Create a table (see page 215).

- The number of columns = the number of fields.
- The number of rows = the number of records + 1 (for the field names).

3 Type the field names into the first row.

4 Type the records into the subsequent rows.

5 Save the data document.

6 Close the data document.

Assessor's tip

Lynne says:

Enter the address as it will be laid out on the letter, with hard returns after each line.

8.43 Carrying out a Mail Merge

8.43.1 The Main Document

As part of carrying out a merge, you create a main document. This will look exactly like a normal letter except at the points where information needs to be retrieved from the data document, where you will see merge fields.

8.43.2 Carrying out a Merge

1 Create a new, blank document.

2 Type all of your standard text as normal, leaving blank spaces where you normally type the name, address, etc.

3 Click on the Tools menu.

4 Click on Letters and Mailings.

5 Click Mail Merge Wizard – the Mail Merge Task Pane will appear.

8

6 Select the type of merge you want to do – normally this will be Letters.

7 Click Next.

Click Next to continue.
Step 1 of 6

➡ Next: Starting document

8 Select Use the current document.

Select starting document

How do you want to set up your letters?

◉ Use the current document

9 Click Next.

10 Click Browse.

Use an existing list

Use names and addresses from a file or a database.

▦ Browse...

11 Change the Look in box to the folder where your data document is saved.

12 Select your data document.

13 Click Open.

Mail Merge Recipients					? X

To sort the list, click the appropriate column heading. To narrow down the recipients displayed by a specific criteria, such as by city, click the arrow next to the column heading. Use the check boxes or buttons to add or remove recipients from the mail merge.

List of recipients:

	▼ N...	▼ Address	▼ Salutation	▼ Previous_Course	▼ Date_Attend
☑	Mr Fre...	13, Cheese...	Mr Bloggs	Word Essentials	12/6/2005
☑	Mrs Bi...	27, Salt Av...	Mrs Watford	Excel Advanced	5/2/2005
☑	Mr Art...	57, Smokey...	Mr Mitchell	Access Intermediate	3/1/2005

Select All	Clear All	Refresh		
Find...	Edit...	Validate		OK

14 Click OK.

15 Click Next.

16 Place the cursor where you want the address to go.

17 Click Address Block to insert the address.

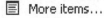 Address block...

```
Insert Address Block                          [?][X]

Specify address elements
   ☑ Insert recipient's name in this format:
   ┌─────────────────────────────────────┬─┐
   │ Joshua                               │▲│
   │ Joshua Randall Jr.                   │ │
   │ Joshua Q. Randall Jr.                │ │
   │ Mr. Josh Randall Jr.                 │ │
   │ Mr. Josh Q. Randall Jr.              │ │
   │ Mr. Joshua Randall Jr.               │▼│
   └─────────────────────────────────────┴─┘
   ☑ Insert company name
   ☑ Insert postal address:
      ⦿ Never include the country/region in the address
      ○ Always include the country/region in the address
      ○ Only include the country/region if different than:
      ┌─────────────────────────────────────┐
      │                                     │
      └─────────────────────────────────────┘

Preview
   ┌─────────────────────────────────────┐
   │ Mr. Joshua Randall Jr.              │
   │ Blue Sky Airlines                   │
   │ 1 Airport Way                       │
   │ Kitty Hawk, NC 27700                │
   │                                     │
   └─────────────────────────────────────┘

   [Match Fields...]        [  OK  ]  [ Cancel ]
```

18 Click OK.

19 Click More items to insert other fields, making sure your cursor is placed where you want the fields to be inserted.

    ▤ More items...

20 Select the field you wish to insert.

21 Click Insert.

22 Click Close.

23 Click Next.

```
Insert Merge Field                            [?][X]

Insert:
   ○ Address Fields          ⦿ Database Fields
Fields:
   ┌─────────────────────────────────────┬─┐
   │ Name                                 │▲│
   │ Address                              │ │
   │ Salutation                           │ │
   │ Previous_Course                      │ │
   │ Date_Attended                        │ │
   │                                      │ │
   │                                      │ │
   │                                      │ │
   │                                      │ │
   │                                      │ │
   │                                      │▼│
   └─────────────────────────────────────┴─┘

   [Match Fields...]     [ Insert ]  [ Cancel ]
```

24 Preview your letters using the arrows – you can click Previous at any time to go back and correct mistakes.

25 Click Next.

26 Click Print to print the merge, or Edit individual letters to merge to a file.

Merge

📇 Print...

📄 Edit individual letters...

27 Choose the records you wish to merge.

28 Click OK.

8.44 Test Your Knowledge

The questions below will test what you know of the knowledge and understanding requirements of this unit. All the answers to these questions are contained or referred to within this chapter.

1 What important questions should you ask before beginning work on a document?

2 What are styles?

3 When would you use a template?

4 What would you do if you needed to send a letter to ten customers?

5 What software would you use if you wanted to send a personalised letter to a large number of people?

6 In which format would you save a file if it is to be used on the Web?

7 What is RTF and why would you use it?

8 What checks can you do when you have finished your document?

9 Describe a proofreading technique.

10 How could you improve your efficiency?

8.45 Evidence

The tasks you undertake as evidence for your ITQ should be work-related. Therefore, your supervisor at work should be able to give you guidance on the type of tasks you should take on. Below are some ideas of possible tasks for this unit. Consider how you can adapt these ideas to make them more relevant for your own workplace and to ensure you cover all the skills requirements.

- Write a short report that explains how you will make sure your documents are suitable for the intended audience and that they clearly communicate the correct information.

- Write a report explaining some numerical data. Include a chart from Excel and any images to back up your report. Save this file in an appropriate format.

- Write a report on the appropriate procedure to carry out in an emergency. Include a list with bullets or numbering, insert a table and make any appropriate formatting changes.

- Work on an existing document that has multiple pages. Add page numbering and a header or footer; adjust the margins, indents and orientation. Remember to take screenshots at each point.

- Write a letter to your colleagues, use the mail merge feature and take a screenshot to show the use of this.

8

CHAPTER 9

Spreadsheet Software

9.1 About This Unit

What you need to know

To gain ITQ Level 2 in this unit, you should demonstrate the following competency:
Use spreadsheet software effectively to produce more complex spreadsheets.
To achieve this you should know and understand:

1 How to produce information that is clear and appropriate.

2 More complex spreadsheets.

3 How to analyse and interpret more complex data.

You should also be able to display the following skills and techniques:

1 Handling files appropriately.

2 Combining information of different types.

3 Entering and editing spreadsheet data:

- Formatting spreadsheets.
- Checking spreadsheets using a range of tools.

4 Using functions and formulas in more complex types of spreadsheet.

5 Analysing and interpreting:

- Presenting more complex data.

6 Improving efficiency through the use of shortcuts.

How to prove your skills

You need to carry out at least two work-based tasks which demonstrate the skills and knowledge listed above. In order to show your competency, it may well be necessary for you to complete more tasks than this.

Make sure you have plenty of evidence that shows how you completed each task, such as a copy of the file you worked on, or a document with screenshots of the processes you followed. You can back this up by producing a report which shows your knowledge of the subjects covered within the unit.

Excel is a spreadsheet program. Spreadsheets are basically big tables that hold text and numbers. Calculations can then be performed on those numbers, to help you manage your accounts, work out sales figures, or calculate interest payments on loans. Excel can be used for:

- Formulae or calculations.

- Storing information (as a database).

- Creating tables.

9.2.1 For Formulae (Calculations)

Here is a very simple domestic budget using Excel.

	A	B	C
1	**Income**	£ 1,200.00	
2			
3	**Outgoings**		
4	Rent	£ 250.00	
5	Food	£ 150.00	
6	Social	£ 85.00	
7	Gas	£ 30.00	
8	Electricity	£ 30.00	
9			
10	**Total**	£ 545.00	
11			
12	**Left Over**	£ 655.00	
13			

This cell contains a formula to add up the total outgoings

This cell contains a formula which takes the total outgoings away from the income, which gives you the amount left over

9.2.2 For Storing Information (as a Database)

The diagram below shows part of a database in Excel. The columns represent the fields in the database and the rows hold the records.

	B	C	D	E	F	G
1	**Surname**	**First Name**	**Sex**	**Date of Birth**	**Department**	**Number**
2	Jekyll	Abigail	Female	23-May-60	Design	1
3	Akinlotan	Abimbola	Female	12-Mar-58	Sales	5
4	Hyde	Alexander	Male	23-May-28	Finance	3
5	Richards	Anna	Female	27-Mar-68	Sales	6
6	Dalloway	Anne	Female	15-Jun-59	Personnel	8
7	Olivelle	Anthony	Male	21-Nov-67	Technology	5

Excel has a simple database facility that allows you to:

- Sort information into any order (e.g. by surname).

- Extract the information you wish to see (e.g. only the females).

9.2.3 For Creating Tables

Excel can also be used very much like word-processing tables, i.e. for laying out information neatly in rows and columns. Spreadsheets can then be formatted to look very impressive!

	A	B	C	D
1	Competitor	Current Share	Share in 2 years	
2	Largest competitor	50%	30%	
3	Second competitor	25%	20%	
4	Third competitor	15%	10%	
5				

Practise this!

Think about either a spreadsheet that you have recently created or have been asked to work on. Try to figure out what the information is for: what is its purpose?

Assessor's tip

Lynne says:

Other questions to ask yourself include:

- Who is it is for? (Customers, staff, clients)
- How will it be used? (Hard copy, website, email attachment)
- When is it needed?

All of these things will help you in either planning or working on your spreadsheet.

9.2.4 Common Excel Jargon

There are a number of words used when describing Excel that you may not have come across before.

- **Spreadsheet** – an electronic table or tables used to store data and make calculations. These tables appear as 'sheets'. Spreadsheet can mean either the application (e.g. Excel), or the file created by a spreadsheet application (known in Excel as a workbook).

- **Workbook** – an entire file of sheets. A workbook is the term given to a file created in Excel.

- **Worksheet or sheet** – these are the separate pages contained within a workbook.

- **Cell** – a single space on a spreadsheet, used to enter information.

- **Formula** – an equation used to calculate values from the data on a spreadsheet. For example, a simple formula could add together the value of two cells.

- **Column** – spreadsheets are divided into vertical columns, each represented by a letter at the top.

- **Row** – spreadsheets are also divided into rows, with each represented by a number on the left of the screen.

- **Cell reference** – each cell has its own reference, taken from the column and row it is in. So, an example of a cell reference might be B2 (B for the column it is in, 2 for the row).

Starting and Closing Excel

9.3.1 Starting Excel

Microsoft
Excel

1 Click on the Start button.

2 Click on the All Programs.

3 Click on Microsoft Excel.

Or, if you have a shortcut:

Double click on the shortcut on the desktop.

9.3.2 Closing Excel

1 Click on the File menu.

2 Click on Exit.

Or

Click on the X at the top right-hand corner of the screen.

9.3.3 What are Workbooks?

- Excel files are known as workbooks.

- Workbooks are made up of sheets, or spreadsheets.

9.4 **Opening and Closing Workbooks**

9.4.1 Opening Your Workbook

1 Click on the Open icon.

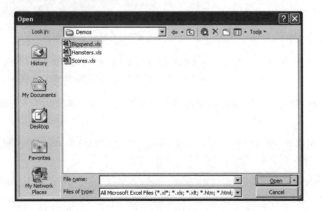

2 Change the folder Excel is looking in if required.

3 Click on the name of the workbook you wish to open, scrolling across if necessary.

4 Click on Open.

Or, if you see your file in the Task Pane, you can click on it there to open it. If you don't see it, then click on More workbooks, and you will be taken to the Open Workbook box (see above).

9.4.2 Multiple Workbooks

In Excel you can open more than one workbook at a time. If you find that you need to open another workbook, simply open it in the normal way (see previous section). You may wish to have more than one workbook open if you want to copy information from one workbook to the other.

If you know that you will want to use more than one workbook when you start, you can select all the workbooks that you will need from the Open dialog box, and then click on Open. From the Open dialog box:

1 Click on the first file you wish to open.

2 Hold down the Control (Ctrl) key on the keyboard.

3 Click on the next file you wish to open.

4 Continue clicking on all the files you wish to select.

5 Release the Control key.

6 Click Open – all the selected files will be opened in separate windows.

How can I switch between more than one open workbook?

1 Click on the Window menu – a list of open workbooks can be seen at the bottom of the menu.

2 Click on the file you wish to switch to.

9.4.3 Switching Between Open Workbooks

1 Click on the Window menu – a list of open workbooks can be seen at the bottom of the menu.

2 Click on the file you wish to switch to.

Or

Click on the button on the taskbar for that workbook.

9.4.4 Closing Your Workbook

[×]

Click on the *bottom* X at the top right of the Excel screen (see below) – **not** the top one!

Or

1 Click on the File menu.

2 Click on Close.

What happened? Excel closed completely!

You must have clicked the top X instead of the bottom one. Clicking the top one closes Excel completely, so make sure you only click the bottom X to close your workbook.

9.5 Creating a New Workbook

9.5.1 Creating a New Workbook

[▯]

Click on the New icon.

Or

1 Click on the File menu.

2 Click on New.

3 Click on General Templates in the Task Pane.

4 Ensure you are on the General tab.

5 Click Workbook.

6 Click OK.

9.6 Saving Your Workbook

9.6.1 Saving Your Work for the First Time

[💾]

1 Click on the Save icon.

2 Type in a name for your workbook (up to 255 characters).

3 Change the folder to save in, if required.

4 Click on Save.

Shortcut

Press Ctrl (Control) + S on the keyboard to save.

9.6.2 Saving Your Workbook After You Have Made Changes

Click on the Save icon to save your work after you have made changes. The file will be saved in the same place with the same name.

Save your work regularly!

Keep clicking on the Save icon as you are working to ensure that you do not lose your work!

9.6.3 Creating a Copy Using Save As

Using Save As will allow you to make a copy of your workbook with a different name and/or in a different location.

1 Click on the File menu.

2 Click on Save As.

3 Type in a new file name for the workbook if required.

4 Change the folder if required.

5 Click Save.

9.7 | Using Shortcuts

Why use shortcuts?

Shortcuts are invaluable for improving your efficiency. Not only will you be able to work more quickly but the chances of your hand falling off from 'click exhaustion' are much reduced.

9.7.1 Shortcuts for Moving Around

Press this on the keyboard	You will move
Up arrow key	Up one cell
Down arrow key	Down one cell
Left arrow key	Left a cell
Right arrow key	Right a cell
Ctrl + right arrow key	To the furthest right column of the current spreadsheet
Ctrl + left arrow key	To the furthest left column of the current spreadsheet
Ctrl + up arrow key	To the top row of the sheet
Ctrl + down arrow key	To the bottom row of the sheet
Home	To column A
Ctrl, Home	To cell A1
Ctrl, End	To the bottom right cell of the current spreadsheet
Page Up	The active cell up one screen
Page Down	The active cell down one screen

9.7.2 Other Shortcuts

Press this on the keyboard	This will happen
Ctrl + C	Copy
Ctrl + V	Paste
Ctrl + X	Cut
Ctrl + Z	Undo
Ctrl + Y	Redo

9.8 Entering Text and Numbers

9.8.1 What Happens When I Enter Text and Numbers?

- When you enter text or numbers into a cell, the state of the cell changes.

- When you have finished typing you must confirm that you have finished by pressing Enter or clicking on the green tick.

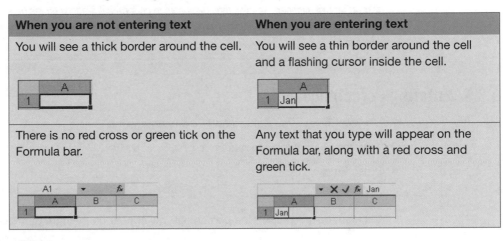

When you are not entering text	When you are entering text
You will see a thick border around the cell.	You will see a thin border around the cell and a flashing cursor inside the cell.
There is no red cross or green tick on the Formula bar.	Any text that you type will appear on the Formula bar, along with a red cross and green tick.

9.8.2 Entering Text

1 Click on the cell you want to enter text into.

2 Type the text you require.

3 Press Enter.

Or

Click on the green tick – the text will appear on the left-hand side of the cell.

9.8.3 Entering Numbers

1 Click on the cell you want to enter a number into.

2 Type the number you require.

3 Press Enter.

Or

Click on the green tick – the number will appear on the right-hand side of the cell.

9.8.4 Entering Dates

1 Click on the cell you want to enter a date into.

2 Type the date you require with forward slashes around it, e.g. 1/1/2000.

3 Press Enter.

Or

Click on the green tick – the date will appear on the right-hand side of the cell.

Assessor's tip

Sheena says:

Always enter dates with slashes. If you enter dates with dots, e.g. 1.1.2000, then Excel will see them as text rather than numbers. You will then be unable to perform calculations on the date. Performing calculations on dates is very common when you wish to calculate how many days there are between two dates.

9.8.5 Entering Percentages

1 Click on the cell you want to enter a percentage into.

2 Type the percentage you require, e.g. 10%.

3 Press Enter.

Or

Click on the green tick – the percentage will appear on the right of the cell.

9.8.6 What is the Difference Between Enter and the Green Tick?

- If you press Enter, you move down one cell after you have pressed it.

- If you click on the green tick, you remain in the same cell after you have clicked it.

9.8.7 Why do Numbers go on the Right?

When Excel puts data on the right it confirms that calculations can be performed on the data you have entered. Any data that appears on the left cannot be used in a calculation.

9.8.8 What if I Make a Mistake?

If you make a mistake, and you have not yet confirmed the entry:

Click on the red cross on the Formula bar.

Checking your work

After a while your spreadsheet can seem like a blur of numbers, even for a spreadsheet demon. It's important to get into the habit of checking your figures and knowing how to correct them when they go wrong.

9.9.1 Deleting the Contents of a Cell

1 Click on the cell you wish to delete.

2 Press the Delete key.

Or

1 Click on the cell you wish to delete.

2 Click on the Edit menu.

3 Click Clear.

4 Click Contents.

9.9.2 Replacing the Contents of a Cell

1 Click on the cell you wish to replace.

2 Type in the new text – the original contents will disappear.

9.9.3 Editing the Contents of a Cell

There are three ways of editing the contents of a cell.

1 Double click on the cell you wish to edit – a cursor will appear inside the cell.

2 Enter or amend the text.

3 Press Enter or click on the green tick.

Or

1 Click on the cell you wish to edit.

2 Press F2 on the keyboard – a cursor will appear inside the cell.

3 Enter or amend the text.

4 Press Enter or click on the green tick.

Or

9

1. Click on the cell you wish to edit – the formula bar will show the contents of the cell.

2. Click on the text on the Formula bar.

   ✗ ✓ *fx* =SUM(A1:A7)|

3. Enter or amend the text.

4. Press Enter or click on the green tick.

9.10 Selecting Cells

To select, your mouse must look like a big white cross!

✛

9.10.1 Why Select Cells?

If you want to work with just a part of your spreadsheet, you must select the part you wish to work with. The list below shows some of the situations in which you may need to select cells.

- When you are formatting part of the spreadsheet, e.g. making it bold, italic, changing the size.

- When you are copying or moving part of the spreadsheet.

- When you are adding or deleting rows and columns.

- When you are choosing the cells you wish to use in a calculation, or formula.

- When you are printing part of your spreadsheet.

9.10.2 Selecting a Range of Cells

1. Position the mouse over the middle of the cell, at the top left-hand corner of the area you wish to select.

2. Make sure your mouse looks like a big white cross.

3. Click and drag the mouse pointer over the cells you require.

What do cells look like when they are selected?

All the cells, apart from the first one you selected, will go black. The first cell remains white (this indicates the active cell of the selection).

5	Female	27-Mar-68	Sales
6	Female	15-Jun-59	Personnel
7	Male	21-Nov-67	Technology
8	Female	02-Apr-74	Manufacture

9.10.3 Selecting Columns

Click on the grey column letter you require (see below).

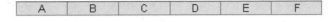

Or

Click and drag over the column letters to select several columns.

9.10.4 Selecting Rows

Click on the grey row number you require.

Or

Click and drag over the row numbers to select several rows.

9.10.5 Selecting the Whole Spreadsheet

Click on the grey square at the top left of the spreadsheet.

9.10.6 Selecting Cells which are Not Next to Each Other

1 Select the first range of cells you require.

2 Hold down Control (Ctrl) on the keyboard.

3 Select the second range of cells you require.

4 Release the mouse.

5 Release Control.

9.10.7 Deselecting Cells

Click onto a cell outside of the selection.

Or if you have selected the whole spreadsheet:

Click into the middle of the sheet.

9.11 Adding Up Numbers with AutoSum

9.11.1 What is AutoSum?

AutoSum is a quick and easy way of adding up a list of figures.

9.11.2 Using AutoSum

Σ

1 Click on the cell where you would like to put the answer.

2 Click on the AutoSum icon – moving lines will appear around the figures you are adding up.

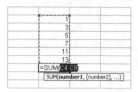

3 The formula will appear in the cell (see below).

4 Press Enter or click on the green tick.

What does the Sum formula mean?

When you use AutoSum, you will see a formula similar to the one shown below in the cell.

=SUM(A1:A6)

SUM means that Excel is going to add up numbers. The cell references in brackets show the range of cells which will be included in the addition. The last cell reference (A6 in the example above) should always be a blank cell (see below).

Assessor's tip

Rudy says:

Always include a blank cell between the figures and the answer. This ensures that if you need to add any more figures to the list you are adding up, the answer will update to include the new information. If you do not leave a blank line, you may end up with an incorrect answer.

9.11.3 What if AutoSum Has Put Moving Lines Around the Wrong Figures?

1 Ensure that you can still see the moving lines around the wrong figures (if you can't, click on the cell and click on the AutoSum icon again!).

2 Click and drag over the correct figures, remembering to include the blank cell.

3 Press Enter or click on the green tick.

9.11.4 What is a Circular Reference?

A circular reference occurs when the cell which contains the formula is used in the formula. Excel can't give you the answer because the answer is part of the calculation. This can happen when you correct AutoSum after it has put moving lines around the wrong figures, if you have selected the formula cell by mistake. You will see this error message after you confirm the formula.

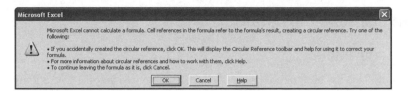

The diagram below shows an example of a spreadsheet with a circular reference.

	A	B	C	D
1	1			
2	3			
3	5			
4	7			
5	11			
6	13			
7	0			
8				

A7 ▼ *fx* =SUM(A1:A7)

To correct a circular reference:

1 Click on the cell which contains the formula.

2 Press the Delete key.

3 Enter the formula again, without including any reference to the cell which the formula is in!

9.12 Typing the Sum Function to Add Up Numbers

9.12.1 The Sum Function

Typing the Sum function gives you exactly the same result as using the AutoSum icon. It just means that you type in the formula yourself, rather than getting AutoSum to do it for you. This can save you having to correct AutoSum when it guesses at the wrong cells. Here's how:

1 Select the cell you want to put the answer into.

2 Type =SUM.

3 Type an open bracket, like this (.

4 Type in the first cell reference from the list you want to add up.

5 Type a colon, like this : .

6 Type the last cell reference from the list you want to add up (this should be a blank cell).

7 Type a closed bracket, like this) .

8 Press Enter or click on the green tick.

So if you wanted to add up the cells from cell A2 to D6, you would type in =SUM(A2:D6)

9.13 Entering Simple Formulae

9.13.1 What is a Formula?

Formula is the term used for a calculation in a spreadsheet. The diagrams below show an example formula being entered.

To work out the surplus, we need to do a calculation by taking away the expenditure from the salary. You can see this being entered on the left-hand side. On the right-hand side, you can see what happens after the formula has been entered.

	SUM ▾ ✕ ✓ *fx* =B3-B12		
	A	B	C
1	*Home Budget*		
2			
3	*Income*	£2,000.00	
4			
5	**Expenditure**		
6	Rent	£ 200.00	
7	Food	£ 150.00	
8	Social	£ 35.00	
9	Bills	£ 50.00	
10	Loan	£ 100.00	
11			
12	*Total*	£ 535.00	
13			
14	*Surplus*	=B3-B12	
15			

	B14 ▾ *fx* =B3-B12		
	A	B	C
1	*Home Budget*		
2			
3	*Income*	£2,000.00	
4			
5	**Expenditure**		
6	Rent	£ 200.00	
7	Food	£ 150.00	
8	Social	£ 35.00	
9	Bills	£ 50.00	
10	Loan	£ 100.00	
11			
12	*Total*	£ 535.00	
13			
14	*Surplus*	£1,465.00	
15			

9.13.2 How is the Formula Made Up?

- Formulae always start with an equals (=) sign – that's how Excel knows it's a formula.

- Cell references are used in the calculation instead of numbers. This means that if the number inside the cell changes, the answer to the formula will update!

- A mathematical symbol is used to denote the type of calculation.

Here is the formula from the example above which found us the surplus (or money left over).

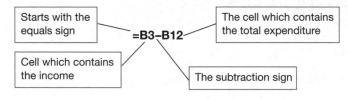

Starts with the equals sign	The cell which contains the total expenditure

=B3–B12

Cell which contains the income	The subtraction sign

9.13.3 Types of Calculation

There are four main types of calculation:

Addition	For adding numbers together, e.g. finding totals.
Subtraction	For finding the difference between two numbers, e.g. subtracting expenses from income.
Multiplication	For multiplying two numbers together. This is commonly used in spreadsheets to find VAT and other percentages – if you see the word of, then you need a percentage multiplication: e.g. 20% of £100 is 20% multiplied by £100 ¾ of 200 is ¾ multiplied by 200.
Division	Used when you wish to divide an amount by another number. For example, finding the amount per month for a loan would involve dividing the total amount of the loan by the number of months you need to repay it.

Addition is usually carried out by using AutoSum or typing the Sum function. If you need to do another sort of calculation, you will have to create a formula, as detailed below.

9.13.4 Creating a Formula

1 Click on the cell where you require the answer.

2 Type the = sign.

3 Type the first cell reference you require.

Or

Click on the first cell you require – flashing lines will appear around the cell, and the cell reference will be inserted.

4 Type in the mathematical symbol you require (see next page).

5 Type the next cell reference you require – flashing lines will appear around the cell, and the cell reference will be inserted.

Or

Click on the next cell you require.

6 Press Enter.

Or

Click on the green tick to confirm the formula – the answer will appear in the cell, and the formula will appear on the Formula bar.

9

9.13.5 Mathematical Symbols

Press +   To perform an addition

Press –   To perform a subtraction

Press *   To perform a multiplication

Press /   To perform a division

9.13.6 Precedence of Calculation

Calculations are not simply done from left to right, as you might expect. Below is the order in which all calculations are performed:

Priority	Symbol	Explanation
1	( )	Anything in brackets is done before anything outside the brackets is even considered.
2	^	Raises a number in order of magnitude: raises it to the power of something else, e.g. 3^3
3	* /	Multiply and divide are on the same level. Whichever is the furthest left in the formula is done first.
4	+ –	Plus and minus are on the same level. Whichever is the furthest left is done first.

The acronym for this is **BODMAS**:

Brackets **O**rder **D**ivide **M**ultiply **A**dd **S**ubtract

9.14 Error Messages

9.14.1 What do the Error Messages Mean?

When something goes wrong with a formula, Excel produces messages that attempt to describe what the problem is:

#DIV/0!	You have attempted to divide by zero – make sure all the cells being used in the formula have numbers in them.
#N/A!	Part of your formula is using a cell that does not have information in it, or the information is not yet available.
#NAME?	There is some text in the formula that does not mean anything to Excel. There may be a range name in the formula that Excel does not recognise.
#NULL!	Two areas do not intersect. You may have forgotten to include a comma between two ranges of cells.
#NUM!	You have used text instead of numbers whilst performing a function, or the result of the formula is too big or too small to be shown by Excel.
#REF!	One of the cells being used in the formula does not exist. It may have been deleted after you created the formula.
#VALUE!	A cell containing text has been used in the formula.

You may also see error messages about circular references (see page 256).

9.14.2 Correcting Formulae

1 Select the cell containing the formula.

2 Click on the formula on the Formula bar.

3 Amend the formula as required (see below).

✗ ✓ *fx* =SUM(A1:A7)

4 Press Enter.

Or

Click on the green tick.

Amending the formula

You can delete the parts of the formula you do not want with the Delete or Backspace keys on the keyboard.
If you want to enter new cell references, you can either type them in, or click on the cells you require.

To use drag and drop, your mouse pointer must look like a white arrow with four smaller arrows at the tip.

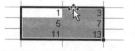

9.14.3 Moving Text with Drag and Drop

1 Select the cells you wish to move.

2 Position your mouse at the edge of the selection – the mouse pointer will change to a white arrow.

3 Click and drag to the new postion – a fuzzy grey line will show you where you are going.

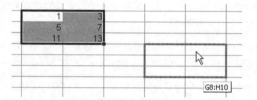

4 Release the mouse when you are in the correct place.

9.14.4 Copying Text with Drag and Drop

1 Select the cells you wish to copy.

2 Position your mouse at the edge of the selection – mouse will change to a white arrow.

3 Hold down Control (Ctrl) on the keyboard – a plus sign will appear next to the white arrow.

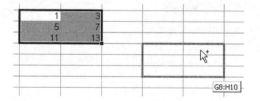

4 Click and drag to the new position – a fuzzy grey line will show you where you are going.

5 Release the mouse button when you are in the correct place.

6 Release Control.

9.15 Cut, Copy and Paste

The clipboard

When you copy or cut anything it is temporarily stored on an area called the clipboard until you need it again. The clipboard can hold only one item at a time, and when you copy or cut a new item it will overwrite what was previously there.

9.15.1 Moving Data

1 Select the cells you wish to move.

2 Click on the Cut icon – the selection will have flashing lights around it, and will be moved to the Windows clipboard.

3 Select the cell you wish to move to – this cell will become the top left-hand corner of the cells you cut.

4 Click on the Paste icon.

9.15.2 Copying Data

1 Select the cells you wish to copy.

2 Click on the Copy icon – the selection will have flashing lights around it, and will be moved to the Windows clipboard.

3 Select the cell you wish to copy to – this cell will become the top left-hand corner of the cells you copied.

4 Click on the Paste icon.

9.16 Using AutoFill to Copy Text and Formulae

Your mouse must look like the small black cross to use AutoFill

9.16.1 What is AutoFill?

AutoFill is a quick way of entering standard information, such as the months or days of the week, onto your spreadsheet. You can also use it to copy text or formulae very quickly.

9.16.2 Using AutoFill

1 Click on the cell(s) you wish to copy.

2 Position the mouse pointer over the small square at the bottom right-hand corner of the active cell – your mouse pointer will change to a small black cross.

3 Click and drag over the cells you wish to copy to – a fuzzy grey line will appear around the cells, and labels will appear to show you what is being copied.

4 Normally, this is all you have to do – but if the results are not what you expect, click on the Smart Tag (an Office XP feature) that appears at the bottom right of the cells, and choose Fill Series.

9.16.3 Special Lists

Certain text works well with AutoFill, such as months, days or dates. Have a look at the examples below, which were all created using AutoFill:

January		Qtr 1		01/05/2005
February		Qtr 2		02/05/2005
March		Qtr 3		03/05/2005
April		Qtr 4		04/05/2005
May				05/05/2005
June				06/05/2005
Monday	Tuesday	Wednesday	Thursday	Friday

Practise this!

Use AutoFill to create a list of salary or customer payment dates.

9.16.4 Starting Off the Sequence for AutoFill

Sometimes you may want to start off a sequence of numbers or dates for AutoFill, e.g. when you want to enter a list of dates that go from week to week, rather than day to day. To achieve this, you must first start off the sequence for AutoFill.

1 Type in the first date or number you require.

2 Type the second date or number you require in the next cell.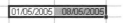

3 Select both of the cells.

4 AutoFill as normal.

| 01/05/2005 | 08/05/2005 | 15/05/2005 | 22/05/2005 | 29/05/2005 | 05/06/2005 |

9.17 Find and Replace

9.17.1 Using Find

1 Select the cells you wish to search, or click in any cell to search the entire sheet.

2 Click on the Edit menu.

3 Click on Find.

4 Type the text or number you are searching for into the white box.

5 Click Find Next.

6 Keep clicking Find Next until you have found what you are looking for.

7 Click Close.

9.17.2 Find and Replace

1 Select the cells you wish to search, or click in any cell to search the entire sheet.

2 Click on the Edit menu.

3 Click on Replace.

4 Type what you are searching for into the Find what box.

5 Type what you want to replace it with into the Replace with box.

6 Click Find Next and Replace to replace individual occurrences.

7 Keep clicking Find Next until you have found what you are looking for.

Or

Click Replace All to replace all occurrences.

8 Click Close.

9.18 Sorting

9.18.1 Sorting Data

Sorting is usually used to sort a database by one or more of its fields, e.g. name, date, cost, etc. (see section 9.2.2).

1 Click into any cell in the column you wish to sort (*do not* select the whole column).

2 Click Sort Ascending icon.

Or

Click Sort Descending icon.

What is the difference between ascending and descending?		
If you are sorting this	**Ascending means**	**Descending means**
Text	A to Z	Z to A
Numbers	Lowest to highest	Highest to lowest
Dates	Earliest to latest	Latest to earliest

9.18.2 Sorting the Right Data

If you select an entire column before you sort, rather than just clicking into the column, only the data in that column moves. The rest of the information on the sheet stays still. If you are working with a database this can cause the information to become mismatched and data to end up with the wrong record. This catastrophe can be avoided by a few simple steps.

If you select an entire column before you click on Sort you will see this message:

1. Make sure that Expand the selection option is selected.

2. Click Sort.

Excel will expand your selection so that all your data is sorted.

9.18.3 Sorting by More Than One Column

Sometimes you may wish to sort by more than one bit of information. This tends to happen when you have a certain field which people can be *grouped* by, e.g. Department, Gender, etc., and you want to sort them within their groups. The spreadsheet below has been sorted by Department initially, and then within this, people have been sorted by their surname.

	A	B
1	**Department**	**Surname**
2	Design	Jekyll
3	Design	Jospin
4	Design	Pullen
5	Design	Robinson
6	Design	Sierra de la Guerra
7	Finance	Corwall
8	Finance	Hyde
9	Finance	Minniver
10	Finance	Ross
11	Manufacture	Al Said
12	Manufacture	Duck
13	Manufacture	Hull
14	Manufacture	Scot
15	Manufacture	Sutherland
16	Manufacture	Zhivago
17	Personnel	Brown
18	Personnel	Dalloway
19	Personnel	Day
20	Personnel	Huntington
21	Personnel	Lazarus
22	Personnel	Mulley
23	Personnel	Plod

1. Click into any cell within the database you wish to sort.

2. Click on the Data menu.

3. Click Sort – the text in the spreadsheet will become highlighted.

4. Click the down arrow underneath Sort by.

5. Click on the field you wish to sort.

6. Click next to Ascending or Descending for the first field.

7. Click on the down arrow underneath Then by.

8. Click on the next field you wish to sort.

9. Click next to Ascending or Descending for the second field.

10. Enter sort information for a third field if required.

11. Click in the circle next to Header row if the fieldnames are held in the top row.

12. Click OK.

9.19 Filtering

9.19.1 How to Add Filters

To switch the AutoFilter on or off:

1 Select a cell in the list you wish to filter.

2 Click on the Data menu.

3 Click on the Filter submenu.

4 Click on AutoFilter.

Drop-down arrows appear on the column headers.

	A	B	C	D
1	Clown ▾	Cheese ▾	BucketofWater ▾	Custard Pies ▾
2	Koko	Gorgonzola	Yes	8
3	Coco	Cheddar	Yes	10

To use the filter:

1 Click the drop-down arrow.

2 Select the data you wish to display.

Only that data is now shown.

	B
	Cheese ▾
	(All)
	(Top 10...)
	(Custom...)
	Brie
	Camembert
	Cheddar
	Edam
	Gorgonzola
	Gouda
	Gruyere
	Mozzarella
	Port Salut
	Red Leicester
	Stilton
	Wensleydale

	A	B	C	D
1	Clown ▾	Cheese ▾	BucketofWater ▾	Custard Pies ▾
2	Koko	Gorgonzola	Yes	8
4	Roro	Gorgonzola	No	7
5	Polo	Gorgonzola	Yes	5
6	Lolo	Gorgonzola	No	6
7	Solo	Gorgonzola	No	3
8	Moko	Gorgonzola	No	5

3 You can filter the data further by using another drop-down arrow.

	A	B	C	D
1	Clown ▾	Cheese ▾	BucketofWater ▾	Custard Pies ▾
5	Polo	Gorgonzola	Yes	5
8	Moko	Gorgonzola	No	5

9.20 Subtotals

9.20.1 Creating Subtotals

1 Select the list you wish to create subtotals for.

2 Click on the Data menu.

3 Click on Subtotals.

4 Choose the column header you want to divide into subtotals.

5 Choose the function you wish to apply to the totals, e.g. SUM, MIN, etc.

6 Click OK.

1 2 3		A	B	C
	1	Vegetable	Size	Cost
	2	Cabbage	Large	45
	3	Cabbage	Medium	11
	4	Cabbage	Large	40
	5	**Cabbage Total**		96
	6	Carrot	Small	9
	7	Carrot	Large	38
	8	Carrot	Large	35
	9	**Carrot Total**		82
	10	Swede	Medium	15
	11	Swede	Small	6
	12	Swede	Small	3
	13	Swede	Small	5
	14	**Swede Total**		29
	15	Turnip	Small	5
	16	Turnip	Medium	10
	17	Turnip	Large	50
	18	Turnip	Medium	12
	19	**Turnip Total**		77
	20	**Grand Total**		284

Assessor's tip

Rudy says:

It might help to sort your list before applying subtotals – if you have a list of different types of vegetable, for example, the subtotal function will work better if you have all the identical items next to each other.

9.20.2 Using Subtotals

Excel puts automatic outlines onto your subtotals. Click on the plus/minus symbols or the numbers at the left of the spreadsheet to display different sections.

In this example only the subtotals and grand total are displayed:

1 2 3		A	B	C
	1	Vegetable	Size	Cost
	5	**Cabbage Total**		96
	9	**Carrot Total**		82
	14	**Swede Total**		29
	19	**Turnip Total**		77
	20	**Grand Total**		284

Sorting is usually used to sort a database by one or more of its *fields*, e.g. name, date, cost etc.

1 Click into any cell in the column you wish to sort (*do not* select the whole column).

2 Click on the Sort Ascending icon.

Or

Click on the Sort Descending icon.

If you select a column before you sort, only the data in that column moves. The rest of the information on the spreadsheet stays still. If you are working with a database this can cause the information to become mismatched. Have a look at the spreadsheet below.

	A	B	C	D	E
1	Payroll Number	Title	Surname	First Name	Sex
2	5	Mr	Olivelle	Anthony	Male
3	23	Miss	Duck	Caroline	Female
4	19	Mr	Dodgson	Charles	Male
5	26	Miss	Richards	Anna	Female

You want to sort this spreadsheet by order of sex. If you select column E before you sort (which contains the sex), look at what happens.

	A	B	C	D	E
1	Payroll Number	Title	Surname	First Name	Sex
2	5	Mr	Olivelle	Anthony	Female
3	23	Miss	Duck	Caroline	Female
4	19	Mr	Dodgson	Charles	Male
5	26	Miss	Richards	Anna	Male

The information in column E gets sorted, but everything else stays in the same place – so Anthony Olivelle in row 2 is apparently female, and Anna Richards in row 5 is apparently male!

If you do accidentally select the whole column, you will see this message:

If you want to sort the whole list, make sure to select Expand the selection, and then click Sort.

9.21 Importing Data

9.21.1 Paste Special

When you copy information you can paste it into Excel in different ways – unformatted text, as a picture, or as a link that updates. When copying Excel data, you can paste the values, the formulae, or even the formatting.

1 Copy the data you wish to paste into Excel.

2 Click on the Edit menu.

3 Click on Paste Special.

4 Choose the type of formatting you require.

5 Click OK.

For Excel data:

For Word data:

9.21.2 Exporting Your Spreadsheet to Word

You have just found out that you need to present a report to the board! The figures are all in Excel. How can you get them into your Word document quickly and easily and how then can you make sure that the figures are all up to date? What if the board want you to make an immediate change? Don't panic! Excel has the perfect solution.

There are four ways to share data between different applications.

1 Use Cut, Copy and Paste.

2 Paste with a Link.

3 Embed a document.

4 Open a file in a different file format.

What is the difference between the four ways of sharing data?

- Copy and Paste will put a picture of the data you wish to copy in your document.

- Paste Link will connect your document to the source file and it will be updated when the source file changes.

- Embedding a document puts the document you wish to copy right into your application. The toolbars will change and you can edit your document where you are.

- Open a file in a different format – check which file formats are supported by both applications.

9.21.3 To Paste a Picture of Your Spreadsheet into Word

1 Open Word.

2 Switch back to Excel using the taskbar.

3 Select the information you wish to copy.

4 Click on Copy icon.

5 Switch to Word using the taskbar.

6 Move the cursor to the position you wish to insert your Excel spreadsheet.

7 Click on Paste icon.

8 A picture of your spreadsheet is pasted in.

9.21.4 To Paste Your Spreadsheet in Word with a Link

1 Open Word.

2 Switch back to Excel using the taskbar.

3 Select the information you wish to copy.

4 Click on Copy icon.

5 Switch to Word using the taskbar.

6 Move the cursor to the position you wish to insert your Excel Spreadsheet.

7 Click on Edit menu.

8 Click on Paste Special.

9 Click in the Paste link circle.

10 Select a format.

11 Click in the box before Display as Icon.

12 Click OK.

Your spreadsheet will be pasted into a Word document.

What will happen when I change information in Excel?

When you make any changes in Excel they will be reflected in the copy in your Word document.

What happens if the original spreadsheet is moved or renamed?

Your link will be lost! You may need to perform the copy and paste again.

9.22 Using Absolute Cell References

9.22.1 What are Absolute Cell References?

- Formulae usually use relative cell references. When you AutoFill a relative cell reference it adjusts as you move down or across (see section 9.16, using AutoFill to copy text and formulae). This is, on the whole, what you need in order for your spreadsheet to make sense.

- Occasionally, however, you will want one of the cell references to stay the same when it is AutoFilled. A cell reference that does not adjust when it is AutoFilled is an absolute cell reference.

The spreadsheet below shows an absolute cell reference in action. Everyone's salary is due to increase by 10%. The first formula, to find Bloggs' new salary, has been created. We multiply his current salary (cell C4) by 10% (cell B1).

	D4	▼	ƒ× =C4*B1		
	A	B	C	D	E
1	Salary Rise	10%			
2					
3		*Name*	*Old Salary*	*Increase*	
4		Bloggs	£67,895.00	£6,789.50	
5		Richards	£15,678.00		
6		Dalloway	£26,748.00		
7		Olivelle	£20,000.00		
8		Duck	£12,500.00		
9					

However, everyone's salary is being increased by 10%. If we AutoFill the formula as it is, then the cell reference B1 will be adjusted to B2, then B3 etc, and we'll end up with some funny answers.

		▼	ƒ×		
	A	B	C	D	E
1	Salary Rise	10%			
2					
3		*Name*	*Old Salary*	*Increase*	
4		Bloggs	£67,895.00	=C4*B1	
5		Richards	£15,678.00	=C5*B2	
6		Dalloway	£26,748.00	=C6*B3	
7		Olivelle	£20,000.00	=C7*B4	
8		Duck	£12,500.00	=C8*B5	
9					

		▼	ƒ×		
	A	B	C	D	E
1	Salary Rise	10%			
2					
3		*Name*	*Old Salary*	*Increase*	
4		Bloggs	£67,895.00	£6,789.50	
5		Richards	£15,678.00	£ -	
6		Dalloway	£26,748.00	#VALUE!	
7		Olivelle	£20,000.00	#VALUE!	
8		Duck	£12,500.00	#VALUE!	
9					

AutoFill has adjusted the reference to the 10% in cell B1.

The answers don't make sense, because Excel has changed the B1 reference.

We actually need cell B1 to remain constant or absolute as it is AutoFilled down. In other words, we need to tell Excel that this is an absolute cell reference! The diagrams below show what happens when you make B1 absolute.

		▼	ƒ×		
	A	B	C	D	E
1	Salary Rise	10%			
2					
3		*Name*	*Old Salary*	*Increase*	
4		Bloggs	£67,895.00	=C4*B1	
5		Richards	£15,678.00	=C5*B1	
6		Dalloway	£26,748.00	=C6*B1	
7		Olivelle	£20,000.00	=C7*B1	
8		Duck	£12,500.00	=C8*B1	
9					

		▼	ƒ×		
	A	B	C	D	E
1	Salary Rise	10%			
2					
3		*Name*	*Old Salary*	*Increase*	
4		Bloggs	£67,895.00	£6,789.50	
5		Richards	£15,678.00	£1,567.80	
6		Dalloway	£26,748.00	£2,674.80	
7		Olivelle	£20,000.00	£2,000.00	
8		Duck	£12,500.00	£1,250.00	
9					

B1 stays the same all the way down.

Now the answers make sense!

9.22.2 Creating Absolute Cell References

1 Click on the cell where you require the answer.

2 Enter the formula as normal.

3 Position the cursor next to the cell reference which you need to make absolute.

4 Press F4 on the keyboard – dollar signs will appear around the cell reference.

✕ ✓ *fx* =C4*B1

5 Press Enter or click on the green tick.

6 AutoFill the formula as normal.

Existing formulae can be changed to have absolute cell references

Place your cursor in the Formula bar and follow the instructions from step 3 above!

Not sure whether you need an absolute cell reference?

Absolute cell references are needed only when you want to AutoFill formulae. If you aren't sure, just AutoFill your formula and see if it works. If you find that you are getting strange answers, you may very well need an absolute cell reference.

9.23 Relative Cell References

9.23.1 What are Relative Cell References?

Relative cell references are used in formulae where you do not wish the reference to remain constant as the formula is AutoFilled. Relative cell references do not contain the $ sign that is found in absolute cell references.

9.24 Finding the Average

9.24.1 What are Functions?

Some calculations can become a bit long-winded if you try to create them with straightforward formulae, such as finding the average of a group of numbers. Functions let you perform complex calculations, like finding the average of a group of cells, quickly.

9.24.2 Finding the Average

1 Select the cell where you want to put the answer.

2 Type =.

3 Type Average.

4 Type an open bracket, like this (.

5 Type the first cell reference you require.

6 Type a colon, like this :.

7 Type the last cell reference you require – this should be a blank cell.

8 Type a closed bracket, like this).

9 Press Enter, or click on the green tick.

E.g. =AVERAGE(A1:A6)

Practise this!

Create a list of your colleagues' salaries (you can guess if you don't know). Use the Average function to find the average salary.

9.24.3 Using the Count Function

This function counts the amount of cells that contain numbers.

1 Select the cell where you require the answer.

2 Type =.

3 Type COUNT.

4 Type an open bracket, like this (.

5 Type the first cell reference you require.

6 Type a colon, like this :.

7 Type the last cell reference you require.

8 Type a closed bracket, like this).

9 Press Enter, or click on the green tick.

E.g. =COUNT(A1:A6)

9.24.4 The If Function

This function returns one value should a condition you specify prove to be true, and another if the condition should prove to be false. For instance, imagine you are preparing a budget sheet. You could use the IF function to tell Excel:

IF the total expenditure is over a certain level, then enter 'Over Budget' into the cell. But IF total expenditure is not over a certain level, then enter 'Within Budget' into the cell.

The true condition should be entered before the false condition. So a formula including the IF function will take this format:

=IF(logical test, "value if true", "value if false")

e.g. =IF(B10>450, "Over Budget", "Within Budget")

The above formula will have the results below, depending on the value of cell B10:

B11	▾	fx =IF(B10>450,"Over Budget","Within Budget")		
A	B	C	D	E
1 Expenses				
2				
3				
4 Rent	200			
5 Food	150			
6 Social	100			
7 Bills	35			
8 Monkeys	10			
9				
10 Total	495			
11 Within Budget?	Over Budget			
12				

B11	▾	fx =IF(B10>450,"Over Budget","Within Budget")		
A	B	C	D	E
1 Expenses				
2				
3				
4 Rent	200			
5 Food	150			
6 Social	100			
7 Bills	35			
8 Monkeys	10			
9				
10 Total	395			
11 Within Budget?	Within Budget			
12				

9.24.5 Using the If Function

1 Select the cell where you require the answer.

2 Type =IF.

3 Type an open bracket.

4 Type the condition for the function.

5 Type a comma.

6 Inside quotation marks, type the data to be entered into the cell if the condition is true.

7 Type a comma.

8 Inside quotation marks, type the data to be entered into the cell if the condition is false.

9 Press Enter, or click on the green tick.

Practise this!

Create a table that displays the names and years' experience of your colleagues. (Be sure to include those with both under and over five years' experience.) In a third column use the IF function to display either 'Senior' (for those who have worked longer than five years) or 'Junior' (for those with less than five years' experience).

9.24.6 Using the Minimum Function

This function finds the smallest number from a range of values.

1 Select the cell where you require the answer.

2 Type =MIN.

3 Type an open bracket.

4 Type the first cell reference you require.

5 Type a colon.

6 Type the last cell reference you require.

7 Press Enter, or click on the green tick.

E.g. =MIN(A1:A6)

9.24.7 Using the Maximum Function

This function finds the largest number from a range of values.

1 Select the cell where you require the answer.

2 Type =MAX.

3 Type an open bracket.

4 Type the first cell reference you require.

5 Type a colon.

6 Type the last cell reference you require.

7 Press Enter, or click on the green tick.

E.g. =MAX(A1:A6)

9.25 Print Preview

9.25.1 Why Check Your Spreadsheet?

The spreadsheet you work with on screen will look very different when you print it out. Before you distribute the spreadsheet you have created, you need to make sure it fits on the page properly, and that the calculations you've used are correct. You can examine the spreadsheet more closely by changing the view you are using.

9.25.2 What is Print Preview?

There are three views in Excel:

1 **Normal view**: used for the majority of the time you are working with Excel.

2 **Print preview**: used to show you how the spreadsheet will print out.

3 **Page break preview**: used to show you where your page breaks are so that you can adjust them if necessary.

Print Preview is especially important in Excel, as Normal view does not give you a clear indication of where your pages begin or end, or whether there is page numbering etc.

9.25.3 Getting a Print Preview

Click on Print Preview icon – *a new toolbar will appear.*

Or

1 Click on the File menu.

2 Click Print Preview – *a new toolbar will appear.*

9.25.4 Moving Between Pages in Print Preview

Preview: Page 2 of 4   You can see how many pages will print out at the bottom left of the screen.

Click on Next or Previous to move through the pages.

Next   Previous   Or

Use the scroll bar on the right of the screen.

9.25.5 Using the Zoom in Print Preview

1 Position the mouse pointer over the page – it will change to a magnifying glass.

2 Click once with the left mouse button – if you are zoomed out, you will zoom in, and if you are zoomed in, you will zoom out.

Or

Zoom   *Click on Zoom.*

9.25.6 Printing from Print Preview

Print...   1 Click on the Print button.

2 Click OK.

9.25.7 Closing Print Preview

Close   *Click on the Close button.*

9.26 Page Break Preview

9.26.1 Getting Page Break Preview

When you check your work in Print Preview you may decide that you want to adjust where the page breaks are so that a new page starts at a sensible point.

1 Click on View menu.

2 Click on Page Break Preview.

The view will now be Page Break Preview (see below).

3 Click on the dotted blue line.

This indicates the edge of your page.

4 Drag to a new position.

9.26.2 Closing Page Break Preview

1 Click on View.

2 Click Normal.

9.27 Printing a Worksheet

9.27.1 Printing a Worksheet

   Click on the Print icon.

Be patient with your printer!

Sometimes it can take a while for your spreadsheet to print out, and it is tempting to click the Print icon again. If you do, you will get two copies!

9.28 Changing the Page Set-up

9.28.1 Opening the Page Set-up

There are two ways of getting into Page Setup – through Print Preview, or from the Normal View. Going to Page Setup from Print Preview means that you can see how your changes have affected the spreadsheet. If you go from Normal View, you will not be able to see the changes.

From Print Preview:

Click on the Setup button.

From Normal view:

1 Click on the File menu.

2 Click Page Setup.

9.28.2 Changing the Margins

If you need to make a bit of extra room on your page, you might want to make the margins a bit smaller:

1 Bring up the Page Setup dialog box (see above).

2 Click on the Margins tab.

3 Type the margins you require into the boxes.

Or

Use the up and down arrows next to the margin sizes.

9.28.3 Changing the Margins from Print Preview

Margins

1 Click on the Margins button.

2 Position your mouse pointer over the margin you wish to resize – the pointer will change to a cross arrow (the dotted lines represent the margins).

3 Click and drag the lines to change the margins.

9.28.4 Changing the Orientation

1 Bring up the Page Setup dialog box (see page 279).

2 Click on the Page tab.

3 Click in the circle next to Portrait or Landscape.

4 Click OK.

Practise this!

Try changing the orientation of a spreadsheet from landscape to portrait and back to landscape again.

9.28.5 Scaling the Size of a Spreadsheet

If your spreadsheet is too big to fit on the page, or it is too small to read, you can scale it up or down in size.

1 Bring up the Page Setup dialog box (see page 279).

2 Click on the Page tab.

3 Increase or decrease the percentage next to Adjust to.

Or

If you want to fit the sheet onto one or more pages:

Click on Fit to.

Enter the number of pages you would like to adjust it to.

4 Click OK.

9.28.6 Changing the Paper Size

1 Bring up the Page Setup dialog box (see page 279).

2 Click on the Page tab.

3 Choose the paper size you require from the drop-down list next to Paper size.

4 Click OK.

9.29 Creating Headers and Footers

9.29.1 What are Headers and Footers?

- Headers and footers contain information which appears at the top and bottom of every page of your spreadsheet when it is printed.

- They usually include things like the date, the name of the file, your organisation name, page numbers etc.

- You can only see headers and footers in Print Preview.

9.29.2 Creating Headers and Footers

1 Bring up the Page Setup dialog box (see page 279).

2 Click on the Header/Footer tab.

3 Click on the drop-down arrow underneath Header.

4 Click on the header you require.

5 Click on the drop-down arrow underneath Footer.

6 Click on the footer you require.

7 Click OK.

9.29.3 Removing Headers and Footers

1 Bring up the Page Setup dialog box (see page 279).

2 Click on the Header/Footer tab.

3 Click on the drop-down arrow underneath Header or underneath Footer.

4 Scroll to the top of the list.

5 Click (none).

6 Click OK.

9.29.4 Creating Custom Headers and Footers

If you want a bit more flexibility, you will need to customise your headers and footers.

1 Bring up the Page Setup dialog box (see page 279).

2 Click on the Header/Footer tab.

3 Click Custom Header.

Or

Click Custom Footer.

4 Click into the section you require.

5 Enter the text you require.

Or

Click on one of the icons shown to enter text (see below).

6 Click OK.

7 Click OK.

Going from left to right, here is what the icons mean:

- Changes the font.

- Inserts the page number.

- Inserts the number of pages.

- Inserts the date.

- Inserts the time.

- Inserts the file name and path.

- Inserts the file name.

- Inserts the sheet name.

- Inserts a picture.

- Formats the picture.

What do the codes mean?

When you enter information from the toolbar, such as the date, you will see a code rather than the actual information, e.g. &[Pages] for number of pages, and &[Tab] for the name of the sheet.

When you look at your spreadsheet in Print Preview, or print it out, however, the real information will appear.

Practise this!

Create a header that includes the date, file name and the name of your company.

9.30 Inserting and Deleting Rows and Columns

9.30.1 Inserting a Row

1 Select the row (or a cell in the row) *below* where you want a new one.

2 Click on the Insert menu.

3 Click Rows – a new row will be inserted above the selection.

Or

1 Select the row *below* where you want a new one.

2 Press Control (Ctrl) and + on the keyboard.

If you select row 5

	A	B
1	Fishcakes	5
2	Monkeysuits	10
3	Stoat polishers	15
4	Cheese wobblers	20
5	Egg spanners	25
6	Chicken dancers	30
7		

a new row is inserted above row 5.

	A	B
1	Fishcakes	5
2	Monkeysuits	10
3	Stoat polishers	15
4	Cheese wobblers	20
5		
6	Egg spanners	25
7	Chicken dancers	30

9.30.2 Inserting a Column

1 Select the column (or a cell in the column) to the *right* of where you want a new one.

2 Click on the Insert menu.

3 Click Columns – a new column will be inserted to the left of the selection.

Or

1 Select the column to the *right* of where you want a new one.

2 Press Control (Ctrl) and + on the keyboard.

If you select column B   a new column is inserted to the left of column B.

	A	B	C
1	Fishcakes	5	
2	Monkeysuits	10	
3	Stoat polishers	15	
4	Cheese wobblers	20	
5	Egg spanners	25	
6	Chicken dancers	30	

	A	B	C
1	Fishcakes		5
2	Monkeysuits		10
3	Stoat polishers		15
4	Cheese wobblers		20
5	Egg spanners		25
6	Chicken dancers		30

9.30.3 Inserting Several Rows and Columns

If you want to insert several rows or columns, you can do them all at once. Let's look at how you would insert six rows:

1 Select six rows *below* where you want the six new ones.

2 Click on the Insert menu.

3 Click Rows – six new rows will be inserted above the selection.

Or

1 Select six rows *below* where you want the six new ones.

2 Press Control (Ctrl) and + on the keyboard.

Inserting columns works the same way – select six columns to the right of where you want the new ones, click on the Insert menu, and click Column (or select the columns and use Ctrl +) .

9.30.4 Deleting Rows and Columns

1 Select the row(s) or column(s) you wish to delete.

2 Click on the Edit menu.

3 Click Delete.

Or

1 Select the row(s) or column(s) you wish to delete.

2 Press Control (Ctrl) and – on the keyboard.

Pressing Delete on the keyboard doesn't work!

This will only delete any text that the row or column contains, rather than the row or column itself.

9.31 | Resizing Rows and Columns

To resize columns or rows

Your mouse must look like the cross arrow. You can see this only if you position your mouse on the grey line between column letters or row numbers.

9.31.1 Resizing Rows and Columns

1 Position your mouse on the grey line to the right of the column letter you wish to resize.

Or

Position your mouse on the grey line below the row number you wish to resize.

2 Click and drag to the size you require.

Assessor's tip

Sheena says:

If you make a column too narrow for the text it contains, you will see hash signs (#) inside the cells. If you make the column a bit wider, you'll be able to read the text clearly again.

E
####
####
####
####
####
####

9.31.2 Using AutoFit

AutoFit will make a column or row just big enough for the information it contains.

1 Position your mouse on the grey line to the right of the column letter you wish to resize.

Or

Position your mouse on the grey line below the row number you wish to resize.

2 Double click.

9.31.3 Resizing Several Rows or Columns at Once

1 Select the rows or columns you wish to resize.

2 Place your mouse on the grey line at the right-hand edge of the selected columns.

Or

Place your mouse on the grey line underneath the selected rows.

3 Click and drag to the required size – all columns and rows will become that size.

9.31.4 Resizing all the Columns and Rows

1 Select the whole of the spreadsheet (see page 255).

2 Resize column A to the desired size.

And/Or

Resize row 1 to the desired size.

3 Click in the middle of the spreadsheet to deselect.

9.32 Changing the Font and Font Size

9.32.1 What is Formatting?

Formatting is changing the appearance of your spreadsheet, either to give emphasis to important parts, or to make it easier to read.

Common types of formatting are: **bold**, *italic*, underline, font (or typeface), size, borders and shading.

9.32.2 Applying Bold

B

1 Select the cell(s) you wish to make bold.

2 Click on the Bold icon – the Bold icon will look 'pushed in'.

9.32.3 Applying Italic

I

1 Select the cell(s) you wish to make italic.

2 Click on the Italic icon – the Italic icon will look 'pushed in'.

9.32.4 Applying Underline

U

1 Select the cell(s) you wish to underline.

2 Click on the Underline icon – the Underline icon will look 'pushed in'.

9.32.5 Removing Bold, Italic or Underline

1 Select the cell(s) you wish to remove bold, italic or underline from.

2 Click on the Bold, Italic or Underline icon to remove it.

9.32.6 Changing the Font Size

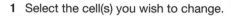

1 Select the cell(s) you wish to change.

2 Click on the drop-down arrow in the Font Size box.

3 Click on the size you require – you may need to scroll through the sizes.

Or

1 Select the cell(s) you wish to change.

2 Click inside the Font Size box – the font size number will go blue.

3 Type in the size you require.

4 Press Enter.

9.32.7 Changing the Font

1 Select the cell(s) you wish to change.

2 Click on the drop-down arrow next to the Font box.

3 Click on the Font you require – you may need to scroll through the fonts.

Or

1 Select the cell(s) you wish to change.

2 Click inside the Font box – the Font name will go blue.

3 Type in the name of font you require.

4 Press Enter.

9.32.8 Changing the Font Colour

1 Select the cell(s) you wish to change.

2 Click on the drop-down arrow next to the Font Colour icon.

3 Click on the colour you require.

4 Deselect the cells – the colour may look strange until you deselect.

9.33 Changing the Number Format

9.33.1 What are Number Formats?

When you enter numbers they are usually unformatted. They may, however, represent money or a percentage. In order to make them look like what they represent, you can apply a number format to them. Common number formats include:

- Currency.
- Percentage.
- Commas.
- Dates.
- Displaying negative numbers in red.

9.33.2 Applying Number Formats

1 Select the cell(s) you wish to change.

2 Click on the number format you require (see below).

Going from left to right, this is what each icon means:

- Currency.
- Percentage.
- Commas.
- Increase decimal places.
- Decrease decimal places.

9.33.3 Changing Number Formats with the Menu

Changing number formats with the menu gives you a much greater choice of formats.

1 Select the cell(s) you wish to change.

2 Click on the Format menu.

3 Click Cells.

4 Click on the Number tab.

5 Click on the category you require from the left-hand side.

6 Click on the style you require on the right – each category has different options, e.g. date.

7 Click OK.

Practise this!

Create a list of numbers and practise changing the number format to currency and then to percentages.

9.33.4 Removing Number Formats

1 Select the cell(s) you wish to remove number formats from.

2 Click on the Edit menu.

3 Click on the Clear submenu.

4 Click Formats.

9.34 Changing the Alignment

9.34.1 What is Alignment?

Alignment refers to the position of data inside the cell. There are three main types in Excel:

1 **Left** (usually for text).

2 **Right** (usually for numbers).

3 **Centre** (usually for headings).

9.34.2 Changing the Alignment

1 Select the cell(s) you wish to change.

2 Click on the alignment icon you require.

9.34.3 Vertical Alignment

If you have tall rows, you may wish to change the vertical alignment (top, centre, bottom, justify) rather than the horizontal (left, centre, right). Look at these cells:

They have been aligned vertically. Cell A1 has the text at the top, B1 has it in the centre, and C1 has it at the bottom. Cell D1 is vertically justified, which means that the text is spaced out so that it touches the top and bottom of the cell.

A	B	C	D
Top			This cell
	Centre		is justified
1		Bottom	vertically

1 Select the cell(s) you want to change.

2 Click on the Format menu.

3 Click Cells.

4 Click on the Alignment tab.

5 Click on the drop-down arrow under the Vertical box.

6 Click on the alignment you require.

7 Click OK.

Vertical:

Top

9.35 Applying Borders

9.35.1 What are Borders?

The lines that you can see around the cells in your spreadsheet don't necessarily print out. They are known as *gridlines*. If you want lines to print out, or you need to add decorative lines to your spreadsheet, then you can use *borders* to format it.

9.35.2 Applying Borders with the Icon

Draw Borders...

1 Select the cell(s) you wish to apply a border to.

2 Click on the arrow next to the Borders icon.

3 Click on the border style you require.

4 Deselect the cells – you can't see the border if the cells are still selected!

Careful which cells you select!

Sometimes you have to think carefully about which cells to select. Imagine that you want to add a double line above the selection of cells shown below.

10	Loan	£ 100.00	
11			
12	*Total*	£ 535.00	
13			
14	*Surplus*	£1,465.00	
15			

There is no option for adding a double line above, only one for adding a double line below:

However, if you select the cells in row 11 above the total, you can apply a double line below those. This has the same effect as applying a double line to the top of the cells containing the total.

10	Loan	£ 100.00	
11			
12	*Total*	£ 535.00	
13			
14	*Surplus*	£1,465.00	
15			

9.35.3 Applying Borders with the Menu

1 Select the cell(s) you wish to apply a border to.

2 Click on the Format menu.

3 Click Cells.

4 Click on the Border tab.

5 Click on the line style you require from the right-hand side.

6 Click on the drop-down arrow underneath Colour and click on a different colour if required.

7 Click on the Border icons to set the borders you require.

8 Click OK.

9.35.4 Removing Borders

1 Select the cells you wish to remove the borders from.

2 Click on the arrow next to the Borders icon.

3 Click on the blank border style.

9.36 Adding Colours to Cells

9.36.1 Changing the Background Colour

You can add colours to cells, rows and columns to make spreadsheets easier to read. Don't go overboard though – too many colours will make into a fascinating, but unreadable, mess. Not very professional.

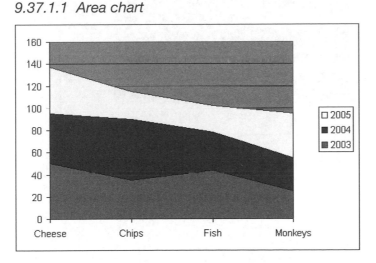

1 Select the cell(s) you wish to change.

2 Click on the Format menu.

3 Click Cells.

4 Click the Patterns tab.

5 Click on the colour you wish to use – or click No Color to remove the colours.

6 Click OK.

9.37 Creating Charts

Creating a chart makes it easier to compare and contrast the figures in a spreadsheet. Charts are also sometimes called graphs.

9.37.1 Which Chart Should I Use?

9.37.1.1 Area chart

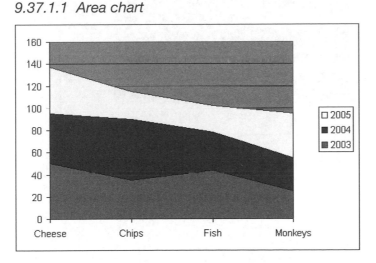

Use this when you want to emphasise change over time.

9.37.1.2 3-D surface

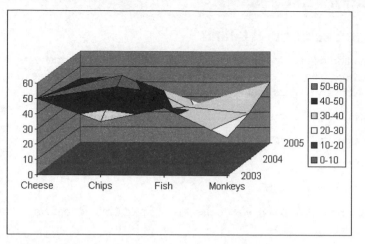

A surface chart is a bit like a 3D map. Colours and patterns show areas that are in the same range of values.

9.37.1.3 Bar chart

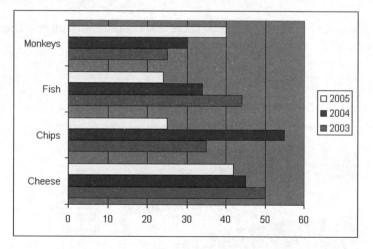

A bar chart simply compares values with each other, by displaying them as lines, or 'bars'.

9.37.1.4 Radar chart

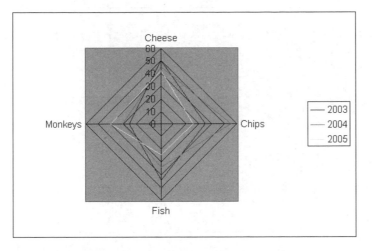

In this chart, each type of information has its own line radiating out from the centre. The further the line comes out from the centre, the higher the value.

9.37.1.5 Column chart

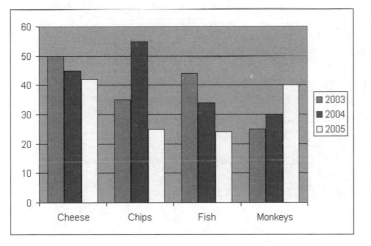

A column chart is the same as a bar chart, except the bars are vertical instead of horizontal.

9.37.1.6 Bubble chart

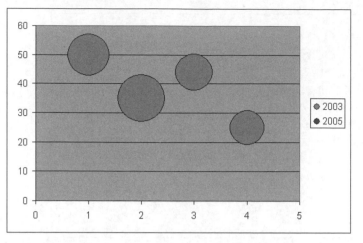

A bubble chart shows three sets of variables, represented by the two axes and the size of the bubble. The bigger the bubble, the higher the value.

9.37.1.7 Line chart

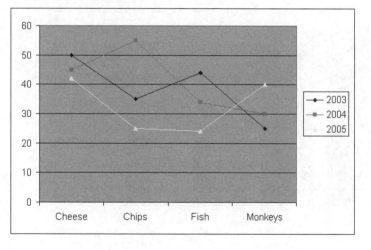

A line chart is useful for comparing overlapping figures.

9.37.1.8 Scatter chart

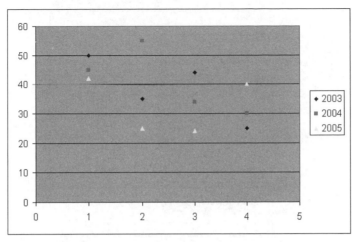

A scatter graph is useful for comparing data with the average or estimated values. This type of chart is usually used for displaying scientific data.

9.37.1.9 Pie chart

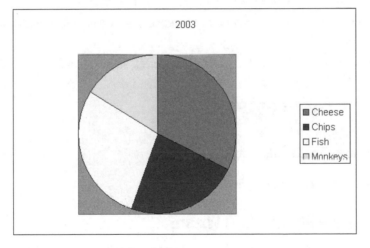

A pie chart is useful for showing one set of figures clearly.

9.37.1.10 Doughnut chart

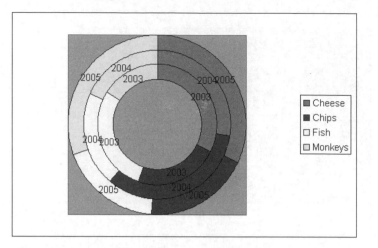

A doughnut chart is similar to a pie chart, but it can show more than one set of figures – each ring of the doughnut represents a set of figures.

9.37.2 Creating Charts with the Keyboard

1 Select the cells you wish to chart – include labels and figures, but do *not* select whole rows or columns.

In this example, the types of product are selected, as are the years, and the numbers themselves:

	2003	2004	2005
Cheese	50	45	42
Chips	35	55	25
Fish	44	34	24
Monkeys	25	30	40

2 Press F11 to create the chart.

9.37.3 Creating Charts with the Chart Wizard

1 Select the cells to be charted – include labels and figures, but do *not* select whole columns and rows, or the results will be quite bizarre – only choose the values and labels (but not the title).

2 Click on the Chart Wizard icon.

3 In step 1 of the wizard, choose the chart type you require (see below).

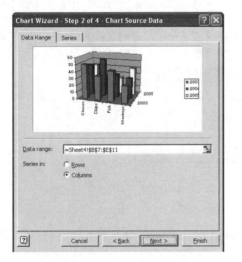

Choose a chart type from the list on the left and then choose a chart format from the examples shown on the right. To see an example of the chart you have selected, click and hold down the mouse button on the Press and hold to view sample button.

4 Click on Next.

5 In step 2 of the wizard, check that the cells you selected have produced the expected chart.

- The large area at the top shows you how your chart will look.

- The Data range box shows you what cells you have selected.

- Change the Series in section to decide whether the chart uses the rows or columns from your cells.

6 Click on Next.

7 In step 3 of the wizard, change the chart options if required (see below).

- Click on the Titles tab to add titles to the axes or to the whole chart.

- Click on the Axes tab to change the scale of the axes.

- Click on the Gridlines tab to choose whether to show major or minor gridlines.

- Click on the Legend tab to decide the position of the legend (the chart key) on the chart.

- Click on the Data Labels tab to show values or percentages around the bars.

- Click on the Data Table tab to include a table of the figures you have charted.

8 Click on Next.

9 In step 4 of the wizard, decide whether you wish your chart to appear on a new sheet or as an object next to your figures.

10 Click on Finish.

9.38 Moving, Resizing and Deleting Charts

This only applies to charts which have been created using the wizard, that are on a sheet as an object.

9.38.1 Moving Charts

1 Click on the white area of the chart to select it – black boxes will appear around the edge.

2 Click and drag from the middle of the chart to a new location – your mouse should look like a white arrow.

9.38.2 Resizing Charts

Your mouse must look like a double-headed arrow to resize a chart!

↕

---

1 Click on the chart to select it – black boxes will appear around the edge.

2 Hover the mouse pointer over a box – your mouse pointer will change to a double-headed arrow.

3 Click and drag to make the chart larger or smaller.

9.38.3 Deleting Charts

1 Click on the white area of the chart to select it – black boxes will appear around the edge.

2 Press the Delete or Del key.

9.39 Using the Chart Toolbar

9.39.1 Displaying the Chart Toolbar

1 Click on the View menu.

2 Click Toolbars – any toolbars currently displayed will be ticked.

3 Click Chart.

9.39.2 Selecting with the Chart Toolbar

1 Click the drop-down arrow next to the Chart Objects icon.

2 Click on the part you wish to select.

9.39.3 Changing the Chart Type

1 Select the white chart background.

2 Click on the drop-down arrow next to the Chart Type icon on the chart toolbar.

3 Click on the chart type you prefer.

9.40 Changing Chart Options

9.40.1 Changing Chart Titles

1 Select the white chart background.

2 Click on the Chart menu.

3 Click Chart Options.

4 Click on the Titles tab.

5 Type in the titles you require.

6 Click OK.

9.40.2 Adding Data Labels

1 Select the chart area.

2 Click on the Chart menu.

3 Click on Chart Options.

4 Click on Data Labels.

5 Choose the type of data label you would like to see, value, label or percentage.

6 Click OK.

9.41 Test Your Knowledge

The questions below will test what you know of the knowledge and understanding requirements of this unit. All the answers to these questions are contained or referred to within this chapter.

1 What important questions should you ask before beginning work on a spreadsheet?

2 Name three things Excel can be used for.

3 Name four different types of charts that you can use in Excel.

4 Name two different ways of transferring your data from Excel to Word.

5 Describe the difference between a bar chart and a line chart.

6 Describe how the IF function works.

7 Explain how sorting works and when you would use it.

8 Give an example of a formula using the Sum function.

9 Name three adjustments you could make to the appearance of a spreadsheet before printing.

10 Name two different number formats that you could use.

9.42 Evidence

The tasks you undertake as evidence for your ITQ should be work-related. Your supervisor at work should be able to give you guidance on the type of tasks you should take on. Below are some ideas of possible tasks for this unit. Consider how you can adapt these ideas to make them more relevant for your own workplace and to ensure you cover all the skills requirements.

■ Create a spreadsheet based on some numerical information that is relevant to you, such as your company's financial data. Make use of the IF, AutoSum, Average, Maximum and Minimum functions. Include your company's name and give the document a title in the header. Create a footer which displays your name and the date.

■ Create an appropriate chart based on some existing numerical data. Resize the chart as necessary and add chart titles and data labels.

■ Create a spreadsheet that makes use of an absolute cell reference, such as VAT or an exchange rate. Export this spreadsheet to Word via one of the methods covered above.

■ Create a list, or use an existing list that you can first sort and then apply subtotals to. Change the orientation of this spreadsheet and then print it.

9

CHAPTER 10

Database Software

10.1 About This Unit

What you need to know

To gain ITQ Level 2 in this unit, you should demonstrate the following competency:
Enter and retrieve a range of information, and create and modify database fields.
To achieve this you should know:

1 What the basic principles of database design are.

2 What field characteristics there may be in a simple database.

3 How to maintain data integrity and why it is important to do so.

You should be able to display the following skills and techniques:

1 Entering data into an existing database.

2 Creating fields in a simple database.

3 Modifying databases by changing field characteristics.

4 Formatting – data and reports.

5 Planning and producing database reports based on multiple criteria database queries.

6 Checking data in databases.

7 Improving efficiency through the use of shortcuts.

10

How to prove your skills

You need to carry out at least two work-based tasks which demonstrate the skills and knowledge listed above. In order to show your competency, it may well be necessary for you to complete more tasks than this.

Make sure you have plenty of evidence that shows how you completed each task, such as a copy of the file you worked on, or a document with screenshots of the processes you followed. You can back this up by producing a report which shows your knowledge of the subjects covered within the unit.

10.2 Access

Access is a database program. That's all well and good, but what is a database? Well, suppose you had a list made up of loads of names and addresses – this is a simple database. Access is a bit cleverer than that, though. It lets you store names and addresses, sure, but you can create clever things called relational databases, that contain lots of little databases linked together. So you could have the names and addresses database, which is linked to an employment record database, which is linked to a holiday/sick day database, which is linked to a database that records the salaries – it's as complex or as simple as you want it to be.

10.2.1 Starting Access

Microsoft
Access

1 Click on the Start button.

2 Click on All Programs.

3 Click on Microsoft Access.

Or, if you have a shortcut on the desktop, double click on the shortcut.

10.2.2 Closing Access

1 Click on the File menu.

2 Click Exit.

Or

Click the top X at the top right of the Access window.

10.3 Opening, Saving and Closing a Database

10.3.1 Opening a Database

When you open Access, the following screen is displayed:

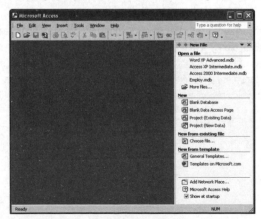

To open a database that is displayed in the Task Pane on the right, just click on the name of the file.

To open a database on your hard drive:

1 Click on the File menu.

2 Click Open.

Or

Click on the Open icon.

Or

Click on More files from the Task Pane.

3 If necessary, click on the drop-down arrow next to the Look in box to change the folder you are in.

4 Double click on the database you require.

Or

Click on the database you require.

Click Open.

I can't see my database!

Check the folder you are looking in.

Look in: Local Disk (C:)

If you need to look in a different folder or drive:

1 Click on the drop-down arrow next to the Look in box.

2 Click on the folder or drive you wish to look in.

To look in a subfolder or folder in a drive:

1 Click on the folder or subfolder required.

2 Click on Open.

New File

Open a file

Word XP Advanced.mdb
Access XP Intermediate.mdb
Access 2000 Intermediate.mdb
Employ.mdb
More files...

10

10.3.2 Closing a Database

1 Click on the File menu.

2 Click Close.

Or

1 Click the X at the top right of the database window – *not* the X at the top right of the Access screen!

10.3.3 Saving a Database

Databases are not saved in the same way as Word documents, or Excel spreadsheets, etc.

- When you create a new database it is automatically saved.

- When you add records to a database they are automatically saved.

- When you delete or modify the information in a database, your changes are automatically saved.

- It is only when you alter the design or structure of a database that you need to save your changes.

10.4 What is a Database?

A database is a collection of information with the *information arranged in a structured way*. You have probably used paper databases to look information up, e.g. a telephone book, card index, or a filing system.

10.4.1 The Advantages of Using Computerised Databases

If you have a lot of information to deal with, it is almost always better to use a computer rather than paper records. The main advantages are:

- You can **sort** your information into any order, e.g. a phone book on computer could be arranged in order of postcode, name of the town, area code etc.

- **Finding** people is much easier. Unlike a paper system, you are not reliant on one key piece of information, e.g. to find someone in a phone book you have to know their surname. If the phone book was on a computer, you could know their address, their first name etc., and still use it to find them.

- You do not have to see all the information at once. The information that you wish to see can be **extracted** from the whole, e.g. all the people who live in London, all the people who are three months late in paying their bill, etc.

- Information can be **cross-referenced**, which would be impossible on paper, e.g. you may want to see everyone who lives in London and is also three months late with paying their bill.

- **Updates** are much easier on a computer. You can quickly delete or edit the information.

- Computers use **less space** than a large paper filing system.

10.4.2 Do You Need a Database?

Consider what you need a database for. Will it help you work more efficiently, or will the effort and time you put in outweigh the benefit of using it?

10.4.2.1 A good example

If you have a list of clients on a database, you could search through and find those clients that meet a specific criteria. For example, those in Warwickshire, who have spent X amount on your product or service in the last year, but have not placed an order in the last three months. You could then send them a letter to see if they want to buy anything.

10.4.2.2 A bad example

A list of suppliers who you only need to look up by name. A simple card file (or table in Word) may be quicker and a lot cheaper, if all the information is simply listed in alphabetical order and is only needed in that order.

10.5 | The Parts of an Access Database

10.5.1 The Database Window

When you first open a database you will see the database window. This is like the 'control centre' of the database – everything you create and use will be done from here. When the database is open, this window will also be open somewhere on the screen.

The name of the database is shown on the title bar – in this case, 'Disaster'. The Objects bar on the left shows you the seven possible parts of a database. At the moment you are looking at the tables – there is one table in this database, called 'tblPlates'.

10.5.2 What Do the Parts of a Database Do?

The seven different parts all work together to make the whole database function. Each part has a specific role in the way the database works. In order to work with databases, you need to know about the four main database components:

1 *Tables* Tables are where **all** the **information** in your database **is stored**. They are the first part to be created, and no other part can function until the tables are in place. You can use tables to input information. Tables also allow you to see lots of information at once. A database with one table is known as a **flat-file** database. Other databases have more than one table. These tables will be related to each other in some way, e.g. one table for employee details, and another table for the training they go on. This is known as a **relational** database.

2 *Queries* Queries allow you to **extract** information from the tables. Tables contain all the information, but you may wish to take out a section from the whole, e.g. all the people who live in London, all the sales staff, etc. You can think of queries as the 'questions' you ask of your tables. Queries appear as 'mini' tables. The query shown below has extracted all the sales staff from a table.

3 *Forms* Forms are based on tables and contain the same information. They are used to input information in a more user-friendly way than tables.

4 *Reports* Reports are used to print information off from the database. They are based on the information found in tables or queries. Reports can also be used to produce mailing labels.

10.5.3 Navigating Around the Database Window

To use different parts of the database, just click on the button you require from the Objects bar on the left. Objects of that type will appear to the right – so if you clicked on Queries, then all the Queries would appear on the right.

10.5.4 Opening a Database Object

1 Click on the button you require, e.g. Tables.

2 Double click on the object you require.

Or

1 Click on the button you require, e.g. Tables.

2 Click on the object you require.

3 Click Open.

You can end up with lots of windows open!

When you open an object, it appears in a new window and the database window remains open behind the object window. If you open up more objects, you can end up with a lot of windows on your screen. Don't panic; this is perfectly natural and not at all bad for your health. If you get worried, just close the windows you don't need – but don't close the main database window, or your whole database will close!

10.5.5 Closing a Database Object

1 Click on the File menu.

2 Click Close.

Or

Click the X at the top of the object window.

10.6 Using Tables

10.6.1 What is a Table?

Tables are the core of your database, and contain all the raw information. No other part of the database can function without tables.

Some databases store all the information in one table. These are known as **flat-file** databases.

Sometimes databases store the information in more than one table. These are known as **relational** databases.

10.6.2 Opening a Table

1 Click on the Tables button.

2 Click on the table you wish to open.

3 Click Open.

Or

1 Click the Tables button.

2 Double click on the table you want to open.

10.6.3 Table Jargon

Each table is made up of rows and columns.

Each row holds one complete piece of information – a record. The picture below shows the record for Geoff Cohen.

EMPLOYEE ID	LASTNAME	FIRSTNAME	INITIAL	GENDER	DEPARTMENT	PHONE
5	Cohen	Geoff	A	Male	SALES	(217)555-4204

Each column holds one piece of information per record – a field, e.g. last name, department, gender, etc. The field names are shown in grey at the top of the table.

Each box of the table is a cell and contains one piece of information.

10.6.4 Moving Around a Table

To move around cells:

Click on the cell you require.

Or

Press the Tab key to move one cell to the right.

Or

Use the cursor keys to move around the cells.

To move around records:

Click on the record you require.

Or

Use the vertical scroll bar to move up and down the records.

Or

Use the record navigation buttons at the bottom left of the screen:

Going from left to right, here is what the navigation icons do:

- Move to the first record.
- Move to the previous record.
- Displays the current record (you can type in a record number and press Return to go to that record).
- Move to the next record.
- Move to the last record.
- Create a new record after the last one.
- The number to the right displays the total number of records – you cannot click on this.

To move around fields:

Click on the field you require.

Or

Use the horizontal scroll bar to move left and right around the fields.

10.6.5 Editing the Information in a Table

1 Move to the cell you wish to change.

2 Make any changes you require.

3 Click outside the record you are in – the changes are automatically saved.

To quickly change everything in the cell:

1 Position the mouse pointer at the left of the cell – it will change to a big white cross.

2 Click the left mouse button once – the cell will be selected.

3 Type in the new information.

4 Click outside the record you are in – the changes are automatically saved.

When are my changes saved?

As soon as you start typing, a pencil will appear to the left of the record.

As long as you can see the pencil, the information is not saved. However, as soon as you move out of this record, the pencil will disappear, and your changes are saved automatically.

When I edit the information, a drop-down arrow appears

This means that you are working with a look-up field. If you click the drop-down arrow, you will get a choice of information which can go in this field, e.g. male or female for a gender field. This saves you time and helps to prevent mistakes.

Assessor's tip

Rudy says:

If you find yourself stuck in a record which Access won't let you get out of, press Escape (Esc) on the keyboard.

10

10.6.6 Entering New Records

1 Click on New Record icon.

2 Type in the new information.

3 Click outside the record when you have finished – the changes are saved automatically.

Assessor's tip

Lynne says:

Sometimes you might find a field with the word AutoNumber in. You don't have to enter information into this field yourself – Access automatically adds a number for you.

Can I add a new record anywhere in the table?

No, only in the last row of the table:

	+	Peterson	John
*			

The asterisk (*) symbol shows you that this is the space for a new record.

10.6.7 Selecting Records

→	+	Beman	

Click on the Record Selector to the left of the record – the mouse pointer will change to a black arrow.

Or, if you would like to select several records:

1 Click on the Record Selector to the left of the first record and hold down the mouse button.

2 Drag over the other records you wish to select.

Can I select records that are not next to each other?

No! Usually, if you select things, then you can use the Control key to select items that are not next to each other. In an Access table, you can only select multiple records if they are next to each other.

10.6.8 Deleting Records

1 Select the record you wish to delete (using the Record Selector to the left of the record).

2 Press the Delete key.

Or

3 Click the Delete icon.

When I try to delete, Access says

Microsoft Access

⚠ The record cannot be deleted or changed because table 'tblTraining' includes related records.

[OK]   [Help]

This means that you have a 'relational' database and your table is linked to another one. The person you are trying to delete has information about them in another table within this database. In order to delete them, you will have to go to the linked table first and delete them from there.

10.7 Changing the View of a Table

10.7.1 What are the Views of a Table?

There are two views to a table:

1 **Design view**: where you can add, edit or delete fields and change the way your table works.

2 **Datasheet view**: where you can input data.

10.7.2 Changing the View

1 Click down arrow next to view icon.

2 Click the view you require.

The View icon looks different depending on which view you are in!

When you are in Design View it will look like this:

When you are in Datasheet View it will look like this:

10

10.8 Creating New Fields

10.8.1 Creating the Fields and Deciding the Data Type

Ensure you are in Design View to start with.

1 Click into the first row under Field Name.

Field Name	Data Type	Description

2 Type in your first field name, e.g. OrganisationID.

3 Press Tab.

Or

Click into the Data Type column.

4 If required, click the drop-down arrow and change the data type (see next section).

5 Press Tab.

Or

Click into the Description column.

6 If required, type in a description for this field (e.g. what the field is for).

Access will not allow the following characters in field names:

. (full-stop)   ! (exclamation point) [ ] (brackets)   ` (grave accent)

It is good practice to not include spaces in field names

Although you can use spaces in field names and it will not usually cause problems, it can cause conflicts if you use Visual Basic for Applications with Access.

10.8.2 Specifying Data Types

You must specify what data type each of the fields in your table should be.

Data type	What does it store?	Example	Extra information
Text	Letters or numbers	First name Last name	Holds up to 255 characters. Most of your fields will probably be text.
Memo	Letters or numbers	Comments	Holds up to 64,000 characters. It is usually used when you need to add a lot of text.
Number	Numbers	Number of staff	Holds numbers which you intend to sort numerically, or perform calculations on.
Date/Time	Dates and times	Date hired Order date	Holds dates which you can then sort into date order and perform calculations on.
Currency	Monetary values	Salary	Formats numbers as currency and allows you to perform calculations on those numbers.

Data type	What does it store?	Example	Extra information
AutoNumber	A number which Access generates automatically for each record	ID Number	Used mostly as a primary key field, because the number will be unique for each record. Even if the record is deleted, the number goes with it.
Yes/No	A field which gives you the choice of 'yes' or 'no'	Full-time	
OLE object	OLE objects are generally graphics, e.g. photographs, logos	Logo Product preview	Holds up to 1 gigabyte (limited by disk space).
Hyperlink	Links to somewhere elsethat your computer has access to, e.g. a Word document, a website	Company website	When you click on the data in this field it will link you to somewhere else.
Lookup wizard	A field that allows you to choose from a drop-down list	Gender Department	

10

Is a phone number a number data type?

No! Phone numbers, part numbers, or numbers on which you don't intend to do calculations are text! If you make them numbers, you will not be able to have a '0' at the start of your phone numbers.

10.9 Field Properties

10.9.1 What are Field Properties?

Field properties are a way of limiting the information which people can type into your table – useful if you want to try to minimise the possibility of mistakes. For example, you can use them to:

■ Limit the number of characters allowed into a field, e.g. allowing only 10 characters for postcode Specify a default, or automatic value, e.g. 'London' in the town field, if most of your addresses are in London.

■ Change the way that data appears, e.g. formatting a date which is typed in as 1/1/06 to appear as 01 January 2006.

10.9.2 Setting Field Properties

You can change the field properties at any time, but...

If you change them after you have already inputted data to the table, you may lose some of the information. If existing data doesn't fit the new requirements, Access may just delete it.

1 Ensure you are in Design View of the table.

2 Click into the field you wish to set properties for.

3 Change the properties as required (see next sections).

General	Lookup	
Field Size	50
Format	
Input Mask	
Caption	
Default Value	
Validation Rule	
Validation Text	
Required	No
Allow Zero Length	Yes
Indexed	No
Unicode Compression	Yes
IME Mode	No Control
IME Sentence Mode	None

4 Click on the Save icon.

Field properties change depending on the data type!

For example, fields with a text data type will have different properties available than a field with a number date type, etc.

10.9.3 Changing Field Size

What does it mean? The maximum number of characters which people can input into a field (including spaces).

When am I likely to use it? For text fields where there is always a limited number of characters, e.g. postcode, phone number.

1 Click into the Field Size box.

Field Size	12

2 Change the number to the maximum number allowed for your field.

10.9.4 Changing Format

What does it mean? Changes the way in which the data appears.

When am I likely to use it? For dates or numbers which you wish to appear differently from the way they have been input, e.g. numbers which you wish to become percentages, dates which you wish to become long dates, 01 Jan 1999.

1 Click in the Format box.

2 Click the drop-down arrow.

Format		
General Number	3456.789
Currency	£3,456.79
Euro	€3,456.79
Fixed	3456.79
Standard	3,456.79
Percent	123.00%
Scientific	3.46E+03

3 Click on the format you require.

10.9.5 Setting an Input Mask

What does it mean? Forces the information which is input to appear in a certain way. The input mask determines how it should appear, for example an input mask of '0000' would force people to enter four numbers into the field.

When am I likely to use it? When there is a standard format for the field in question, e.g. National Insurance numbers which are always two letters, followed by six numbers and then one letter.

1 Click into the Input Mask box.

2 Type in the input mask you require, e.g. LL000000L for a national insurance number.

Input Mask	LL000000L	...

These are the symbols you are most likely to use in your input mask:

0	Number which must be filled in
9	Number which does not have to be filled in
#	Number or space which does not have to be filled in and can include plus or minus signs
L	Letter which must be filled in
?	Letter which does not need to be filled in
A	Letter or number which must be filled in
a	Letter or number which does not need to be filled in
&	Any character or space which must be filled in
C	Any character or space which does not have to be filled in
<	All characters which follow this will be converted to lower case (the symbol does not show when you input data)
>	All characters which follow this will be converted to upper case (the symbol does not show when you input data)

10

10.9.6 Changing the Default Value

What does it mean? Text which is already typed into the field before you start to input data (you can still type something else, though).

When am I likely to use it? When you often type the same data into a field, e.g. if most of your records contain 'London' in the address, you could change the default for town/city to 'London'.

1 Click into the Default Value box.

2 Type the default you require.

10.9.7 Setting the Validation Rule and Validation Text

What does it mean? Setting a rule for the data which can be input into a field. The validation text is the error message which will be displayed if the rule is broken.

When am I likely to use it? One example would be a credit limit. Imagine that nobody can have a credit limit over £50,000. You can set the validation rule as <50000, which forces Access to only accept numbers which are less than 50,000.

1 Click into the Validation Rule box.

2 Enter the validation rule, e.g. <50000.

3 Click into the Validation Text box.

4 Type the error message you wish to appear if people break the rule, e.g. 'You must enter a value of less than £50,000'.

| Validation Rule | <50000 |
| Validation Text | Please enter a figure of less than £50,000 |

10.9.8 Making a Field Required

What does it mean? People must enter something into this field when they create a new record.

When am I likely to use it? When you have a field which you do not want to be left blank, e.g. organisation name, phone number etc.

1 Click into the Required box.

2 Click the drop-down arrow.

3 Click Yes.

If you do not fill in a required field in Datasheet View, Access will display the following message:

Microsoft Access ☒

⚠ The field 'tblTest.Department' cannot contain a Null value because the Required property for this field is set to True. Enter a value in this field.

OK   Help

10.9.9 Allowing Zero Length

What does it mean? It allows you to leave a field blank on purpose.

When am I likely to use it? When you have a field which you know is to be left blank.

1 Click into the Zero Length box.

2 Click the drop-down arrow.

3 Click Yes.

10.9.10 AutoNumber Property: New Values

What does it mean? The way in which AutoNumber generates the next number: usually it goes up by one each time.

When am I likely to use it? When you do not want the AutoNumber to go up by one each time.

1 Click into the New Values box.

2 Click the drop-down arrow.

3 Click Random.

10.9.11 Number Property: Decimal

What does it mean? It determines how many decimal places are to appear to the right of the decimal point

When am I likely to use it? When you need to specify a certain number of decimal points for a number field

1 Click into the Decimal Places box.

2 Click the drop-down arrow.

3 Click on the number of decimal places you require.

10

10.10 Searching and Sorting Records

10.10.1 Searching

Access tables allow you to find one record at a time in order to make amendments, delete, or view a certain record quickly. However, it will not extract records from the whole table, or allow you to search based on more than one piece of information – to do that you will need to use a query.

1 Click into the column you wish to search through, e.g. lastname, department.

2 Click the Find icon.

3 Type the data you wish to find next to Find What.

4 Click the drop-down arrow next to Match and choose the option you require. Imagine that you are searching for someone whose last name is 'Smith', and you have typed the word 'Smith' next to Find What. Here's what will happen with the different match options:

- Any Part of Field: Will find anything that contains the word 'Smith', e.g. 'Smithson', 'Taylor-Smith' and 'Smith' itself.

- Whole Field: Will only find the word 'Smith' and nothing else.

- Start of Field: Will find the word 'Smith' at the beginning of the text, e.g. 'Smithson', 'Smith', but not 'Taylor-Smith'.

1 Click Find Next – the found record is highlighted in the table.

2 Click Find Next again to find the next record.

When Access has finished it will display this message:

3 Click OK.

4 Click Cancel to close the Find box.

10.10.2 Sorting Records

You can sort records to make it easier to view or find information. In an Access table you can only sort on one field. If you want to sort on more than one you will need to use a query.

To sort records, click into the column you wish to sort, and then click on the Sort icon you require:

The first icon sorts in ascending order, the second sorts in descending order.

It depends on what you are sorting. Have a look at the list below to get an idea of how it works.

	Ascending	**Descending**
Text	A to Z	Z to A
Numbers	Smallest to biggest	Biggest to smallest
Dates	Earliest to latest	Latest to earliest

Blanks will appear at the top if you are sorting ascending, or at the bottom if you are sorting descending.

Assessor's tip

Georgie says:

Memo, OLE and Hyperlink fields do not sort. Their 'field types' won't let them.

How do I save the results of my sort?

Close the table and save the layout changes when you are prompted.

10.11 Toolbars

Shortcut

Toolbars help you to be more efficient!

If you get tired of trawling through menus and options then toolbars are for you. They are a one-stop shop for your computing needs. It helps to get to know which icons carry out some of your most frequently used actions.

10.11.1 What are Toolbars?

Toolbars are used to carry out commands in your software. They contain pictures called icons which you click on to carry out an action:

E.g. Database toolbar:

If you cannot see the toolbar you need, you will need to turn it on using the View menu.

10.11.2 Turning Toolbars On and Off

1 Click on the View menu.

2 Click on the Toolbars submenu.

3 Click on name of toolbar you wish to turn on or off – if it is on, it will be switched off, and if it is off, it will be switched on.

If a toolbar name has a tick next to it

It means that the toolbar is turned on.

```
| ✓ | Database   |
|   | Task Pane  |
|   | Web        |
|   | Customize… |
```

Setting up shortcuts

You can also use keyboard shortcuts instead of toolbar buttons. It's possible to set up your own keyboard shortcuts. To do this in Access, you can follow the same instructions listed in Chapter 8, Word-processing software.

10.12 Creating a Simple Query

10.12.1 What is a Query?

Queries allow you to extract information from tables, e.g. all the women in the Sales department, or all the staff who earn between £20,000 and £30,000, listed in alphabetical order.

Queries look exactly the same as tables – which is not surprising, as they are really the same thing – they just show you the information you have chosen to extract.

Queries also let you input information into the table, without having to see the whole table. If you input data into a query, it will automatically go into the table the query was based on.

Most of the time you will be producing *select queries*. These are queries that simply extract and display the information you asked for. There are other types of query which we will deal with in the Advanced Queries section.

10.12.2 Creating a Query

There are four main steps to creating a query:

1 Choosing the table you wish to extract information from.

2 Choosing the fields you wish to see in the query.

3 Running the query to see the result.

4 Saving the query (if required).

10.12.3 Step One: Choosing the Table

1 Click on the Queries button in the database window.

2 Double click on Create query in Design view – the Show Table box will appear.

 Create query in Design view

Or

Click on New.

Click on Design View.

Click OK – the Show Table box will appear.

3 Double click on the table you wish to use – the table will appear in the background.

4 Click Close.

I didn't add a table before I clicked Close

Click on the Show Table icon to bring the box back!

I added the same table more than once

It's very easy to double click on the same table more than once, or forget to close the Show Table box. If you have added the same table twice, click on the second table

and press the Delete key!

10.12.4 Step Two: Choosing the Fields

You are now in the Design View of the query. It is here that you get to ask Access for the fields you wish to see.

Double click on the field you wish to see from the list within the table – the field will jump to the query grid.

Or

Click and drag the field you require to the Field row in the query grid.

I can't see all the fields I've added

If you add lots of fields to the query grid, you will need to use the horizontal scroll bar to see them all.

How can I add all the fields at once?

Double click the * at the top of the list of fields.

10.12.5 Step Three: Running a Query

You are still in Design View, and this is the place where you ask Access for the information you wish to see. You now want to see the answer, and that's where running the query comes in. Running the query takes you out of Design View and into Datasheet View, where you can see the records that match what you've asked for:

Click on the Run icon.

Or

Click the Datasheet View icon.

What is the difference between the Run icon and the Datasheet icon?

At this stage – nothing! It's only when you get to more advanced queries that the difference will become clear.

Why can I see 'expr' next to some of my fields?

You've probably added the same field more than once! You need to return to Design View and delete one of the fields.

What will happen if I change the data I can see in the query?

The table will also change! Think of the query as the same as the table – you are just seeing less of it. So if you change the data in the query, the data in the table will change as well.

10.12.6 Saving a Query

1 Click on the Save icon.

2 Enter a name for the query.

3 Click OK.

Assessor's tip

Rudy says:

Give queries a consistent name i.e. start the name off with the letters QRY, qry or Query. That way you will know that it's a query whenever you come across it.

10.12.7 Closing a Query

1 Click on the File menu.

2 Click Close.

Or

3 Click the X at the top right of the query.

10.13 Changing the View

10.13.1 What are Views?

There are two views which you will need to use in a query:

1 **Design view**: This is where you add the table and the fields that you wish to see in the query. You can think of it as the place where you ask Access what you want to see.

2 **Datasheet view**: This is where you can see the answer. The Datasheet view looks just like the table.

You will also see another view available – **SQL view**. This shows how the query will look in SQL code. However, you will not need to use it unless you are interested in using code to program your database – it's not part of ITQ and, quite frankly, your life is a lot less complicated and more interesting without it. So don't worry about it. You're not missing anything.

10.13.2 Switching to Design View

Click on the Design View icon.

10.13.3 Switching to Datasheet Vew

Click on the Datasheet View icon.

10.14 Adding Criteria to Queries

10.14.1 What are Criteria?

So far you have created queries that have pulled out certain fields from the table. However, it is more likely that you will want to pull out certain records, e.g. all the **females**, all the people in the **Sales** department, all the people who earn **over £20,000**. The text in bold is known as criteria, and they can easily be added to a query.

10.14.2 Searching for Records on One Criteria

1 Create a new query as normal.

2 Add the fields you wish to see in Design View.

3 Type in the criteria you wish to use on the criteria row, under the relevant field name – the criteria will get quotation marks around it when you click outside.

4 Run the query as normal.

For example, finding females. The word 'female' is typed on the criteria row under the Gender field:

For example, finding people in the Sales department. The word 'sales' is typed on the criteria row under the Department field:

Are criteria case sensitive?

No, you can type in whatever case you like, as long as you spell it correctly!

Why is my query not showing anything?

The biggest mistake with adding criteria is spelling the criteria incorrectly, or using a term which is not in the table. For example, let's say you want to find the females in this table:

	EMPLOYEE ID	LASTNAME	FIRSTNAME	INITIAL	GENDER
+	5	Cohen	Geoff	A	Male
+	9	Dean	Christine	W	Female
+	12	Egan	Michelle	P	Female
+	33	Orlando	John	3	Male
+	21	Kaufman	Lisa	C	Female

If you type the word 'females' as your criteria, you won't find anybody, because the text in the table is 'female' without an 's' on the end!

It may also be that you have stray criteria left over from another time when you ran this query and it is affecting your result.

10.14.3 Searching for Records Which do not Meet a Criteria

You may want to find records which are not something, e.g. all the people who do not work in the Sales department.

1 Create a new query as normal.

2 Add the fields you wish to see in Design View.

3 Type the word NOT in front of your criteria underneath the field you wish to find it in – your criteria will get quotation marks around it, once you click outside.

4 Run the query as normal.

DEPARTMENT
tblEmployee
☑
Not "sales"

10.14.4 Searching for Records Where information is Missing

You may have forgotten to add information in various fields when you were inputting them. Or you may have left certain information deliberately blank when you were inputting because you did not have the information to hand at the time. If you would like to find the blanks in a field:

1 Create your query as normal.

2 Add the fields you wish to see in Design View.

3 Type the word 'NULL' into the criteria row of the field you wish to find blanks in (this will change to 'Is null' once you have clicked outside!).

This example will find people whose last name has been left blank:

LASTNAME
tblEmployee
☑
Is Null

4 Run your query as normal.

10.15 Numbers, Dates and Wildcards

So far, the criteria you have added have not allowed you to make comparisons. You may want to find people who earn more or less than a certain figure, or people who started before or after a certain date. This section will show you how to do this.

10.15.1 Using Numbers

Below are examples of criteria which can be added to make comparisons with numbers, e.g. greater than, less than, between, etc. In the examples below, the number 100 has been used to show you how it works:

What do you want to find?	This is what you type in the criteria row:
Numbers greater than 100	>100
Numbers less than 100	<100
Numbers greater than or equal to 100	>=100
Numbers less than or equal to 100	<=100
Between 1 and 100	Between 1 and 100

When using numbers as criteria

Just type the number – you do not have to include pound signs, percentage symbols, etc.

10.15.2 Using Dates

Below are examples of criteria which can be added to make comparisons with dates, e.g. before, after, between, etc. In the examples below, the date 1/1/2000 has been used to show you how it works:

What do you want to find?	This is what you type in the criteria row:
Dates after 1/1/2000	>1/1/2000
Dates before 1/1/2000	<1/1/2000
Dates after or equal to 1/1/2000	>=1/1/2000
Dates before or equal to 1/1/2000	<=1/1/2000
Dates between 1/1/2000 and 31/12/2000	Between 1/1/2000 and 31/12/2000

Can I type dates with full stops?

No! Access won't let you, and you will get an error message. Always use slashes, like this: 1/1/2000.

Access will put hashes (#) around your dates!

In the same way as criteria get quotation marks when you click outside, dates will get hash marks (#) around them.

Assessor's tip

Georgie says:

How to remember whether to use greater than or less than?
Imagine that Access takes the 1/1/1900 as 1. Every subsequent day goes up by an integer of one, so 2/1/1900 is 2, 3/1/1900 is 3 etc. The bigger the number the later the date. So if you want to find earlier dates it will be less than *and if you want to find later dates it will be* greater than.

10.15.3 Using a Wildcard

Wildcards allow you to search for partial information in a field, e.g. finding words that start with a certain letter, finding words that end with a certain letter, finding dates that end in a certain year, etc. A wildcard is just an asterisk (*), and can be placed wherever there is blank information to be filled in. The table below shows examples of wildcards:

What do you want to find?	This is what you type in the criteria row:
Words beginning with **Ke**	Ke*
Words ending in **son**	*son
Dates ending in the year 1984	*/*/84

Access will add the word 'Like' and quotation marks around criteria with wildcards!

In the same way that criteria get quotation marks around them when you click outside, wildcards will display this text.

10.16 Adding More Than One Criteria

10.16.1 What are AND and OR?

Often you will want to add more than one criteria, e.g. all the **females** who work in the **Sales** department, all the **males** who earn **under £20,000** etc. If you have more than one criteria, you must specify whether the relationship between them is AND or OR:

1 **AND** means you will find records which match **both** criteria:

- e.g. only females who work in Sales,

- only males who earn over £20,000.

2 **OR** means that you will find records which match **either** of the criteria:

- e.g. all the females, and all the people who work in Sales,

- all the males, and all the people who earn over £20,000.

You can't have ANDs on the same field!

For example, Female AND Male will not give you anybody, because no one can be both female and male at the same time.

ORs are usually on the same field

For example, Manchester OR London, will return all the records which are either Manchester or London. If you said London AND Manchester, you will not get anything because you are asking Access to find you records which have both Manchester and London in the same field. You can't be in Manchester and London at the same time.

10.16.2 Using AND

1 Create your query as normal.

2 Add the fields you wish to see in Design View.

3 Type your first criteria onto the Criteria row under the relevant field.

4 Enter any other criteria *on the same criteria row as the first* and under the relevant field.

5 Run your query as normal.

The example below will show all the females in the Sales department:

GENDER	DEPARTMENT
tblEmployee	tblEmployee
☑	☑
"female"	"sales"

10.16.3 Using OR

1 Create your query as normal.

2 Add the fields you wish to see in Design View.

3 Type your first criteria onto the first Criteria row under the relevant field.

4 Type any additional criteria *on a different criteria row* under the relevant field.

5 Run your query as normal.

The example below will show all the females and all the people in the Sales department:

GENDER	DEPARTMENT
tblEmployee	tblEmployee
☑	☑
"female"	
	"sales"

10.16.4 Some Examples of Queries with Multiple Criteria

This will find all the females in the Executive department who were hired after 1/1/80 – i.e. Female AND executive AND after 1/1/80:

GENDER	DEPARTMENT
tblEmployee	tblEmployee
☑	☑
"female"	"sales"

This will find all the executive staff and all the sales staff – i.e. executive OR sales:

DEPARTMENT
tblEmployee
☑
"executive"
"sales"

This will find all the females who are executives and all the males who are salespeople – i.e. (female AND executive) OR (male AND salesperson):

GENDER	DEPARTMENT
tblEmployee	tblEmployee
☑	☑
"female"	"executive"
"male"	"sales"

10.17 Sorting Queries

10.17.1 Sorting in Datasheet View

As well as choosing to see certain records, you can also change the order in which the information is displayed. To do this, you need to sort the query. You can sort in either Datasheet or Design View.

What's the difference between sorting in Datasheet View and sorting in Design View?

In Datasheet View you can only sort by one field.

In Design View you can sort on more than one field.

10.17.2 Sorting on One Field in Datasheet View

1 Click into the column you wish to sort.

2 Click on the sort button you require.

Sort ascending:

Or

Sort descending:

10.17.3 Sorting on One Field in Design View

Field:	LASTNAME
Table:	tblEmployee
Sort:	
Show:	Ascending
Criteria:	Descending
or:	(not sorted)

1 Click into the sort row for the field you wish to sort.

2 Click the drop-down arrow which appears.

3 Click Ascending or Descending.

4 Run your query as normal.

How do I remove the sort order?

This is done in the same way as sorting a field. Click the drop-down arrow in the sort box, and then click on Not Sorted to remove the sort order.

10.17.4 What Does Sorting on More Than One Field Mean?

Let's imagine that you wish to sort a query by the Lastname field. If lots of people have the same last name, then you would probably want to sort their first names within that, like the example below:

LASTNAME	FIRSTNAME
Pope	Jan
Rizzo	Ann
Rodan	Bill
Sanders	Kathy
Skye	Jim
Smith	Bob
Smith	Fred
Smith	Jane
Smith	Kim
Young	Sandy
Youngblood	Dick
Zambini	Rick

Imagine that you need to produce a list of the people who work in different departments. You could sort by the Department field first, and then within that sort by the person's last name, like this:

DEPARTMENT	LASTNAME
FINANCE	Collins
FINANCE	Smith
FINANCE	Smith
FINANCE	Smith
SALES	Adams
SALES	Bicksby
SALES	Campbell
SALES	Cohen
SALES	Drasin
SALES	Drendon
SALES	Egan
SALES	Gilbert

10.17.5 Sorting on More Than One Field in Design View

The field which is your first choice for sorting must be to the left!

In the query grid, the field which is your first choice for sorting *must* be on the left of any other fields you wish to sort.

For example, sorting by department and then by lastname – the Department field must be to the left of Lastname:

DEPARTMENT	LASTNAME
tblEmployee	tblEmployee
Ascending	Ascending
☑	☑

1 Ensure that the field which is your first choice for ordering is on the left.

2 Click into the Sort row for your first field.

3 Click the drop-down arrow.

4 Click Ascending or Descending.

5 Click into the Sort row for your second field.

6 Click Ascending or Descending.

7 Run your query as normal.

10.18 Using Forms

10.18.1 What are Forms?

Forms are based on tables or queries. They show the same information, but they look nicer. Okay, they're more useful than that – you can use them to:

■ Input data in a more user-friendly way than inputting data directly into a table or query.

■ View individual records on the screen (rather than multiple records like a table or query).

- Input data into more than one table at once.

- Prevent users from having to access the tables in your database. The tables are the structure of your database, and if they are accidentally deleted, or their design is accidentally changed, it could ruin everything. Forms give people a way of inputting data without giving them access to the tables.

10.18.2 Opening a Form

Forms

1 Click on the Forms button.

2 Click the form you wish to open.

Open

3 Click Open.

Or

1 Click on the Forms button.

2 Double click the form you wish to open.

10.18.3 Navigating Around Records

Click the required button at the bottom of the form:

Page: |◄ ◄ [2] ► ►|

Going from left to right, here is what the buttons do:

- Move to the first record.

- Move to the previous record.

- Move to the next record.

- Move to the last record.

10.18.4 Editing a Record

1 Go to the record you wish to edit.

2 Click on the field you wish to change.

3 Make your changes as required.

When are my changes saved?

Just like in a table, as soon as you move onto another record the changes will be saved. So be careful!

10.18.5 Adding a New Record

Click on the New Record icon.

10.18.6 Printing a Form

Click on the Print icon.

10.18.7 Closing a Form

Click the X on the form window.

You will not be asked to save!

If you have only typed data in, Access will not ask you if you want to save the form.

10.18.8 Deleting a Form

1 Click on the Forms button.

2 Select the form you want to delete.

3 Click on the Delete Form icon.

4 Click Yes.

10.18.9 Deleting a Record

1 In Form View, go to the record you wish to delete.

2 Click on the Delete icon on the toolbar.

10.19 Using Reports

10

10.19.1 What are Reports?

Reports are used to print off the information from your database in a presentable format. They are based on Tables or Queries. Base a report on a query if you only want to show certain records in your report, rather than every record in the tables. You can use reports to:

- Group information under key headings.

- Calculate totals and work out statistical information.

- Produce mailing labels.

10.19.2 Opening a Report

Reports

1 Click on the Reports button.

2 Click on the report you wish to open.

3 Click Open.

Or

1 Click on the Reports button.

2 Double click the report you wish to open.

10.19.3 Changing the Print Preview

When you open a report you will be taken to the Print Preview. To change the way the Print Preview looks, use the toolbar:

Going from left to right, this is what each icon means:

- Zooms in or out of the report.
- Shows one full page.
- Shows two full pages.
- Click this icon and drag over the grid to view multiple pages.
- Click the drop-down arrow to change the zoom level.
- Closes the report.
- Goes to the page set-up.

10.19.4 Moving Between the Pages

Click the navigation buttons at the bottom of the screen:

Going from left to right, this is what each icon means:

- Go to the first page.
- Go to the previous page.
- Displays the current page – you can type in a page number and press Return to go to that page.
- Go to the next page.
- Go to the last page.

10.19.5 Printing a Report

To print the whole report, just click once on the Print icon.

10.19.6 Printing a Selection of Pages

1 Click on the File menu.

2 Click on Print.

3 Click in the circle before Pages.

4 Change the page numbers in the From and To boxes.

```
┌─ Print Range ──────────────────────────┐
│  ○ All                                  │
│                                         │
│  ⦿ Pages  From: [    1  ]  To: [   3| ] │
│                                         │
│  ○ Selected Record(s)                   │
└─────────────────────────────────────────┘
```

5 Click OK.

10.19.7 Changing the Orientation of Your Report

1 Click File.

2 Click Page Setup.

3 Click Page tab.

4 Click the circle next to Landscape.

Or

Click the circle next to Portrait.

5 Click OK.

10.19.8 Changing the Paper Size

1 Click File.

2 Click Page Setup.

3 Click Page tab.

4 Click the down arrow next to Size.

5 Select the Paper Size you require.

6 Click OK.

10.19.9 Closing a Report

Click on the X icon at the top of the report window.

Or

Click Close.

10.20.1 The Ways of Creating a Report

There are several different ways of creating a report:

- **Design View**: will allow you to create the report from scratch with no help from Access.

- **Report Wizard**: will allow you to create a report with help from the Access Report Wizard. You can choose which fields you wish to see on the report.

- **AutoReport Columnar**: will create an instant report based on the query or table you specify, with the each record laid out in a column. You cannot choose which fields you wish to see.

- **AutoReport Tabular**: will create an instant report based on the query or table you specify, with all the records laid out in tabular format. You cannot choose which fields you wish to see.

- **Chart Wizard**: will create a chart with help from the Chart Wizard.

- **Label Wizard**: will create mailing labels with help from the Label Wizard.

10.20.2 Creating a Report with the Report Wizard

1 Click on the Reports button.

2 Double click Create Report by Using Wizard.

    Create report by using wizard

Or

Click New.

Click Report Wizard.

Click OK.

3 Click the drop-down arrow under Tables/Queries.

4 Click on the table or query you wish to base the report on.

5 Double click the fields you wish to see on your report from underneath Available Fields – they will jump over to the Selected Fields column.

6 Click Next.

7 If required, double click on the field(s) you wish to group by, e.g. Department.

Report Wizard

Do you want to add any grouping levels?

DEPARTMENT

FIRSTNAME, LASTNAME

FIRSTNAME
LASTNAME

Priority

Grouping Options ...   Cancel   < Back   Next >   Finish

8 Click Next.

9 If required, click the drop-down arrow and click on the field you wish to sort by.

Report Wizard

What sort order do you want for detail records?

You can sort records by up to four fields, in either ascending or descending order.

1 LASTNAME   Ascending
2   Ascending
3   Ascending
4   Ascending

Cancel   < Back   Next >   Finish

10 Click Next.

11 Click the circles next to the layout options you require for your report (the options will be slightly different if you are grouping by a field).

Report Wizard

How would you like to lay out your report?

Layout
○ Stepped
○ Block
○ Outline 1
● Outline 2
○ Align Left 1
○ Align Left 2

Orientation
● Portrait
○ Landscape

A

☑ Adjust the field width so all fields fit on a page.

Cancel   < Back   Next >   Finish

12 Click Next.

13 Click on the style you require for your report.

14 Click Next.

15 Type in a title for your report (this will appear as the title of the report).

16 Click Finish.

When is my report saved?

As soon as you have typed a title and clicked on Finish, your report is saved.

10.21 Summary Options on a Report

10.21.1 What are Summary Options?

You can use the report wizard to summarise number or currency fields on your report. They will allow you to produce:

- Totals.

- Averages.

- Maximum number.

- Minimum number.

If your report is grouped, you can also obtain subtotals, sub-averages etc. based on each group.

For example, the report below has used Summary Options to find the total salary, the average salary, the maximum salary, and the minimum salary for each department:

DEPARTMENT	FIRSTNAME	LASTNAME	SALARY
EXECUTIVE			
	Christine	Dean	14500
	Debbie	Anderson	12000
	Debbie	Anderson	12000
	Loni	Dickerson	49000
	Vicky	Goreman	59000
	Lena	Barnett	12250
	Mary	Hamby	11500
	Rick	Zambini	79500
	Robert	Newman	52000
	Marilyn	Keagan	16500
	Sandy	Berman	35000
	Harry	Eiven	10500

Summary for 'DEPARTMENT' = EXECUTIVE (12 detail records)

Sum	363750
Avg	30312.5
Min	10500
Max	79500

The Summary Options for salary are shown at the bottom right of the report – the Sum, the Average, the Minimum and the Maximum.

10.21.2 Creating Summary Options

1 Click on the Reports button.

2 Click Create report by using wizard.

3 Click the drop-down arrow under Tables/Queries.

4 Click on the table or query you wish to base this report on.

5 Double click the fields you wish to see on the report.

6 Click Next.

7 Double click the field(s) you wish to group by if required.

If you wish to create subtotals for a set of records, you will have to group by the field you wish to find subtotals for.

8 Click Next.

9 If required, choose the field(s) to sort by if required by clicking the drop-down arrow.

10 Click the Summary Options button.

11 Tick the boxes next to the field summary values you require.

Field	Sum	Avg	Min	Max
SALARY	☑	☑	☑	☑

12 Choose the options you require underneath Show.

13 Click OK.

Show
- ◉ Detail and Summary
- ○ Summary Only

☐ Calculate percent of total for sums

Summary Options ...

10

14 Click Next.

15 Choose the layout you require.

16 Click Next.

17 Click the style you require.

18 Click Next.

19 Type the title you require for your report.

20 Click Finish.

10.21.3 Checking Your Report

It's important to do a final check of your report before you print of hundreds of copies of send it to the big boss. Things to check for include:

- Formatting – are the fonts readable, do they look professional and suitable?

- Layout – is the layout clear for your purposes?

- Spelling – have you carried out a spell check?

- Page Setup – does the report fit the page?

- Data – is this the most up-to-date version, has it changed since you created the form?

- Have you tried sorting the data to find errors?

10.22 Data Integrity

Make sure there is a separate field for each piece of data you wish to sort or extract

For example, if you create a field called Name which includes both the first name and the last name, you will not be able to sort it alphabetically by the last name. It will also be difficult to extract people whose last name is, for example, 'Smith'. When you create the query you will have to use wildcards.

10.22.1 The Golden Rule

The golden rule is:

Information should *NEVER* need to be entered twice!

The greatest mistake in designing a database is creating something where information is duplicated in different places. This makes your database almost impossible to work with. Here are some examples. Let's suppose you need a database to do the following:

- Hold information about employees and which training course(s) they are going on.

- Be able to produce a list of the people's names and the course(s) they are going on.

- Be able to produce a list of the courses and the people that are going on that course.

10.22.2 Example One – Duplicating Records

The temptation is to cram all this information into one table. You would probably decide that the following fields are crucial: *Lastname*, *Firstname*, *Course*.

However, look what happens when you create a table with these fields and start to input data – Honor Blackman is going on three courses, which means her details have to be entered three times:

Firstname	Lastname	Department	Course
Bob	Hoskins	Geezer	Word 2000
Roger	Moore	Espionage	Excel XP
Honor	Blackman	Aerial Display	Word XP
Honour	Blackman	Aerial Display	Excel XP
Honor	Blackman	Geezer	Access 2000
Michael	Caine	Geezer	Word XP

This can cause all sorts of difficulties. Consider the following.

- You will have to enter the same details again and again. This wastes time and increases the chances of you making mistakes – as in the above table.

- You will have to make multiple changes. Imagine you want to update the details for Honor Blackman. You will have to change her details three times for each record that she appears in.

- It will be difficult to sort records. You will not be able to produce a coherent alphabetical list of the people, because they will be duplicated again and again.

- It will be difficult to count records, because they are duplicated so many times.

10.22.3 Example Two – Duplicating Fields

In the last example you saw how duplicating records causes problems. However, it is still tempting to get all the information into one table. At this point, people may decide to duplicate the course field instead, like this:

Firstname	Lastname	Department	Course1	Course2	Course3
Bob	Hoskins	Geezer	Word 2000		
Roger	Moore	Espionage	Excel XP	Word 2000	
Honor	Blackman	Aerial Display	Word XP	Excel XP	Access 2000
Michael	Caine	Geezer	Word XP		

Although this may solve the problem incurred by duplicating the records, it creates plenty more problems of its own.

- Let's say you want to find all the people on the Word 2000 course. When you create a query, you don't know whether 'Word 2000' has been input into Course 1, Course 2, Course 3 etc., so you have to add all the course fields to the query and add the criteria 'Word 2000' to all of them. The relationship between the criteria has to be OR so you will have to add each criteria on a different line. If you have 60 course fields, this is going to make a very complicated query!

- You can't create an alphabetical list of all the courses, as the course names are spread out over several different fields.

- Look at the number of blank fields which there are in this table. Most people may only be going on one or two courses, and yet you have a table with three course fields, and most of them are blank! This creates a very unwieldy table.

- You probably won't just want the course name, as in the picture above, but the date, the location, the price etc. You will end up having to create several duplicated fields for all this information as well.

If you are in this situation

Speak to your techies or the person who created the database – you may well need a *relational* database.

10.22.4 Some Solutions

A good solution is to use a **form** (see Section 10.18 on forms) for data input. This ensures that you, or whoever else has their hands on the database, are always entering the same type of information.

Another solution is **field properties** (see Section 10.9, Field properties). You can set fields to have drop down menus or default values to avoid misspellings or incorrect entries.

10.23 Checking Your Work

10.23.1 Spelling and Grammar Check

Nobody's perfect – even the best of us makes the odd spelling mistake now and again. Luckily, we can get Access to check the spelling of our documents for us.

1 Click on the Spell Check icon.

- A word highlighted in red inside the white box at the top indicates a misspelling – just above this, Access says what it thinks is wrong (e.g. Not in Dictionary).

- A word or sentence highlighted in green at the top indicates a grammatical error.

- In the Suggestions box, Access offers you some words to choose from that might be correct.

- On the right-hand side, there are buttons that let you change the spelling, ignore the word, and so on – see Chapter 8 for more details.

2 Click on the appropriate icon on the right-hand side.

3 Click Cancel to finish the spell check early.

Or

Click OK once the spell check is complete.

Access is not perfect!

Don't just casually let Access change whatever it likes – keep an eye on it, otherwise it will try to change someone's name, use American spellings, or mess up all your grammar.

Don't skip this bit!

No matter how confident you are in your typing abilities, checking your work is a must. Otherwise your readers could end up reading gobbledygook.

10.23.2 Other Ways to Check Your Database

If you want to check that the content, rather than the spelling, of your database is correct, it's a good idea to sort your data. See Section 10.10, Sorting records, for more details.

10.24 Test Your Knowledge

The questions below will test what you know of the knowledge and understanding requirements of this unit. All the answers to these questions are contained or referred to within this chapter.

1 What is a query?

2 What four things do you need to do to create a query?

3 Name four data types.

4 What is an advantage of a computerised database?

5 Why is it important to maintain data integrity?

6 Name two ways of ensuring data integrity.

7 How could you avoid either yourself or other people wrongly entering data into your database?

8 What are field properties?

9 How would you retrieve information from your database?

10 How can you order the data in your table to make it easier to find things?

10.25 Evidence

The tasks you undertake as evidence for your ITQ should be work-related. Therefore, your supervisor at work should be able to give you guidance on the type of tasks you should take on. Below are some ideas of possible tasks for this unit. Consider how you can adapt these ideas to make them more relevant for your own workplace and to ensure you cover all the skills requirements.

- Using an existing database, modify some of the field properties to help ensure data integrity.

- Create a report based on a query with more than one criterion to present to your line manager. Make appropriate changes to the summary options and set up of the form. Print and save a copy of the report.

- Create a query based on multiple criteria. Save it with an appropriate name.

- Write a report on the importance of maintaining data integrity and how this can be achieved. Include as many aspects as possible such as data entry, field types and properties and forms.

CHAPTER 11

Website Software

11.1 About This Unit

What you need to know

To gain ITQ Level 2 in this unit, you should demonstrate the following competency:

Use software effectively to produce multiple-page websites that communicate clearly and accurately.

To achieve this you should know and understand:

1   How to produce information that is clear and appropriate.

2   Multiple-page websites.

3   How to review website features for the user.

4   What laws and guidelines affect the use of IT and how they affect it.

5   User issues for websites.

You should also be able to display the following skills and techniques:

1   Handling files appropriately.

2   Combining information of different types.

3   Planning and producing multiple-page websites.

4   Editing, formatting and laying out oontont for multiple-page websites.

5   Checking text and checking images for multiple-page websites.

6   Uploading and maintaining content.

How to prove your skills

You need to carry out at least two work-based tasks which demonstrate the skills and knowledge listed above. In order to show your competency, it may well be necessary for you to complete more tasks than this.

Make sure you have plenty of evidence that shows how you completed each task, such as a copy of the file you worked on, or a document with screenshots of the processes you followed. You can back this up by producing a report which shows your knowledge of the subjects covered within the unit.

11.2 Introduction to the World Wide Web

The Internet is the physical connection of lots and lots of computer networks around the world, joined by cables, telephone lines and satellite links, etc.

The Internet hosts the less tangible World Wide Web (WWW). The WWW consists of millions of websites that can be reached and moved between by clicking on 'hyperlinks' (usually blue and underlined) when you visit a web page.

Websites are files stored on computers that are written primarily in a code called Hypertext Mark-up Language (HTML).

The Joy of FrontPage!

With FrontPage you do not need to learn HTML to produce wonderful websites. FrontPage creates the HTML for you.

11.2.1 What do You Need to See a Web Page?

Computer – the most obvious requirement, although there are other ways too, e.g. TV, mobile, PDA.

Modem – allows your computer to communicate with other computers via the telephone.

Browser – software that finds and retrieves the websites that you want to visit. The browser software interprets the HTML and chooses how to display the information on your screen. Internet Explorer and Netscape Navigator are the 'big two' – but there are others.

Internet Service Provider (ISP) – provides you with access to the Internet, and gives you space to store your website.

11.2.2 What Else do You Need to Create a Web Page?

Image editing package – for manipulating or customising pictures.

FTP software – for putting your website up on the World Wide Web for everyone to see!

More Joy of FrontPage!

FrontPage allows you to publish your site to the World Wide Web *without* any additional FTP software. FrontPage is an all-round package.

11.2.3 Download Speed

You know when you're trying to access a website and it takes ages to load? It's very annoying. That's because of the download speed: literally the speed it takes to download. Here are a few reasons why download speeds might vary:

- Type of internet connection the user has (slower dial-up or faster broadband).

- Connection speed the user has.

- Available memory on the user's computer.

- How many people are using the same connection.

- Amount and size of information on the web page.

- Amount of traffic on the web page.

11.2.4 Interactive Features

Websites are not just about information. They can be fun; they can invite you to participate and allow you to contact people. Here are a few examples:

- **Message boards** – a place where people can post messages and respond to each others' messages. A bit like a conversation, but not in real time. This is useful if you want to communicate with people who are not online at the same time. Message boards are often based around a theme or interest, such as chess or extreme roller skating.

- **Chat rooms** – similar to message boards but conducted in real time. You can chat to whoever else is online at the same time. You'll often need to register your details before entering a chat room.

- **Forms** – can be used for a variety of things. They are basically a way for the user to submit information to a website. Often online newspaper articles offer a form which allows readers to leave comments on the issues discussed.

Practise this!

What other interactive features have you come across on a website? Have a brainstorming session and write down as many as you can think of.

11

11.2.5 Multimedia Features

You can get anything on the Web these days. There are websites where you can view and upload photos, watch and upload videos, catch a TV programme, watch a movie, listen to the radio, listen to music… the possibilities are almost endless.

11.3 Creating Webs

11.3.1 What is a Web?

A web is the name FrontPage gives to an entire website. A website can consist of web pages, files and images.

11.3.2 Creating a Web

To create a web:

1 Click the drop-down arrow beside the New icon.

2 Select Web.

The Web Site Templates dialog box appears.

3 Select Empty Web.

4 Enter a location for the new web (you will usually just want to change the bit after the single \).

5 Click OK.

11.3.3 Restricting Features in a Web

New features are always coming out on the World Wide Web. Not all browsers will support all these new features. To only allow features that will work with certain browsers:

1 Click on the Tools menu.

2 Click on Page Options.

3 Click on the Compatibility tab.

4 Decide which browsers you are designing for (choose 'Both Internet Explorer and Netscape' unless you are on an intranet).

5 Decide which browser versions you are designing for.

6 Let FrontPage know what server your site will be hosted on (if in doubt, ask your ISP).

7 If you wish to exclude any other technologies, uncheck the appropriate boxes.

8 Click OK.

Greyed out features

Oh no, it's broken! Not really. If a feature you wish to use is greyed out in most programs, It usually means you have not done something yet.

11.4 Creating and Saving Web Pages

11.4.1 Creating New Pages

1 Click the drop-down arrow beside the New icon.

2 Select Page.

3 Select Normal Page.

4 Click OK.

11.4.2 The Homepage

All webs need a homepage, just like all people need a home. The homepage is usually the first page people will see when they visit your site. It's a bit like the front page of a magazine. It is usually welcoming and gives people a clear idea of what the site is about – including links to the contents inside.

Make your homepage sparkle

Your homepage is the first port of call for weary web visitors. It needs to look inviting; it needs to clearly communicate its purpose and appear user-friendly. If your site looks too complicated, your visitors will probably get bored and go off somewhere else.

Here's a rather nice example:

Screenshot provided courtesy of Happy (www.happy.co.uk)

11.4.3 Saving a Web Page with a File Name and Title

The first time you save a web page you will need to enter a **filename** and a **page title**.

- The **filename** is the name of the web page and forms part of its address.

- The **page title** appears on the title bar (blue bar at the top of the screen) of the viewer's browser when they look at your page. It is a good idea to make it descriptive and to mention your organisation's name – some search engines categorise sites this way. Oh, and it's a good idea to spell it properly as well.

What do I need to call my homepage?

Unfortunately you can't call it Harry or Bob. You *must* give your homepage the name 'index' or 'default'.
When a browser goes to a website it automatically looks for the index page first, unless otherwise specified.

---

1 Click the Save icon.

   Type in a file name for the document.

2 Click on Change title button.

File name:	Index

3 Enter a title for the document.

Set Page Title   ☒

Page title:

Bobbin's Books: Reading The World

The title of the page is displayed in the title bar of the browser.

OK   Cancel

4 Click OK.

5 Click Save.

11.4.4 Saving Changes

To save later changes:

Click the Save icon again.

11.4.5 Closing a Web

1 Click on the File menu.

2 Click Close.

11.4.6 Opening a Web

To open a web you made earlier:

1 Click on the File menu.

2 Select Open Web.

3 Select the web you wish to open.

Bobbin's Books
images

4 Click Open.

11.5 Opening Pages

11.5.1 Opening Pages Within a Web

If you want to open pages within a web you have opened, make sure you can see the folder list and double click on the files to view them.

11.5.2 Opening an Existing Page

1 Click the drop-down arrow beside the Open icon.

2 Click Open.

3 Navigate to the folder containing the file you wish to open.

4 Select the file.

5 Click Open.

11.6 Formatting Text

11.6.1 Bold, Italic, Underline

To make text bold, italic or underlined:

1 Select the text.

2 Click **B**old, *I*talic or <u>U</u>nderline.

11.6.2 Aligning Text

To align text:

1 Click into paragraph to align.

2 Click the appropriate icon.

> This is left aligned for normal text
>
> This is centre aligned for headings
>
> This is right aligned for dates
>
> And this is a piece of fully justified text that has straight edges at both sides. It looks very neat and tidy, doesn't it?

11.6.3 Changing Font

To change font:

1 Select the text to change.

(default font)

2 Choose font from drop-down list.

11

11.6.4. Sizing Text

To change the font size:

1 Select the text to change.

Normal ▾

2 Choose size from drop-down list.

The bigger the number, the bigger the text.

Be consistent when sizing text

When text is sized using the drop-down list as above and also sized using the heading styles, they may look the same in FrontPage but when viewed elsewhere may not. Choose one way or the other.

What does Normal mean?

Normal is equivalent to font size 3.

11.7 Horizontal Lines

11.7.1 Inserting Lines

1 Click on the Insert menu.

2 Select Horizontal Line.

11.7.2 Formatting Lines

1 Right click on the line.

2 Select Horizontal Line Properties.

3 Choose a width for the line using the arrows.

4 Choose a height for the line using the arrows.

5 Decide where the line should be aligned.

6 Choose a colour for the line.

7 Click OK.

11.7.3 Deleting Lines

1 Select the line.

2 Press the Delete key.

11.8 Colour

11.8.1 Changing Text Colour

To change the colour of text:

1 Select the text to change.

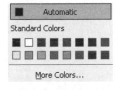

2 Click the drop down arrow next to the Font Color icon.

3 Either choose a colour.

Or

Click More Colors.

Pick the colour you require.

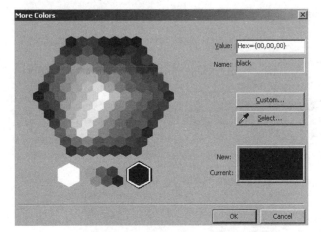

4 Click OK.

Practise this!

Write a sentence about your favourite colour. Try changing the colour of the text to red and then back to its original colour.

11.8.2 Setting the Default Font Colour

To set a text colour for the whole page:

1 Right click anywhere on the page.

2 Click on Page Properties.

3 Click on the Background tab.

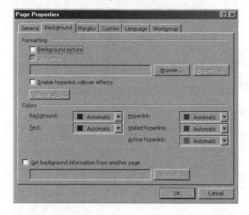

4 Click the drop-down arrow on the Text box.

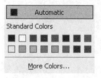

5 Either choose a colour.

Or

Click More Colors.

Pick the colour you require.

6 Click OK.

11.8.3 Background Colour

To set a background colour for the page:

1 Right click anywhere on the page.

2 Click on Page Properties.

3 Click on the Background tab.

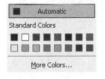

4 Click the drop-down arrow on the Background box.

5 Either choose a colour.

Or

Click More Colors.

Pick the colour you require.

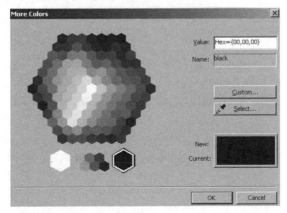

6 Click OK.

11.9 HTML Tags

If you are interested in learning a little bit of HTML, or would like help in knowing where formatting begins and ends, the reveal tags mode can help. Compare the following two screens.

This is what you normally see:

This screen has the tags revealed:

11.9.1 Revealing Tags

1 Click on View menu.

2 Click on Reveal Tags.

11.9.2 Hiding Tags

Once you've had a good look at the tags, or if you're thoroughly confused, you might want to hide the tags.

1 Click on the View menu.

2 Click on Reveal Tags.

Are the tags already revealed?

A tick next to Reveal Tags will tell you if tags are currently revealed.

11.9.3 Viewing HTML

Click the HTML tab at the bottom of the page.

11.9.4 Altering Basic HTML

Want to feel like a computing genius? HTML has some very simple rules that make it easy to understand and make basic changes. These are some of the core principles:

`<html>`

- All tags are enclosed in angle brackets.
- All tags come in pairs: one to start, one to finish.   `<p><b>This is bold</b></p>`
- The second or closing tag is preceded by /.
- The tags enclose the text that they affect.
- `<b>` Is the tag for bold.
- `<i>` Is the tag for italic.

If I was writing 'Hello' in HTML and I wanted to make it bold I would write:

```
<b>hello</b>
```

If I changed my mind and thought it looked stupid, I would go back and take out the bold tags:

```
hello
```

Assessor's tip

Lynne says:

*Remember the closing tag. If you start with this **** you must finish with this ****. Make sure you have clicked on the HTML tab, otherwise you'll be writing nonsense in normal text!*

Practise this!

Go to the HTML tab and write the following sentence: My website is the best website in the world. Using tags, make the word 'best' italic. Click back onto the Normal tab to see if it has worked.

11.10 Managing Your Files

11.10.1 Folders View

Files are managed in Folders View. To get to Folders View:

1 Click View.

2 Click Folders.

11.10.2 Creating Subfolders

Make sure you are in Folders View. To create a subfolder:

1 Right click the Folders pane.

2 Choose New.

3 Choose Folder.

4 Enter a name for the folder.

5 Press Enter.

11.10.3 Moving Files

When you move files, all hyperlinks are redirected so that they remain valid. Make sure you are in Folders View.

1 Make sure the files you want to move are visible in the Files pane.

2 Click and drag the files to their new folder.

11.10.4 Deleting Files

Make sure you are in Folders View. To delete a file:

1 Select the file to delete.

2 Right click the file.

3 Click Delete.

4 Click Yes.

11.10.5 Renaming Files

Make sure you are in Folders View. To rename files:

1 Select file to rename.

2 Right click the file.

3 Click Rename.

4 Type the new name for the file.

5 Press Enter.

11.11 Understanding Templates and Wizards

11.11.1 What is a Template?

A template is a document shell. It contains features and formatting, but it will lack personalised content. Templates are useful for speeding up the process of document creation, as they get a lot of the repetitive tasks out of the way, and let you get on with the business of creating a great site.

See below for different types of templates.

11.11.2 What is a Wizard?

Wizards are similar to templates, except they ask a number of questions about the document before creating it. The advantage of this is that the document is more tailored to what you require by the time it is finished.

FrontPage has two types of wizards and templates!

One type creates entire websites; the other type creates individual pages.

11.12.1 The Personal Web Template

If you have ever been tempted to create a site about yourself, including photos and your interests, then the personal web template may be of use.

These are the pages and folders this template creates for you:

Name	Title	Size	Type
_private			
images			
photogallery			
aboutme.htm	About Me	8KB	htm
favorite.htm	Favorites	12KB	htm
feedback.htm	Feedback	11KB	htm
index.htm	Welcome to my Web site	16KB	htm
interest.htm	Interests	14KB	htm
photo.htm	Photo Gallery	12KB	htm

11.12.2 The Corporate Presence Wizard

The corporate presence wizard is probably the most sophisticated wizard available. It allows you to provide information on the company, news, products and contact information. It also includes pages for searching and providing feedback as well as an automatic table of contents page.

11.12.3 Creating a Website Using a Template

Website templates are useful when you are first creating a web, but are not so practical when you have a site you are already working on and wish to add to.

1 Click on the File menu.

2 Click New.

3 Select Page or Web.

   The task pane on the right-hand side opens.

4 Click Web Site Templates.

5 Web Site Templates dialog box appears.

6 Choose the template you require.

7 Select the location of the new website using the drop-down arrow.

8 Click OK.

   Your new web will be created.

11.13 | Page Templates and Wizards

A page template is simply a pre-designed page that contains page settings, formatting and content. There are lots of page templates that are already part of FrontPage, or you can create your own page templates.

11.13.1 Feedback Form Template

The Feedback Form template creates a form asking for comments and contact details. While there is nothing unusual about the form it can provide a useful head start when you are creating forms for yourself.

11.13.2 Form Page Wizard

The Form Wizard is another way of getting a head start on your forms. It takes longer than the form template but asks for a lot more detail, and so should be nearer to the form you require at the end of the creation process.

11.13.3 Guest Book Template

A Guest book is a way of allowing users to leave comments on your site. The template contains a form for submitting comments, which then appear at the bottom of the page for all to see.

11.13.4 The Table of Contents Template

The table of contents template displays a list of all the pages in your site. The text it displays depends on the title of the page (as opposed to the filename). This is useful as an alternative navigational aid, allowing people to get to what they want more rapidly.

11.13.5 Creating a Web Page Using a Template

1 Click the drop-down menu on the New icon.

2 Click Page.

   Page Templates dialog box appears.

3 Double click the template you require.

   Template opens as a new web page.

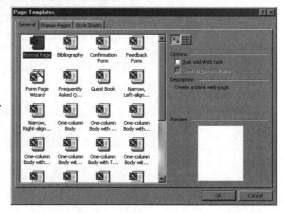

11.14 Understanding Links

11.14.1 Source and Destination Documents

Hyperlinks allow you to 'join' pages. People viewing your pages in a browser can jump from one area of interest in your site to another. Hyperlinks can also take someone to a page on another website.

The page that contains the link is known as the **source document**.

The page the link points to is known as the **destination document**.

Assessor's tip:

Georgie says:

Hyperlinks control how visitors experience your site; they are the only way to get around. At the very least every page should have a link to the home page, so visitors don't get stuck in dead ends.

11.15 Links Between Pages in a Site

These sort of links let the reader jump around from page to page, within your site. They don't send them travelling into other areas of the World Wide Web.

11.15.1 Creating a Link

1 Select the text you wish to be a hyperlink ('hot zone').

Click the Insert Hyperlink icon.

2 Select the page you want to link to.

3 Click OK.

11.15.2 Removing Links

1 Select the current link.

2 Click the Hyperlink icon.

3 Click on Remove Link.

11.16 Linking to Other Websites

11.16.1 Creating a Link by Typing in the Address

If you already know the address:

1 Select the text that is to be the link.

2 Click the Insert Hyperlink icon.

3 Type the address that you want to link to in the Address box.

> Address: http://www.google.co.uk|

4 Click OK.

If you don't know the address:

1 Select the text that is to be the link.

2 Click the Insert Hyperlink icon.

3 Click the Browse button.

4 Browse to the page you wish to link to.

> G http://www.google.co.uk/

5 Use the Taskbar to switch back to FrontPage.

The address should now be entered in the Address box.

> Address: http://www.google.co.uk/|

Be polite

It is generally considered polite to let people know when you have linked to them. You will usually find a contact email address on their website.

11.17 Linking to an Email Address

11.17.1 Why Link to an Email Address?

This is a quick way of letting visitors to the site email you. The link normally says something like 'Contact Us' or 'Talk to Me'. When they click on the link, their browser's email package will open with a new email addressed to you. This means people don't need to mess around with typing in email addresses and potentially getting it wrong.

11.17.2 Creating a Link

1 Select the text that will be the link.

2 Click the Insert Hyperlink icon.

3 Click the Email Addresses button.

4 Type in the email address being linked to.

This will either be yours or the person who will deal with the enquiry.

5 Type a subject line if required.

6 Click OK.

Practise this!

1 Write the text: Say hello.

2 Make it a hyperlink to an address that, when clicked, sends an email to bluehair@punky.co.uk.

3 Add the subject line: I like your hair.

11.18 Linking to a Bookmark

11.18.1 Why Use Bookmarks?

Links to a new page normally take you to the top of that page. If the information you are linking to is a long way down that page, people might think they've come to the wrong place or that the information isn't very good. A link to a bookmark will take you to the right place on the right page. Lovely.

11.18.2 Creating Bookmarks

To create a bookmark:

1 Select the text you wish to bookmark.

2 Click the Insert menu.

3 Click Bookmark.

Bookmark dialog box will appear.

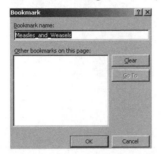

4 If necessary, change the bookmark name.

5 Click OK.

11.18.3 Creating a Link to a Bookmark

Assessor's tip

Rudy says:

To link to a bookmark, both the source (where you're linking from) and the destination (where you're linking to) documents must be open and saved.

---

1 Select the text that is to be the hyperlink.

2 Click the Insert Hyperlink icon.

3 Click the Existing File or Web Page button.

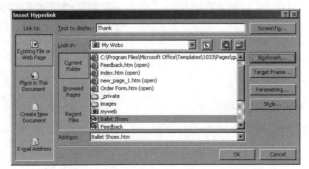

4 Click once on the page that contains the bookmark.

5 Click on Bookmark button.

6 Select required bookmark from list.

7 Click OK.

8 Click OK.

Save and refresh!

Remember to save in FrontPage and refresh in your browser – especially if what you expect to happen doesn't!

11.19 Hyperlink Colours

11.19.1 Why Change Hyperlink Colours?

You may need to change the colour of hyperlinks if your colour scheme makes it difficult to spot them. It's also good practice to set a different colour for visited hyperlinks. That way your audience can tell where they've already been and won't end up reading the same thing again and again and again.

11.19.2 Changing the Colour of Hyperlinks

To change the default colour of hyperlinks:

1 Right click anywhere on the page.

2 Choose Page Properties.

3 Click on the Background tab.

4 Use the drop-down boxes to change colours.

5 Click OK.

- **Hyperlink** changes the colour of hyperlinks before use.
- **Visited Hyperlink** changes the colour of hyperlinks you have been to.
- **Active Hyperlink** changes the colour of hyperlinks you are in the process of visiting.

11.20 Testing Hyperlinks

11.20.1 Testing in a Browser

The best way to check your links is to preview them in a browser and have a go at browsing your site. If they don't work, you know something hasn't quite gone according to plan.

11.20.2 Checking for Broken Links

As the number of links increases, it becomes more and more likely that you may have broken links (links which no longer point anywhere). FrontPage lets you check for these.

1 Check all pages have been saved (unsaved changes will not be checked).

2 Click on the View menu.

3 Click on Reports.

4 Click on Problems.

5 Select Broken Hyperlinks.

Broken Hyperlinks			
Status	Hyperlink	In Page	Page Title
? Unknown	http://www.happy.co.uk	new_page_3.htm	New Page 3
Broken	nothing.htm	new_page_3.htm	New Page 3

11

Don't worry!

External links may be listed as Unknown. That's OK.

11.20.3 To Correct Broken Links

In FrontPage's broken hyperlinks report:

1 Double click a broken link.

Edit Hyperlink dialog box will appear.

2 Type the correct address in the Replace Hyperlink with box.

3 Click Replace.

11.21 Clear Navigation

One of the most important aspects of your site is the navigation scheme. It's been said that the best scheme is one that never requires the audience to think – they should instinctively be able to get around your site. If they have to stop and consider using your navigation, it may well need a redesign.

11.21.1 How to Create Clear Navigation

- If you use text as links, do your links show up clearly amongst your normal text? Make sure you haven't underlined anything that isn't a link.

- Are your links clearly and consistently labelled? If two links from two separate pages end up at the same place, it's good practice to label both links the same.

- Is there an easy and obvious way of getting back to your homepage from every other page? It's comforting for your audience to always feel that they can find their way back to the beginning if they've made a wrong turn somewhere.

- If you have several internal links (i.e. links to other pages in the site), it's best to arrange them visually into a kind of navigation bar. If you are consistent about where it goes on your page, for example, always on the left side, your audience will always be able to find it.

11.21.2 Navigation: Hub or Hierarchy?

There are two common schemes for navigation used on websites, and which one you choose depends very much on the kind of site you're creating.

A **hub**-style site has a central page (normally the homepage) from which a large number of branching links are created (see the diagram below). To move around it, you return to the hub page and take another branch. Hub schemes work best if none of your pages are necessarily more important than any other.

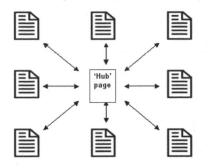

A **hierarchical** site has several 'levels': for example – beneath the homepage might be a page for each department, beneath each department page more pages for various teams, and so on. This design works best if your site is organised into categories and subcategories of lesser importance.

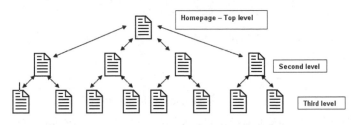

11.22 Creating Tables

11.22.1 Tables for Data and Layout

Tables can be used to display data. For web pages they have the extra special ability to control the layout of pages. You'll find the majority of snazzy-looking websites use tables for their layout. Join the party.

Is there a difference?

The only difference between tables for data and tables for layout is that those used for layout usually have their border size set to 0. That's all.

11.22.2 Creating a Table

To create a table:

1 Click and hold the Table icon.

2 Drag to select the number of rows and columns you want.

11.22.3 Setting Border Size

1 Right click within the table you have created.

2 Click on Table Properties.

Table Properties dialog box will appear.

3 Use the arrow keys to select the border size you require.

4 Click OK.

Using tables for layout?

If your table is being used for controlling page layout, the border size should be set to 0. Nothing more, nothing less.

11.22.4 Inserting Extra Rows and Columns

To insert rows or columns:

1 Place your cursor in a cell where you want a row or column inserted.

2 Click on the Table menu.

3 Click on Insert.

4 Click on Rows or Columns.

Insert Rows and Columns dialog box will appear.

5 Choose Rows or Columns.

6 Choose the number of rows or columns that should be inserted.

7 Choose where the new rows or columns should be inserted, in relation to the cursor.

8 Click OK.

11.22.5 Colouring Borders

1 Right click within the table.

2 Click on Table Properties.

Table Properties dialog box will appear.

3 Select a colour.

Or

Select a light border (for the top and left edges) and a dark border (for the right and bottom edges).

4 Click OK.

Don't get carried away!

You can't have three colours for your borders. The light border and dark border settings will override the colour setting.

11.22.6 Table Background Colour

Table backgrounds can either be blocks of colour, or an image of your choice.

To set the table background:

1 Right click within the table.

2 Click on Table Properties.

Table Properties dialog box will appear.

3 Select a colour.

4 Click OK.

11.22.7 Table Background Image

1 Right click within the table.

2 Click on Table Properties.

 Table Properties dialog box will appear.

3 Select the Use Background Image box.

4 Click Browse.

5 Navigate to your image.

6 Click on your image.

7 Click Open.

8 Click OK.

My images are tiled!

Unfortunately they will be tiled unless you use cascading style sheets. That's too big a subject to cover properly in this chapter, so have a chat with your techies if this is an issue.

11.22.8 Cell Background Colours

You can give each cell in a table a different colour.

1 Right click within the table.

2 Click on Cell Properties.

Cell Properties dialog box will appear.

3 Select a colour.

4 Click OK.

11.23 | Working with Frames

11.23.1 What are Frames?

Frames are a way of seeing more than one page at a time. A page called the **Frameset** acts as a container, laying out the pages and giving them an overall structure. Frames are classically used for navigation purposes, but this is by no means their only possible application.

This website uses frames:

11.23.2 Why use Frames?

Using frames allows you to:

- Display more information at any particular time.
- Use a single page for navigation, meaning less work for you and quicker loading times for users.
- Link to other sites without the viewer actually leaving your site

11.23.3 What are the Disadvantages of Using Frames?

Unfortunately it's not all fun and games when using frames. The following points can be potential traps for users:

- Many of the commands that you are used to carrying out on a page will be applied to the frameset, not the framed pages.
- Not all browsers are capable of seeing frames.
- You need to be extra careful that your pages fit onto any size screen as you are now showing two pages on screen at once.
- The Reload/Refresh icon on users' browsers will reload the frameset, not pages within it, sending the user right back to the beginning page layout. Oh dear.

11.23.4 Framesets

There are a number of different combinations of frames. For example, you can have a frame at the top of the page and one down the left side or just a frame down the left side of the page. It's totally up to you.

Assessor's tip

Sheena says:

When using framesets, it is a good idea to first create the pages that will be used in the frameset. Create them as you would create ordinary web pages.

11.23.5 Creating a Contents Frameset

This frameset will allow you to add a list of links in the left frame and the contents of the page you have clicked in the right frame.

This is probably one of the most commonly used framesets.

1 Click on the File menu.

2 Click New.

3 Select Page or Web.

Dialog box appears.

4 Click on the Frames Pages tab.

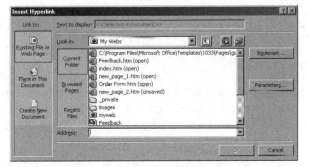

5 Click on the Contents icon.

6 Click OK.

An empty frameset appears.

11.23.6 Filling the Frameset

Set Initial Page...

1 Click the Set Initial Page button in the left-hand frame.

Insert Hyperlink dialog box appears.

2 Navigate to the page which will be in this frame.

Insert Hyperlink dialog box appears.

3 Click OK.

4 Click on the Set Initial Page button in the right-hand frame.

Insert Hyperlink dialog box appears.

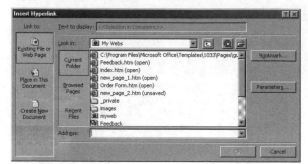

5 Navigate to the page which will be in this frame.

6 Click OK.

11.23.7 Saving the Frameset

1 Click on the Save icon.

Save dialog box appears.

2 Type a new name for the frameset.

Call me frameset

It's a good idea to have the word 'frameset' in the name, so that the file can be easily identified.

11.24 Images in Your Web Page

11.24.1 Image File Types

You can use any image created in any graphics package so long as the image is stored in the correct file format. The Internet only supports images stored as .gif or .jpeg file formats – these are both compression formats. (They summarise some of the image's data so that the file can be as small as possible.)

- **GIF** – image data is summarised in a way that is good for images containing sharp areas of contrast. Use it for graphics such as logos or text.

- **JPEG** – image data is summarised in a way that is good for images with lots of shading and blurred edges such as photographs.

11.24.2 Acquiring Images

Any image on any website can be used on your site. Most images will be protected by copyright, but if you search the Web you will also find many sites that provide free images to use.

To save an image to your hard drive:

1 Open your browser.

2 Browse to the page the image is on.

3 Right click on the image.

4 Select Save Picture As.

5 Choose a place to save the image to.

6 Give it an appropriate filename.

7 Click on Save.

11.24.3 Inserting Images onto the Page

To insert the images you have acquired onto your web pages:

1 Open the page where you want to insert the images.

2 Place the cursor where you want the image to go.

3 Click on Insert Picture From File icon.

4 Navigate to the required folder.

Select your image.

5 Click Insert.

11.24.4 Inserting Clipart Images

1 Position cursor where you require the picture.

2 Click Insert.

3 Click Picture.

4 Click Clip Art.

The Clip Art Task Pane will appear.

5 Type the sort of picture you are looking for into the Search text box, e.g. chicken.

6 Click Search.

Some pictures will be displayed in the Task Pane.

7 Click on the picture you require to insert it.

8 Click X at the top right of Clip Art Task Pane to close it.

Shortcut!

To insert a clipart image, simply click the Insert Clip Art icon on the Drawing toolbar.

11.24.5 Saving Images with the Page

The images you place on the page must be saved as part of the Web, and not simply left as images on the hard disk. FrontPage automatically creates an images folder for this.

Once you have inserted an image:

1 Click on the File menu.

2 Click Save.

3 Click on Change Folder button.

4 Select the images folder in your web.

5 Double click the images folder.

6 Click OK.

7 Click OK.

What if I copy and paste images?

Don't worry. If you copy and paste images into your web, FrontPage will prompt you to save your image when you close the page and give your image an appropriate file format.

11.24.6 Resizing Images

To resize images:

1 Select the image.

White handles will appear around the image.

2 Click and drag one of the corner handles.

My image looks strange!

If you use the handles in the middle of the sides, your image will become distorted. Use the corner to keep the image in proportion.

11.24.7 Cropping Images

Cropping is the process of removing parts of a picture that you don't want to see.

1 Select the image.

2 Select the Crop icon on the Pictures toolbar.

3 Click and drag over the area of your picture you wish to see.

4 Click the Crop icon a second time to crop.

11.24.8 Viewing the Pictures Toolbar

If you can't see the Pictures toolbar when working with images:

1 Click the View menu.

2 Click Toolbars.

3 Select Pictures.

Pictures Toolbar will appear.

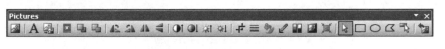

How do I know if it is already displayed?

A tick will indicate when a toolbar is displayed. Click again to hide it.

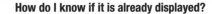

11.24.9 Rotating and Flipping Images

To rotate or flip an image.

1 Select the image.

2 Select the icon you need on the Pictures toolbar.

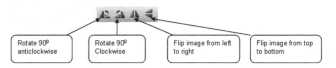

Rotate 90° anticlockwise | Rotate 90° Clockwise | Flip image from left to right | Flip image from top to bottom

11.24.10 Aligning Images with Text

The alignment settings let you choose where you want your image in relation to the text. These are the most common:

- Default alignment

- Left alignment

- Right alignment

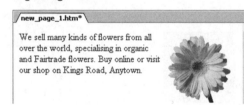

To align your text:

1 Select the image.

2 Right Click.

3 Click Picture Properties.

Picture Properties dialog box will appear.

4 Click the Appearance tab.

5 Choose an alignment from the Alignment drop-down list.

6 Click OK.

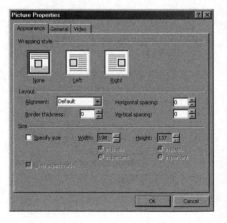

11.25 Customising Images

11.25.1 What is Transparency?

Transparency is where one colour in an image is made to be see-through.

Before the image has been made transparent:

After the image has been made transparent:

11.25.2 Making your Images Transparent

To make a colour transparent:

1 Select the image.

2 Choose the Set Transparent Color icon on the Pictures toolbar.

3 Click on the colour to be made transparent.

One colour and one colour only

When you use transparency only one colour can be affected: this may lead to confusion if a colour is actually made up by mixing two similar but different colours. You will also find that everywhere that the colour occurs in the image will be made transparent, not just the bits around the edges. Use with care!

Why isn't it working?

Your image must be saved as .gif file for this to work.

11.25.3 Adding Text to Images

Text can added to images. This is useful if you want to label an image or if it's a link, you could say where it points to.

1 Select the image.

2 Click the Text icon on the Pictures toolbar.

   Text box will appear on the image

3 Type the text you want.

4 If necessary resize the text or change the font using the Formatting toolbar.

5 Click away from the image to finish.

Why isn't it working?

Your image must be saved as .gif file for this to work.

11.25.4 Wash Out

When wash out is applied to an image, it looks faded.

Caring for a pet is never easy

To apply wash out to an image:

1 Select the image.

2 Click on the Colour icon on the Pictures toolbar.

3 Click Wash Out.

11.26 Placing Text in Your Web Pages

11.26.1 Copy and Paste

The easiest way to move small amounts of text into FrontPage is by copying and pasting. This retains some formatting, and is also capable of copying more advanced features like tables and graphics. The results can be a little unpredictable at times.

1 Select the text you want to copy.

2 Click on the Edit menu.

3 Select Copy.

4 Switch to FrontPage and open the destination page in Page View.

5 Click on Edit menu.

6 Click on Paste.

You may have to do a little tidying up of the layout and formatting if things don't look quite right.

11.26.2 Inserting Files

For placing entire documents on the page, inserting is the easiest approach. This retains most formatting.

1 Click on Insert menu.

2 Select File.

3 Ensure the type of file, e.g. Word 2000, is showing in the Files of Type box (or All Files).

4 Select the file you wish to insert.

5 Click Open.

11.27 Importing Files

11.27.1 Importing Files into your Web

Web pages created elsewhere and other documents such as Word files can be imported into your FrontPage web.

Imported files are added to the folder list.

If a Word document is imported the viewer must have Word on their computer to see the document. (Most people, but by no means all, would have Word.)

Importing is great for intranets where everyone in the organisation uses the same software.

In Folders view:

1 Click on File menu.

2 Click on Import.

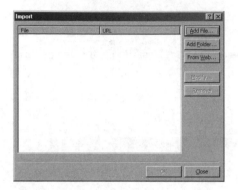

3 Click on Add File.

4 Ensure the type of file, e.g. Word 2000, is showing in the Files of Type box.

5 Select the file.

6 Click Open.

7 Repeat steps 3–6 for each file you are interested in.

8 Click OK.

The files you selected should now be visible in the Folders view as documents in their original format. Double clicking them will open them in the appropriate programme.

11.27.2 Linking to a File

Once you have imported the files to the folder list, it's time to create a link on your web page.

1 Select the text that is to be the hyperlink.

2 Click the Insert Hyperlink icon.

3 Click the Existing File or Web Page button.

4 Navigate to the file you wish to link to.

5 Click OK.

11.28 Publishing

11.28.1 Checking your Site

Before publishing your site it's really important to check the following:

- Spelling.
- Links.
- Images.
- General look and 'feel'.

Proofreading

For general tips on proofreading techniques, take a look at the relevant section in Chapter 8, Word-processing software.

11.28.2 Thinking About Accessibility

Remember that some of your visitors will have different needs. It's important to make sure that your site can be accessed by someone with a visual impairment, for example. Some people use special equipment such as screen readers to help them read websites.

These things can make sites more accessible:

- A reasonable sized font.
- Good navigation system.
- Text labels for images.
- Pages have page titles.
- Clear colour scheme.

11.28.3 Checking Your Images

It's easy to play around with your images, flipping and cropping, and to leave them not quite as you intended. A quick check is vital to ensure images are displayed as your want visitors to see them.

Things to consider:

- Is the size too big or too small?

- Has the image become distorted when resized?

- Check the alignment and orientation of images.

- Is your image stored as a .jpeg or .gif file?

Keep it legal

Before you publish your site, you should take care to ensure you're not breaking any laws. A common problem that many people fall foul of is breach of copyright. That often happens when people reuse images on their own sites that they have found online – without realising they are copyright protected. For more on copyright and other IT laws, check the Laws and guidelines section of Chapter 5.

11.29 Spell Checking

11.29.1 Spell Checking the Document

Don't miss this out!

Even if you were the champion of the spelling tests at school, it is essential to spell check your work. It's easy to overlook typos if you've been working on a document and mistakes can have a big effect on the appearance and professionalism of the website.

To spell check a single document:

1 Click the Spelling icon.

The Spelling dialog box will appear.

2 For each word not recognised choose one of the following options:

- **Ignore** – will leave the word as it is.

- **Ignore all** – will leave all future instances of that word as they are.

- **Change** – will replace the word with the one highlighted in the Suggestions box.

- **Change all** – will replace all examples of the word with the one highlighted in Suggestions.

- **Add** – will add the word to the dictionary.

11.29.2 Spell Checking the Site

To check the entire site:

1 Click View.

2 Click Folders.

3 Click the Spelling icon.

4 Select Entire Web.

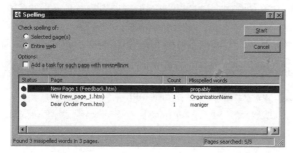

5 Click Start.

6 The report shows all unrecognised words in the site.

7 Double click on a page in the list to open that page and correct it.

8 Click Back To List when you have corrected it.

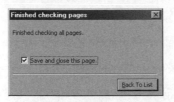

Spelling mistake now shows as edited.

9 Click X to close.

11.30 Uploading Your Site

If your Internet service provider (ISP) has the Microsoft FrontPage Server Extensions you can publish to the web server using the methods described below.

Otherwise, you can use Microsoft FrontPage to publish your website to an FTP server.

11.30.1 What Information do You Need from Your ISP

There are a few things you need to know:

- Web location (e.g. www.badgersbooks.co.uk).
- User name.
- Password.

11.30.2 Publishing Your Site

1 Click on the File menu.

2 Click on Publish Web.

3 Enter the address you wish to publish to.

4 Click OK.

Name and Password dialog box will appear.

5 Enter your Name and Password.

6 Click OK.

7 Click on Publish.

Publishing time

Publishing can take some time. Wait till the end of the day or possibly lunch before doing it.

11.30.3 Publishing to an FTP Server

FTP stands for File Transfer Protocol and is a set of rules that enable your computer to communicate with a server. What that means for you is that it makes it possible for you to upload files to a server and publish them for all to see.

If your ISP does not have FrontPage server extensions you will need to transfer your files using FTP.

1 Click on the File menu.

2 Click on Publish Web.

3 Type ftp://your publishing destination/ (e.g. ftp://10.1.1.1.12/.)

4 Click OK.

Name and Password dialog box will appear.

5 Type in user name and password.

6 Click OK.

7 Click Publish.

What is my publishing destination?

This should be given to you by whoever is hosting your website. It will look a bit like a website address or a string of numbers (as in the example above). If you're not sure, ask your techies, they will know.

What if I only want to publish a certain page?

When you get to step 3, you can enter the folder name for the page you wish to upload (e.g. ftp://10.1.1.1.12/About Me/).

If you don't know the name of the folder, follow step 3 and then navigate to the required folder.

11.31 Test Your Knowledge

The questions below will test what you know of the knowledge and understanding requirements of this unit. All the answers to these questions are contained or referred to within this chapter.

1 What different types of hyperlink can you find on multiple-page websites?

2 Why might some users have difficulty accessing your site? How can it be made more accessible?

3 What are the two main ways to lay out a web page?

4 Give two examples of multimedia features that you might find on a website.

5 Give an example of a multiple-page website. What type of information is on each page?

6 Why might the download speed vary from user to user?

7 In which two formats must image files be saved, in order to use them on the internet?

8 How would you make a sentence bold in HTML?

9 Name three important things to check before publishing your site.

10 What information would you need to know to upload your site to an FTP server?

11.32 Evidence

The tasks you undertake as evidence for your ITQ should be work-related. Therefore, your supervisor at work should be able to give you guidance on the type of tasks you should take on. Below are some ideas of possible tasks for this unit. Consider how you can adapt these ideas to make them more relevant for your own workplace and to ensure you cover all the skills requirements.

- Create a web page for your company. Include a clipart image that relates to your industry or products. Change the order, size and rotation of the image. Take a screenshot of the image before and after each change. Include a hyperlink to a similar company's website as well as an email link for people to contact the manager of the company. Save the web page.

- Using a programme such as Word (see Chapter 8), write a short report on the different features that can be found on a website. Save this file and import it into a new web page. Create a hyperlink to the file you have imported and save the web page.

- Upload a web or web page that you have created. Take a screenshot of a published web page.

- Change some of the HTML on an existing web page. Take a screenshot of the code before and after any changes.

11

CHAPTER 12

Artwork and Imaging Software

12.1 About This Unit

What you need to know

To gain ITQ Level 2 in this unit, you should demonstrate the following competency:

Use software effectively to produce more complex artwork and images that communicate clearly.

To achieve this you should know:

1 How to produce information that is clear and appropriate.

2 More complex artwork and images.

3 What file formats are appropriate for different tasks.

4 What and how laws and guidelines affect the use of IT.

You should also be able to use the following skills and techniques:

1 Handling files appropriately.

2 Creating drawings, artwork and images that are more complex.

3 Inserting, manipulating and editing more complex artwork and images.

4 Combining information of different types.

5 Checking text.

6 Checking images.

12

How to prove your skills

You need to carry out at least two work-based tasks which demonstrate the skills and knowledge listed above. In order to show your competency, it may well be necessary for you to complete more tasks than this.

Make sure you have plenty of evidence that shows how you completed each task, such as a copy of the file you worked on, or a document with screenshots of the processes you followed. You can back this up by producing a report which shows your knowledge of the subjects covered within the unit.

12.2 Thinking About Your Work

12.2.1 Planning

Planning your work is an important part of the creative process, and you need to provide evidence that you have thought ahead before starting on your work.

Things you need to consider include:

- Who is the work for?

- What is the purpose of the work?

- How is the work going to be used?

- When is the work needed?

- What kind of work is required? As well as thinking about how it should look, think also about its size and what format it should be.

Assessor's tip

Rudy says:

Before you start work, compile a written statement of your objectives. Add sketches of how the completed work will look. This is all useful for showing you have given thought to the production process.

12.3 What File Format Should I Use?

12.3.1 Do your Work in the PSD Format

The PSD file format is Photoshop's own and is the only format that supports all of Photoshop's features. For this reason, you should always work in this format when using Photoshop. The only problem is, many programs (for instance QuarkXPress) will not accept information stored in this format. So, once your work is complete you need to save a copy of it in the appropriate format (such as EPS, JPG or TIFF) so it can be opened in other programs.

12.3.2 Choosing a Saving Format

Once you come to save your finished work, there are several different file formats from which you can choose. Your ideal format depends on what you want to do with your image now it's finished. Here are some questions that you need to ask yourself before you select one of the formats:

- Is the image intended for print or for the Web?

- Do you intend to use the image in another application, e.g. Quark or PageMaker?

- Is the image going to be used on a Mac, a PC or both?

- Do you plan to share your files with someone who does not have Photoshop?

- Is memory an issue? If so, do you want your images to be of a high quality or would you prefer to sacrifice this in favour of a smaller file size?

- If you are not sure which format you should use and are going to use a Print Bureau, ask them what file format they require.

12.3.3 EPS (Encapsulated Postscript)

EPS format is used for transferring files between applications. It is intended for vector images (see Section 12.5 for more on these), as more complicated images can become up to three times as large as the same image stored as a PSD. This format is normally used in the print process.

12.3.4 TIFF (Tagged Image File Format)

TIFFs are the most common format used to store high-quality images, primarily photographs. They can consist of many millions of colours at very high resolution, and are the only file format for high-quality glossy printing. This format was created to allow for the sharing of images between Macs and PCs.

12.3.5 JPEG (Joint Photographic Experts Group)

JPEG files are used for saving images with continuous colour, such as photographs. This format uses a space-saving compression format to reduce file size. It takes all the information contained in an image and squeezes it into the smallest possible file size. This format is widely used on the Web, and increasingly for email and printing. However, be careful of highly compressed JPEGs – they can drastically lose quality, and often look ugly when enlarged.

12

12.3.6 GIF (Graphics Interchange Format)

GIF files use a space-saving compression format to reduce file size. Unlike JPEGs, GIFs do not lose quality on saving. GIF files are widely used on the Web. They are fine for line art or cartoon-type images with solid colours but not for photographic images (as the maximum number of colours they can have is 256). These images can support transparency and they can be made into basic animations. They also support interlacing (the process of downloading an image gradually so that the viewer has something to look at as the image appears).

12.3.7 Web Considerations

Only GIFs and JPEGs are guaranteed to show up on web browsers. Both formats use a form of compression to reduce the file size of images, so web pages are quicker to download.

GIF compression works by reducing the number of colours in the image, although not the quality or sharpness, while JPEG compression reduces the sharpness and detail while retaining the number of colours.

Choose GIFs if:

- The image must have transparent areas (is irregularly shaped).

- The image is a simple RGB image containing 256 (8-bit) colours or less.

- The image is intended for animation.

Choose JPEGs:

- For continuous-tone images.

- For rectangular images that don't need transparency.

Assessor's tip

Georgie says:

Familiarise yourself with the different file formats and make sure you know which you should use and when. It's important that you are able to show that you know the difference between the formats.

12.4 What is a Colour Mode and Which Should I Choose?

12.4.1 What are Colour Modes?

Colour modes are palettes of different colours. Before you begin any project you should choose a colour mode that suits your needs. There are five modes you should be aware of in order to use Photoshop to its full potential.

RGB (red, green, blue)	Images in this mode consist of three colours: red, green and blue. This is the type of colour seen in everyday life and should be used on any images that are destined for the screen (i.e. the Web).
CMYK (cyan, magenta, yellow, black)	Images in this mode consist of four colours: cyan, magenta, yellow and black. This mode should be used on any images destined for print, as RGB colours cannot be recreated in print.
Greyscale (black, white, grey)	A lot of colour images end up getting printed in greyscale rather than colour. Often referred to as 'black and white', this colour mode is actually made up of 256 shades of grey. Using this mode is the quickest way to remove the colour from coloured images. After you have created a greyscale image, you can convert it to RGB or CMYK so it can be used on the Web or printed.
Duotone	This colour mode is made up of 256 shades of grey and one other colour as an overlay. This creates a greyscale image with another colour washed over it, so the image appears grey but has increased warmth. For instance, it can be used to simulate old sepia-toned photos. After you have created a duotone image, you can convert it to RGB or CMYK so it can be used on the Web or printed. Note: it's also possible to overlay more colours. Two more gives a 'Tritone', three more gives a 'Quadratone', and so on.
Indexed	GIF images for use on the Web can be saved in indexed colour mode (up to 256 colours). This is not suitable for photographic images that need lots of colours to show their subtleties, but is fine for line art or cartoon-type images.

12

Changing colour mode

Always save a back-up copy of the original image before changing its colour mode.

22.4.2 Changing Modes to Greyscale

If you have an image in either RGB or CMYK mode, you can change it to greyscale at any time.

1 Click on the Image Menu.

2 Choose Mode.

3 Click on Grayscale.

4 Click OK on the box that appears.

12.4.3 Changing Modes to CMYK

This mode should be used on any images destined for print. If you have an image in RGB mode, you can change it to CMYK at any time.

1 Click on the Image menu.

2 Choose Mode.

3 Click on CMYK.

12.5 Graphic Types

Computer graphics fall into two main categories; *vector* and *raster* (*also known as bitmap*). You can work with both types within Photoshop. Understanding the difference between the two categories will help you on the road to creating, editing, and importing your artwork.

Vector graphics	Raster graphics
Image make-up: Made up of mathematically defined lines and curves called vectors.	**Image make-up**: Made up of a fixed number of coloured squares called pixels.
Scaling: Scalable. Images can be increased or reduced in size without losing detail or clarity.	**Scaling**: Non-scalable. Images cannot be resized without losing detail. If you make a raster graphic bigger it will become blurry.
Image type: Cartoon-like. Good at representing bold graphics that must retain crisp lines when scaled to various sizes (e.g. logos).	**Image type**: Photo-realistic images depicted by continuous subtle tones.
Sample usage: Clipart.	**Sample usage**: Photographs.

Working with raster images

When you work with raster (bitmap) images you work with pixels rather than lines and curves. Photoshop CS2 does have some vector features, but vector shapes remain vectors only if they are saved in EPS or PSD format (see Section 12.3.2 on using different file formats).

Saving in other file formats will automatically 'rasterize' vectors. The most common reason for wanting to convert a vector to a raster by rasterizing would be for use on the Web.

12.6 Starting with Photoshop

12.6.1 Starting Photoshop from within Windows

1 Click Start button.

2 Select Programs.

3 Click on Adobe.

4 Click on Adobe Photoshop CS2.

12

Shortcut

You might have a Photoshop Icon on your Desktop (the screen you see when Windows starts up). If you do, just give it a double click and Photoshop will start up.

12.6.2 Exiting Photoshop

When you want to close Photoshop

1 Click on File menu.

2 Click on Exit.

12.6.3 Elements of the Photoshop Screen

Here is a picture of the Photoshop screen with a blank canvas open.

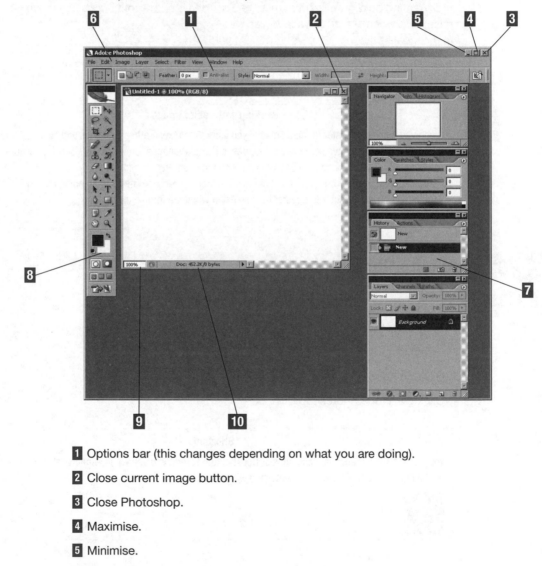

1 Options bar (this changes depending on what you are doing).

2 Close current image button.

3 Close Photoshop.

4 Maximise.

5 Minimise.

6 Menu bar.

7 Palettes (to hide or display these: click on the Window menu and then on the relevant palette).

8 Toolbox.

9 Current view size.

10 Size bar.

Choosing different tools

If a Toolbox tool has a black arrow in its bottom right corner, there are other options for that tool. Click on the icon and hold down the mouse button to see the other options. Select the option you want, then let go of the mouse button.

12.6.4 Changing Views

Photoshop allows you three different screen displays using the View Icons at the bottom of the toolbox. Click on the button for the view you require.

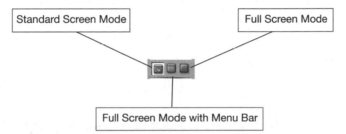

12.6.5 Standard Screen Mode (default)

Standard view displays your images in a window with a title bar and scroll bar on the side and bottom. It gives you full access to the menu bar, as well as the ability to see other images if you have them open.

12.6.6 Full Screen Mode with Menu Bar

Full screen with menu bar view hides other open images and your desktop. The title bar and scroll bars disappear and your image is placed on a grey background. You still have access to all options on the menu bar.

12.6.7 Full Screen Mode

This full screen view is similar to the previous one, except the background colour your image is placed on is black instead of grey. Also, you will not have access to the menu bar.

12.6.8 Page Preview – How Will My Image Look on the Page?

To find out how big your image is in comparison to an A4 page:

1 Click on the Size Bar (bottom of image window) and hold down the mouse button.

The square with a cross indicates your image on an A4 piece of paper.

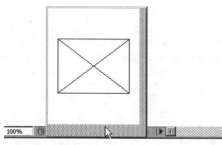

12.6.9 How Big is My File?

The size of your active file is shown on the Size Bar at the bottom left-hand corner of the screen.

If the size is not showing:

1 Click the right-facing arrow on the Size bar (bottom of the image window).

2 Choose Show.

3 Click on Document Sizes.

Two figures show on the Status bar.

■ The first size indicates how big the file will be when all layers are flattened (see Section 12.8 for more on layers).

■ The second size indicates how big the file is when the layers are separated.

12.6.10 Getting Information About Your File

1 Click on the Image menu.

2 Click on Image Size.

3 Look at the settings.

4 Click on Cancel.

12.6.11 Undoing the Last Thing You Did

To undo the last thing you did:

Press Ctrl + Z.

12.6.12 Revert to Saved

If you have made changes to your file that you do not want to save, choose the 'revert' option. All the changes made since the last save will be undone.

1 Click on the File menu.

2 Click on Revert.

12.6.13 Undoing up to 20 Steps: the History Palette

You can use the History palette to undo up to the last 20 things you did. On the History palette:

Click on the step in the list you want to revert to (all steps below this action are also undone).

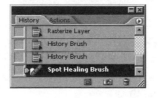

12.6.14 Stepping Forward Through the History Palette

If you make a mistake and undo too far, you can redo:

Click back on the step you just undid.

Shortcut

You can use Ctrl+Shift+Z again to redo the actions you have just undone.

12.7 Handling Files

12.7.1 Creating a New Image

When you create a new image/file, you can choose the size of the image, the background colour, and the image resolution.

1 Click on the File menu.

2 Click on New.

3 Type a name into the 'Name' box.

4 Click on the arrow next to Preset and choose a preset size.

Or

Type dimensions into the Width and Height boxes.

5 Type in a Resolution setting.

6 Choose a Colour Mode and choose a Bit Depth.

Bit depth

Bit depth (also called pixel depth or colour depth) measures how much data is available for colour information on each pixel. The higher the bit depth, the more bits of information available per pixel.

That means more available colours and more accurate colour representation in an image. RGB images use three colours, to reproduce colours on-screen. The three colours translate to 24 bits of colour information per pixel (8 bits × each colour). With 16 bits per colour, even more colours can be reproduced.

Resolution

The resolution you choose for your file is important as it has a major effect on the size of your file. Resolution is measured in pixels per inch (ppi).

The higher the resolution, the more detail in your image. That means there's more data and therefore the image takes up more memory. High resolutions (300 ppi and upwards) are used when the file is intended for printing, as it enables the image to be printed at a large size without a loss of quality.

Lower resolutions (typically 72 ppi) are used for graphics intended for web publication. Most computer monitors can only display at this resolution anyway, and the images are then also smaller and therefore load quickly.

7 Choose a Background Contents colour.

Content colour

White fills the background with solid white.

Background Colour makes the background the same colour as the one displayed in the toolbox background colour box.

Transparent makes the background blank. You will see a checkerboard effect, which represents transparency.

Transparent content

In print: transparency is useful if you have an image around which you want text to run. You must save the Photoshop file in the EPS file format.

On web pages: transparency is useful when you are putting an image on a coloured background. It stops a solid white rectangle appearing around the image and you see the background page colour instead.

8 Click on OK.

12.7.2 Opening Files

1 Click on the File menu.

2 Click on Open.

3 Use the Look in box to navigate to the folder containing the file you want.

4 Click on the File.

5 Click on the Open button.

12

12.7.3 Closing Files

1 Click on the File menu.

2 Click on Close.

Or

Click on the X at the top left of the file's window.

12.7.4 Saving a File for the First Time as a PSD File

To store the newly created/enhanced image:

1 Click on the File menu.

2 Click on Save As.

3 If necessary, click on Save in: down arrow.

4 Choose where you want to save the file.

5 Type in a name in the File name box.

6 If required click on Format down arrow.

7 Choose a new file format (if necessary).

8 Click on Save.

9 Click on OK.

12.7.5 To Save Changes Made to an Existing File

To store changes you have made to your image:

1 Click on the File menu.

2 Click on Save.

Or

Press Ctrl +S.

12.7.6 Saving for the Web

1 Click on the File menu.

2 Click on Save for web.

3 Click on the 4 up tab.

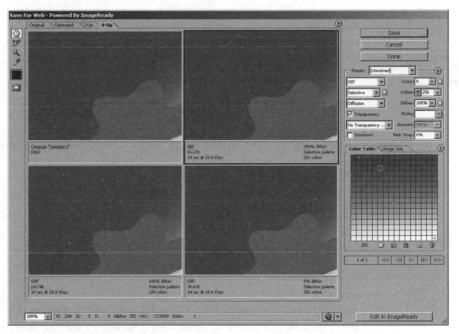

Four different versions of the image will now be displayed. Each has different quality settings. If you make changes to the quality settings, they will be displayed on the individual image.

4 Click on the version you want to make changes to.

5 Make changes to the options on the right of the screen.

6 Click OK.

7 Give the file a name and save location.

8 Click Save.

12.7.7 Saving in Another Format

1 Click on the File menu.

2 Click on Save as.

3 Click on the Format drop-down menu.

4 Choose the format you require.

5 Click Save.

12.7.8 Printing

1 Click on File.

2 Click on Print.

3 Adjust the print settings as required.

4 Click on OK.

12.8 Layers

12.8.1 Using Layers

Layers are one of the most important features of Photoshop. A new image has just a single layer. As you add elements to the image, they are produced on new layers that are laid on top of the original. Think of these layers as being like a stack of acetate sheets. They are transparent, other than the detail they contain. You can make changes to a single sheet without affecting the contents of the others, and you can change their order.

Whenever you add a new element to a Photoshop file, it's good practice to do it on a new layer. That way, if you don't like the change, you can simply delete the layer. If you add something to an existing layer and then save the file, you won't be able to remove it.

Automatic layers

Layers are automatically created when you move or copy part of an image, when you insert text or draw something – basically any time you add anything to the image a layer is created.

12.8.2 To See the Layers Palette

The easiest way to work with layers is to use the Layers palette. If you cannot see the Layers palette, this is how you show it.

1 Click on the Window menu.

2 Click on Layers.

12.8.3 Working with Layers

You can see the name of the active layer on the title bar. If you look at the layers palette, you will also see the active layer is highlighted in blue.

Layers have transparent pixels

Remember layers are transparent where there is no drawing/image – you will only be able to see elements you add in the non-transparent parts of the layer (i.e. where pixels are already coloured in).

12.8.4 Showing and Hiding Layers

To show or hide a layer:

Click on the eye next to the layer in the Layers palette (if the eye is visible, the layer is displayed).

12.8.5 Creating a New Layer

Click on the Create a new layer button at the bottom of the Layers palette. The new layer will be added directly on top of the selected layer.

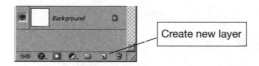

12.8.6 Deleting a Layer

Click and drag the layer onto the trash can at the bottom of the Layers palette.

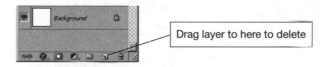

12.8.7 Locking a Layer

You can lock layers so you don't accidentally make changes to them:

1 Click on the correct layer in the Layers Palette.

2 Click on the padlock (top of the palette).

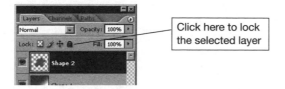

3 The Layer is now locked and cannot be moved.

A padlock will appear next to the layer to show it is locked. To unlock the layer, just click on the padlock at the top again.

12.8.8 Unlocking the Background Layer

The background layer is locked by default. If you want to unlock it:

1 Click on the word Background on the Layers palette.

2 Double click on the Layer.

3 If you like, type in a more meaningful name for the layer.

4 Click on OK.

The background is now called Layer 0 unless you typed in a new name for the layer before clicking on OK.

12.8.9 Moving layers

The layer at the top of the Layers palette will be displayed in front of all the other layers. By moving layers, you can change how the images are displayed.

For example:

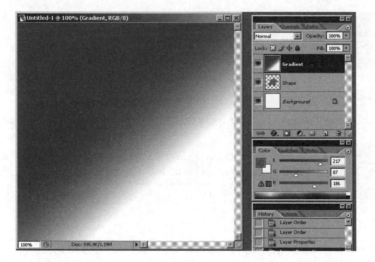

Here the gradient layer is above the shape layer – so the shape cannot be seen.

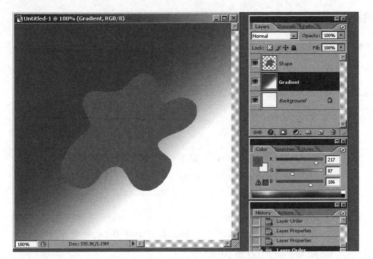

Now the shape layer is above the gradient layer – so the shape is on top with the gradient behind it.

To move a layer:

Click and drag the layer on the Layers palette to its new position.

Assessor's tip

Rudy says:

Practise with creating new layers and moving layers about. Layers are a simple way to make very complex-looking images. By getting to know this feature you will be able to create very professional work.

12.9 Selecting

12.9.1 Selecting a Large Area with the Marquee Tool

Use the Marquee Tools to select a part of the image that you wish to work on. The Marquee Tool comes in different shapes – Rectangular or Elliptical (oval), Single Row or Single Column.

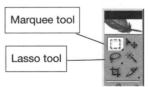

These tools share the same space on the Toolbox – whichever tool you used last will be visible. These tools can also be used to create square and circular selections.

12.9.2 Using the Rectangular/Elliptical Shaped Marquee Tool

1 Click on the Marquee Tool.

2 Point to the top left of area to select.

3 Hold down the mouse button and drag.

4 Release the mouse button.

Creating a perfect square or circle

Hold down the Shift key as you drag the shape.

Making a selection from the centre

Hold down the Alt key as you drag outwards.

12.9.3 Using the Single Row/Column Marquee Tool

Use this to select just one row of pixels horizontally across the image:

1 Click on the Single Row or Single Column Marquee Tool.

2 Point at the row/column you want to select.

3 Click once.

Deselecting selections

Click anywhere on your image away from the selected area.

12.9.4 The Lasso Tools

For greater precision, use the lasso tools. Three of them share the same space on the toolbox; a freehand lasso tool for selecting areas with a steady hand, a polygonal tool for angular selections and a magnetic lasso for making more accurate selections.

12.9.5 The (Freehand) Lasso Tool

Use the lasso tool to make precise 'freehand' selections.

1 Click on the Lasso Tool button.

2 Click and drag over the area you want to select *without releasing the mouse*.

3 Move over the start point to complete selection.

12.9.6 Polygonal Lasso

The polygonal lasso works a bit like a 'join the dots' game and is useful for making selections around objects with straight edges.

1 Click on the Polygonal Lasso Tool button.

2 Click where you want to start the selection.

3 Move and click again to join the dots (repeat).

4 Click on the start point to complete selection.

Assessor's tip

Lynne says:

It can sometimes be difficult to see where your selection begins and ends. If you have Caps Lock on while selecting, your cursor will change into a cross making it easier for you to see what you are selecting.

12.9.7 Magnetic Lasso

The magnetic lasso is the smartest of the lasso tools. It finds an edge and traces around it. This tool works best on images that have strong contrasting borders.

1 Click on the Magnetic Lasso Tool button.

2 Click where you want to start the selection.

3 Move the mouse along the 'line' of the object – the outline 'follows' you.

4 Click along the way to anchor the small boxes that appear when necessary.

5 Double click to complete.

Correcting mistakes

Pressing the Delete key on the keyboard will take you back one magnetic point at a time.

Shortcut

To select your whole image, press Ctrl + A.

To deselect everything, press Ctrl + D.

To turn off the flashing selection border, without losing your selection, press Ctrl + H.

12.10 Drawing Tools

12.10.1 What are Vector Shapes?

Vector shapes are clear, crisp shapes such as rectangles, circles, stars and polygons (multi-sided shapes) that are edited in a different way to the rasterized pixels produced when using tools such as the Paintbrush, Pencil or Airbrush.

12.10.2 Why would I use Vector Shapes?

Here are some facts about vector shapes:

- They are used when you need to keep sharp edges around a shape.
- Vector shapes can be saved in a format such as EPS that can be used in a vector-type program like Adobe Illustrator.
- They are resolution-independent (they can be resized without losing quality, unlike raster shapes).
- When you print them they stay crisp.
- You can save them into a PDF file for the Web.

12.10.3 What is a Shape Layer?

When you draw a shape in Photoshop it can have its own layer known as a shape layer. A shape layer is made up from:

- A fill colour.
- A shape or several shapes that use the same fill colour.

12.10.4 Drawing Basic Shapes on a Shape Layer

Vector shapes appear on the toolbox above the eyedropper tool.

1 Click on a Shape tool (e.g. a rectangle or custom shape).

2 Click and drag to draw a shape.

(A shape layer called Shape 1 appears in the Layers palette.)

3 Draw any more shapes you want (each shape appears on a new layer).

Perfect circles/squares

Hold Shift to draw a perfectly proportioned shape (e.g. square or circle).
Note: when you hold down the Shift key the shape will be created in proportion but it will not be placed on a new shape layer: it will be added to the layer that you are currently on.
Hold Alt to draw from the centre of the shape.

Renaming layers

Rename a shape layer by right-clicking its name (e.g. Shape 1). Choose Layer Properties, then type a new name into the box that appears and click OK.

12.10.5 Filling Shapes on a Shape Layer

1 Double click the fill thumbnail next to the shape layer.

Double click
here to change
the colour

2 Drag the slider to the colour range you want.

3 Click a colour in the left of the box.

4 Click on OK.

This will change the colour of all shapes on that shape layer.

12.10.6 Drawing Custom Shapes

1 Click the Custom Shape tool.

2 Click the Shape: down arrow on the Options bar.

3 Click the custom shape you want to draw.

4 Click the Shape: down arrow again.

5 Drag diagonally to draw the shape.

6 Draw any other shapes you want.

12.10.7 Adding More Shapes to an Existing Shape Layer

1 On the Layers palette, select the Shape Layer to add the shape to.

2 Click on a Shape tool on the Toolbox.

3 Click on the Add to shape area button on the Options Bar.

4 Draw the shape or shapes to add.

Practise this!

Open a Photoshop file and draw a perfect square on a new layer. On the same layer draw an oval shape. On a new layer, draw your choice of custom shape. Save the file with the name Shapes.

12.10.8 Resizing Individual Shapes

1 On the Layers palette, select the Shape Layer.

2 Click the Path Selection tool on the Toolbox.

3 Click once on a shape.

4 Click Show Bounding Box on the Options bar.

5 Drag a handle on the bounding box.

6 Press Enter.

7 Click Show Bounding Box off on the Options bar.

To keep the shape in proportion

Hold Shift down as you drag the Bounding Box handle.

12.10.9 Rotating Individual Shapes

1 On the Layers palette, select the Shape Layer.

2 Click the Path Selection tool on the Toolbox.

3 Click once on a shape.

☑ Show Bounding Box 4 Click Show Bounding Box on the Options bar.

5 Move the mouse outside one of the corner handles, so it becomes a curved arrow.

6 Click and drag to rotate.

7 Press Enter.

8 Click Show Bounding Box off on the Options bar.

More on rotating

See Section 12.11, Working with images, for more on rotating selections.

12.10.10 Moving shapes

1 Select the Shape Layer on the Layers palette.

2 Click the Path Selection tool on the Toolbox.

3 Drag the shape to a new location.

4 Press Enter.

12.10.11 Deleting a Shape

1 Select the Shape Layer on the Layers palette.

2 Click the Path Selection tool.

3 Click the shape to delete.

4 Press Delete on the keyboard.

The shape is deleted, unless there are no other shapes on the layer. In which case you will see this box:

Delete Vector Mask	✕
This operation will clear the vector mask.	OK
What do you want to delete?	Cancel
⦿ Layer 'Shape 3'	
○ Vector Mask	
○ Vector Mask Contents Only	

1 Click the first option in the 'What do you want to delete?' section (the current layer name).

2 Click OK and the layer will be deleted along with the shape.

12

12.10.12 Identifying the Foreground and Background Colours

You can see the current foreground and background colours in the following locations.

On the Toolbox:

On the Colour Picker palette:

12.10.13 Showing the Colour Picker

If the Colour Picker Palette is not showing:

1 Click on the Window menu.

2 Click on Color.

12.10.14 Reversing the Foreground and Background Colours

You can quickly change round the foreground and background colours.

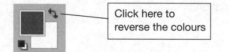

Click on the reverse arrow on the Toolbox.

12.10.15 The Eyedropper – Picking Up a Colour

You can use the eyedropper tool to replicate a colour from elsewhere in the image.

1 Click on the Eyedropper Tool on the Toolbox.

2 Click on an area of colour that you want to use.

3 Paint, type text, or Fill/Stroke a selection.

12.10.16 Which Colours can the Eyedropper Pick Up?

You can pick up colour from part of the image you are working on, from part of a different image or from the Colour Picker palette at the bottom of the colour palette.

12.10.17 Using the Paint Bucket to Fill Areas

You can select an area, or click into a layer to fill it with colour using the Paint Bucket.

1 Use a Selection tool to select an area to fill.

Or

On the Layers palette, select a layer to fill.

2 Choose a Foreground colour.

3 Click the Paint Bucket tool.

4 Point into the area to fill.

5 Click once.

If you cannot see the Paint Bucket on the Toolbox

The Paint Bucket tool appears with the Gradient Fill tool on the toolbox.
   If you cannot see the Paint Bucket, hold the mouse button down on the Gradient Fill tool.

Practise this!

Open your Shapes.psd file (see above). Use the Eyedropper tool to select a colour and then fill in the square with that colour.

12.10.18 Fill Patterns

You can fill areas and layers with patterns, not just colours.

1 Use a Selection tool to select an area to fill.

Or

Click on a layer to fill on the Layers palette.

2 Click the Paint Bucket tool.

3 Click the Fill drop-down arrow on the Options bar.

4 Choose Pattern.

5 Click the Pattern drop-down arrow.

6 Click on a pattern to use as a fill.

7 Point into the area to fill.

8 Click once.

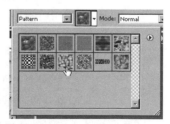

12.11 | Working with Images

12.11.1 Opening Images

1 Click on the File menu.

2 Click on Open.

3 Use the Look in box to navigate to the file you want.

4 Click on the file to be opened.

5 Click on Open.

12.11.2 Placing an Image in an Open File

You can import images into a file you are already working on. To do this:

1 Click on the File menu.

2 Click on Place.

3 Use the Look in box to navigate to the file you want.

4 Click on the file to be imported.

5 Click on Place.

6 Resize the image to the desired dimensions.

7 Press Return on the keyboard.

The imported image will be added on a new layer.

12.11.3 To Move Part of an Image

1 Use a Selection tool to select part of the image.

2 Click on the Move tool.

3 Point to the centre of selection.

4 Click and drag.

12.11.4 To Copy Part of an Image

1 Use a Selection tool to select part of the image.

2 Click on the Edit menu.

3 Click on Copy.

4 Click on the Edit menu.

5 Click on Paste.

Where is the copy?

Photoshop automatically places the copy exactly on top of the original selection!
Click the Move tool and drag the copy to new location.

Shortcut

Hold Ctrl and Alt and drag the selected area to a new location.

12.11.5 Copying Part of an Image to Another Image

To copy part of an image from one file to another:

1 Open up both images.

2 Place the two images side by side.

3 Use a Selection tool to select part of the image.

4 Click on the Move tool.

5 Click in the centre of the selection.

6 Drag the selection to the other image.

12.11.6 Changing the Size of an Image

Photoshop gives you the ability to resize an image by changing its on-screen pixel dimensions or print size.

Enlarging can blur the image

You can increase the size of an image at any time – but bear in mind that increasing the image increases the gaps between each pixel. These gaps are filled with other pixels based on similar colour and tone settings to the original (a process called interpolation).

The image can become less sharp and less detailed.

---

1 Click on the Image menu.

2 Click on Image Size.

3 Make sure there is a tick in the resample image box (this prevents the resolution from changing).

4 Make sure that there is a tick in the Constrain Proportions box (this prevents the image being distorted).

5 Type in a new width measurement.

Or

Type in a new height measurement.

6 Click on OK.

12.11.7 Increasing the Size of the Image with Resampling

By default, when you resize an image, Photoshop will keep the original resolution.

Resampling

Increasing the size of the image with the 'resample' box ticked means that the resolution of the image remains the same. However, the file size will increase when making the image larger because extra pixels are added.

12.11.8 Increasing Image Size without Resampling

An image can be resized without using resampling. Increasing the size of the image and not allowing for resampling means the file size will remain the same but the resolution will drop. The same amount of pixels are spread out over a greater area so the image will lose quality, becoming less sharp and defined.

12.11.9 Let Photoshop Work it Out for you

1 Click on the Help menu.

2 Click on Resize Image.

3 Answer the first question that appears in the Wizard ('what will this image be used for?').

4 Click on the Next button to see the next question.

5 Answer the question.

6 Repeat steps 4 and 5 until the wizard is finished.

7 Click the Finish button.

Practise this!

Open an existing Photoshop file and insert a photographic image into it. Resize the image so it is around half its original size.

12.11.10 The Eraser

The Eraser Tool changes pixels in an image as you click and drag over them. On the Background layer, the tool erases the image and reveals the background colour. On other layers, it removes the colour and replaces it with transparency. You can also use the Eraser Tool to return to a specified location within the History palette.

12.11.11 Erasing Options (Brush and Mode)

1 Click on the Eraser Tool.

2 On the Options Bar, click on the Brush down arrow.

3 Choose a brush size (e.g. 13).

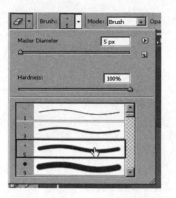

4 On the Options Bar, click on the Mode down arrow (it shows different erasing styles).

5 Choose a mode (e.g. Block – note: some of the options become unavailable).

6 Click and drag on the image to erase.

12.11.12 The Background Eraser

This tool lets you erase areas containing similar colours.

1 Click and hold on the Eraser Tool.

2 Choose the Background Eraser.

3 Choose a Brush size on the Options Bar (the bigger the brush, the easier it is to erase large areas).

4 Choose the sampling on the Options Bar.

Select Continuous	Erases areas containing the colours you clicked on as you drag.
Select Once	Erases areas containing the first colour you clicked on.
Select Background Swatch	Erases areas containing the current Background Colour.

5 Choose a Limits mode.

Select Discontiguous	Erases selected colour from entire Layer.
Select Contiguous	Erases the selected colour in a range where the colour occurs continuously.
Select Find Edges	Erases areas of the same colour as well as maintaining a sharper definition for the edge.

6 Change the tolerance on the options bar (a low tolerance ensures you will erase only areas of very similar colour).

7 If required, tick the Protect foreground box (areas that match the foreground colour in the Toolbox will not be erased).

8 Click and drag over any areas of the same colour that you wish to erase.

12.11.13 The Magic Eraser

This is wonderful when you have a large area you need to erase, and when that area is similar in colour all the way through. It is similar to the Magic Wand tool.

1 Click and hold on the Eraser Tool.

2 Choose the Magic Eraser Tool.

3 Change the Tolerance on the Options Bar (use a low tolerance to choose colours that are very similar).

4 Remove tick in Contiguous box (to ensure the colour chosen changes everywhere).

5 Tick Use All Layers box (this will affect all visible layers in the image).

6 Change the Opacity (100% erases all, 50% erases half the colour).

7 Click once on the colour you wish to erase.

12.11.14 Using the Bounding Box to Rotate/Resize

1 Use a selection tool to select an area.

2 Click the Move Tool.

3 Click in the Show Transform Controls box on the Options Bar, so it is ticked.

4 Point at a corner of your selection.

5 To resize – hold the pointer directly over the corner until you **see** a double-headed arrow.

Or

To rotate – hold the pointer just outside the corner, so you see a curly double arrow.

6 Drag until the selection or image is at the size/angle you want.

7 Press Enter.

8 On the Options Bar, remove the tick from the Transform Controls Box.

12.11.15 Rotating a Specified Amount Using the Edit Menu

1 Use a selection tool to select the image or part of the image.

2 Click on the Edit menu.

3 Choose Transform path.

4 Click on Rotate.

5 Click into the rotate angle box on the Options Bar.

6 Type in the degree of rotation (Enter a number between −180/180).

7 Press Enter.

8 Click the tick on the Options Bar to confirm the rotation.

12.11.16 Rotating a Canvas

You can easily rotate your entire canvas (whole image) using the Image menu.

1 Click on the Image menu.

2 Choose Rotate Canvas.

3 Click on one of the available options on the menu.

12.11.17 The Crop Tool

The Crop tool allows you to select an area of your image that you want to keep and remove the rest.

Make sure you can see the part of the image you want to keep.

1 Click on the Crop tool on the Toolbox.

2 Click and drag to select the area to keep.

3 Click on the tick button on the right of the Options Bar.

Or

Press Enter.

Save a copy!

Once you have cropped an image the cropped pixels are deleted from the file. That's fine if you're sure you want to lose them. If not, save a copy of the file first.

To do this, select Save As from the File menu and click the As a Copy option in the Save As box. This is handy if you think you might want to go back to the original image sometime.

12.11.18 To Resize Your Selection Before Cropping

Once you have selected a cropping area you can resize the selection:

1 Click on the Crop tool.

2 Click and drag to select the area to keep.

3 Move the mouse over the resizing handles.

4 Click and drag to resize the area.

5 Press Enter.

12.11.19 Cancelling the Crop

If you have selected an area with the cropping tool and you then change your mind and do not want to go ahead with the crop:

Press Esc on the keyboard.

12.11.20 Using the Red Eye Tool

This tool removes red eye in flash photos of people and white or green reflections in flash photos of animals.

1 Click on the Red Eye tool on the Toolbox.

2 Change the options on the Options bar, if required.

3 Click in the red eye within the image.

12.11.21 Changing Layer Styles

You can apply subtle effects to layers by using layer styles. To access these options, double click on a layer in the Layers palette.

To set effects on that layer:

1 Click on the effect name on the left.

2 Change the settings as desired.

3 Click on the OK button.

Here are some examples of what you can do with layer styles.

Setting a simple shadow:

1 Open the Layer Style dialog box.

2 Click on the Drop Shadow option on the left.

3 Adjust the Angle figure to change the shadow's angle.

4 Adjust the Distance slider to change how far the shadow is from the shape.

5 Click OK.

Applying a gradient:

1 Open the Layer Style dialog box.

2 Click on the Gradient Overlay option on the left.

3 Click on the arrow on the Gradient drop-down menu and choose the option you want.

Or

Click on the colours on the Gradient drop-down menu and make more detailed changes to the gradient.

4 Click on the Style drop-down menu and adjust the style type.

5 Adjust the Angle figure to change the gradient's angle.

6 Click OK.

12.11.22 Filters

You can use filters to add special effects to your image. The filters are stored in the Filter menu – they are arranged in categories. To apply a filter:

1 Click on the Filter menu.

2 Click on the filter category you want.

3 Click on the filter you want.

4 Set the filter options in the dialog box that opens.

5 Click OK.

What the…?!

Some filters make some pretty drastic changes to your document. Try them out, but be ready to click back through the history palette if you don't like how they turn out!

12.12 Adding Text

In Photoshop you can create horizontal or vertical type. You can type characters or paragraphs. When you create type, a new type layer is added to your image. This means you can edit it as much as you like without affecting the other layers.

12.12.1 Resolution and Type

Type will appear at the same resolution as the picture that it appears in. To create the smoothest possible type for high-resolution output, a resolution of 200dpi is recommended.

Type appears on its own layer!

When you create type, Photoshop will automatically place it on a layer of its own – keep it there if you want to edit the text easily in future.

12.12.2 What is Anti-aliased?

Anti-aliased blends the pixels along the perimeters of hard edges (such as type) to avoid jagged edges. You can choose anti-alias settings for your type using the Options Bar.

12

12.12.3 Typing Characters

The Type tool enables you to decide where you want the text in your image to be located.

1 Click on the Type tool on the Toolbox.

2 Change the settings on the Options Bar if required (you can change the orientation, font, colour and so on).

3 Click on the image where type is to appear.

4 Start typing.

5 Press return when you want to start a new line.

6 Click the tick on the Options Bar to confirm your text.

12.12.4 Typing Paragraph Text

1 Click on the Type tool on the Toolbox.

2 Change the settings on the Options Bar if required.

3 Click and drag in your image to create a bounding box (this will hold your text).Start typing (the text will wrap within the bounding box).

4 Click the tick on the Options Bar to confirm your text.

12.12.5 Character and Paragraph Palettes

These give even more options for your type. Point at each option on a palette and pop-up help tells you what it does.

1 Click on the Window menu.

2 Click on Character or Paragraph.

3 Click on the Character or Paragraph tab.

12.12.6 Editing Character Type

1 Click on the Type tool on the Toolbox.

2 Click the type layer to be edited on the Layers palette.

3 Click on the text in the image.

4 Click and drag over the text to select it.

Or

Click into the existing text and type more text.

5 Make your changes on the Options Bar (if required).

6 Click the tick on the right of the Options Bar.

12.12.7 Editing Paragraph Type

1 Click on the Type tool on the Toolbox.

2 Click the type layer to be edited on the Layers palette.

3 Click on the text in the image.

4 Click and drag over the text to select it.

Or

Click into the image and type more text.

5 Make your changes on the Options Bar (if required).

6 Click the tick on the right of the Options Bar.

12.12.8 Moving Type

While type is still in a layer of its own, use the move tool to move your type to any location.

1 Click on the type layer on the Layers palette.

2 Click on the Move tool on the Toolbox.

3 Click and drag the text to move it to a new location.

12.12.9 Deleting Characters

1 Click on the Type Layer you want to work on.

2 Click on the Type tool.

3 Click before the character to delete and press Delete key.

Or

Click after the character to delete and press Backspace.

Or

Drag across the characters to delete and press the Delete key.

12.13 Warped Type

Warped type is text that is reshaped using a special dialog box.

12.13.1 Applying Warped Type

1 Click on the Type tool on the Toolbox.

2 Type your words.

3 Click on the Create Warped Text button on the Options bar.

4 Choose an option from the Style drop-down list.

5 Click on Horizontal or Vertical.

6 Drag the sliders to the desired levels (the text will change as you change the levels).

7 Click on OK when the text has the look you want.

I can't warp my text

You may find that you have to change the font type of your text in order to warp it.

12.13.2 Rasterizing Type

Some editing options are not available when editing a type layer (e.g. the painting and gradient tools). To be able to use these on type you must first rasterize the type layer so it becomes a normal layer.

Error message

When you try to do certain things on a type layer, you may get an error message that looks something like this.

Click OK and then rasterize your type layer as shown below before you continue.

---

1 Click on the type layer that you wish to rasterize on the Layers palette.

2 Click on the Layer menu.

3 Choose Rasterize.

4 Click on Type.

12.14 Test Your Knowledge

The questions below will test what you know of the knowledge and understanding requirements of this unit. All the answers to these questions are contained or referred to within this chapter.

1 You are to create two images. One will be used on a website, the other will be printed in a magazine. Which should have a higher resolution?

2 When working on a file in Photoshop, why should you always keep a copy of it saved in the PSD format?

3 What legal implications might there be in using an image downloaded from the Internet in your own work?

4 What file format would be most suitable for a file intended for print publication?

5 What colour mode should you use if the file is intended for print publication?

6 What is the primary purpose of layers in Photoshop?

7 What would you use filters for?

8 What does the Eyedropper tool enable you to do?

9 When resizing an image in Photoshop, what effect does resampling have?

10 What is the difference between a vector and raster graphic?

12.15 Evidence

The tasks you undertake as evidence for your ITQ should be work-related. Therefore, your supervisor at work should be able to give you guidance on the type of tasks you should take on. Below are some ideas of possible tasks for this unit. Consider how you can adapt these ideas to make them more relevant for your own workplace and to ensure you cover all the skills requirements.

- Create a new logo for your company. Use basic shapes and text in the design.

- Compile a document that explains how and why you should check the following when creating a file:

  1 Image resolution.

  2 Accuracy of any text used.

  3 File format used.

  4 Colour mode used.

  Also list any other checks you would normally make when creating a file.

- Create a new file that contains a photo of the office where you work. Add a layer on top that contains text (such as your company name or address). Experiment with the filters and layer styles available, until you are happy with the results. Save the file in a format appropriate for the Web.

CHAPTER 13

Presentation Software

13.1 About This Unit

What you need to know

To gain ITQ Level 2 in this unit, you should demonstrate the following competency:
Use presentation software effectively to produce more complex presentations that communicate clearly and accurately.

To achieve this you should know and understand:

1 How to produce information that is clear and appropriate.

2 More complex presentations.

3 How to add images, objects and sound.

You should also be able to demonstrate the following skills and techniques:

1 Handling files appropriately.

2 Editing presentations.

3 Checking presentations.

4 Formatting slides that are more complex.

5 Presenting slides so that others can use them.

6 Producing presentations.

How to prove your skills

You need to carry out at least two work-based tasks which demonstrate the skills and knowledge listed above. In order to show your competency, it may well be necessary for you to complete more tasks than this.

Make sure you have plenty of evidence that shows how you completed each task, such as a copy of the file you worked on, or a document with screenshots of the processes you followed. You can back this up by producing a report which shows your knowledge of the subjects covered within the unit.

13.2 What is PowerPoint?

13.2.1 What is it for?

PowerPoint is used to produce presentations on:

- Acetates (overhead projector slides).

- 35mm slides.

- Paper.

- The computer screen.

- The Internet.

All of these are created in exactly the same way!

The only difference comes at the end when you wish to give the presentation. You could print onto acetate or paper, run the slide show on the screen, upload your presentation to the Internet, or send your presentation to a specialist shop to create 35mm slides.

It can also produce extra documents related to your presentation.

- Speaker's notes.

- Audience handouts.

13.2.2 PowerPoint Jargon

Every presentation you produce is made up of slides. Slide is a generic term that can mean any of the types of presentation listed below.

A presentation

Slide One	Slide Two	Slide Three

13.3 Creating a New Presentation

When you first open PowerPoint, you will be given a new, blank presentation to start with. If you have closed this, or opened another file and then closed it, you will need to create another presentation if you want a new file.

13.3.1 Creating a Blank Presentation

1 Click on the File menu.

2 Click on New.

New

☐ Blank Presentation

3 Click on Blank Presentation from the Task Pane – you will be given a new, blank file.

Or

Click on the New Presentation icon.

Should I use the menu or the icon?

The icon is the quickest way of creating a new presentation, but using the menu gives you access to PowerPoint's design templates, where you can choose colours and pictures for the backgrounds of your slides.

13.3.2 Choosing the Layout

Once you have chosen Blank Presentation, the Task Pane will change to the Slide Layout pane. To choose a slide layout, just pick one that you like, and click on it!

13.4 Applying a Template

13.4.1 What are Design Templates?

Design templates are preset formats that add graphics, colours and fonts consistently to all of the slides in your presentation. The design template will decide how the following elements look.

13

- Fonts and formatting.
- Bullet points.
- Background graphics.

The design template you are currently using will appear on the status bar at the bottom right of the screen.

Blue Diagonal

13.4.2 Applying a Design Template

 Design

1 Click on the Design icon.

   Or

   Click on the Format menu.

   Click on Slide Design.

2 Click on the template you require.

You can change your mind later on – if you have already applied a design template, simply repeat the above steps and choose a different one.

Apply a design template:

13.5 Saving a Presentation

13.5.1 Saving a Presentation

1 Click on the Save icon.

   Or

   Click on the File menu.

   Click on Save.

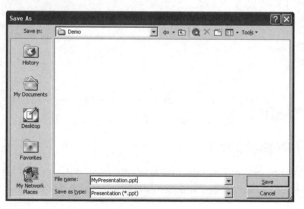

2 Type a filename (maximum of 255 characters) into the File name box.

3 Change the location in the Save in box if required, by clicking on the drop-down arrow next to it.

4 Click Save.

13.5.2 Saving a Presentation After You Have Made Changes

Just click on the Save icon – the previous version is overwritten.

Save regularly!

Click on the Save icon at regular intervals when you are working. If you forget to save for a long time, you are in danger of losing your work if there is a power cut.

13.5.3 Saving a Copy of a Presentation Using Save As

Use Save As if you want to save a copy of your file under a different name, or in a different place.

1 Click File.

2 Click Save As.

3 Type in a new filename (if required).

4 Change Save in box to a different folder (If required).

5 Click Save.

13.6 Opening and Closing a Presentation

13.6.1 Opening a Presentation

1 Click on the Open icon.

2 Click the drop-down arrow next to the Look in box, and go to the drive and folder where your file is saved.

3 Click on the file/folder you require.

4 Click Open.

13.6.2 Opening Multiple Files

To open more than one file, just repeat the process – open one file and then open another one. They will appear as buttons on your taskbar, which you can click to switch between:

Presentati...   Eels.ppt   demopres...

13.6.3 Closing a Presentation

1 Click on the File menu.

2 Click Close.

   Or

3 Click on the bottom X at the top right-hand corner of the screen.

13.7 Adding Text to Slides

13.7.1 What are Slide Layouts?

Every slide has a layout containing placeholders which you can enter text into. Two sample layouts are shown below:

Click to add title

Click to add subtitle

Title slide layout

Click to add title

• Click to add text

Bulleted list layout

13.7.2 What are Placeholders?

Every layout has a placeholder for each item that you will put on your slides. These will always give instructions on how to add information.

Text placeholder

• Click to add text

Chart placeholder

Clipart placeholder

Media clip placeholder

13.7.3 Adding Text to Placeholders

1 Click inside the placeholder you want to add text to – diagonal lines will appear around the edge.

2 Start typing!

3 Click outside the placeholder when you have finished.

PowerPoint does the formatting for you!

PowerPoint comes with preset formatting depending on the template you have chosen. Titles will be bigger, subtitles and bulleted lists will be smaller. There will be different alignments and there will be different fonts.

You can change the formatting on individual slides, but you may lose consistency with the rest of the slides in the presentation.

Moving to the next placeholder with the keyboard

Press Escape (Esc), then press Tab.

13.7.4 Creating Bulleted Lists

1 Click into the bulleted list placeholder.

2 Type your first point.

3 Press return to start a new point.

13.7.5 Changing the Layout

Once a slide is created it is easy to change your mind about its layout.

1   Select the slide you wish to change.

2   Click on the Format menu.

3   Click on Slide Layout.

4   Click on the required new layout in the Task Pane.

13.7.6 Editing the Text in Placeholders

1   Click inside the placeholder you want to change. Diagonal lines will appear around the edge.

2   Make any changes you require.

13.7.7 Creating New Areas for Text

If the placeholders on your slide do not give you all the space you need for text, you can draw a text box.

1   Click on the Text Box icon on the drawing toolbar.

2   Position the mouse on the slide where you require extra text.

3   Click and drag the shape of the text box you require.

4   Start typing – text will wrap inside the box.

13.8 Creating New Slides

13.8.1 Creating New Slides

1   Move to the slide which will appear before the new one.

2   Click on the New Slide icon.

3   Click on the layout you require from the task pane.

Shortcut!

You can also press Ctrl and M to add a new slide.

13.9 The Different Views Within PowerPoint

13.9.1 Changing the View

1 Click on the View menu.

2 Click on the view you require.

Or

Click on the required icon from the bottom left of the screen.

Going from left to right, the icons will take you to a different view:

■ Normal view.

■ Slide Sorter view.

■ Slide Show view (runs the slide show).

13.9.2 Normal View

Normal view is the one that you will work in most of the time. It offers you three different areas:

1 Slide view area where you can see your slide.

2 Thumbnail view area where you can see all the text in your presentation.

3 Speaker's notes area where you can write your own notes on the slides.

Each of these areas can be adjusted according to your preference. In normal view, you can:

■ Add text.

■ Add pictures.

■ Create speaker's notes.

On the left in Normal view is the thumbnail area – it is sometimes called the Outline Pane, although it is still technically the Normal view. This shows you an outline of your presentation. You can click on the slides to switch between them, or just get a general idea of how things look. Click on the icons at the top to switch between the image or text versions.

In the text version, you can add text into the small, outlined slides – just click on them and type as normal, pressing Return to add new lines.

13.9.3 Slide Sorter View

Slide Sorter view shows you all your slides as if they were laid out on a table. You cannot add text or pictures in Slide Sorter view, but you can:

- Change the order of slides.
- Delete slides.
- Add transition and animation effects.

13.9.4 Slide Show View

Slide Show view is used for giving an on-screen presentation. When you have finished creating your presentation, this is what you will use to present the show – and you can use it to make sure it works before standing up in front of 300 people.

13.10 Slide Sorter View

13.10.1 Getting to the Slide Sorter View

1 Click on the View menu.

2 Click Slide Sorter.

Or

Click on the Slide Sorter View icon.

13.10.2 Selecting Slides in Slide Sorter View

Click on the slide you require.

A dark border will appear around the edge.

Or, if you would like to select several slides:

1 Click on the first slide you require

2 Hold down the Shift key

3 Click on the other slides you require

Or, if you would like to select all of the slides:

Press Ctrl and A.

13.10.3 Moving Slides in Slide Sorter View

1 Select the slide you wish to move.

2 Click and drag to a new location.

A vertical grey line indicates where your slide will be placed.

13.10.4 Deleting Slides in Slide Sorter View

1 Select the slide(s) you wish to delete.

2 Press Delete.

13.11 Adding Slide Transitions

13.11.1 What are Slide Transitions?

This refers to the way that the slide comes onto the screen in an on-screen show.

13.11.2 Creating Slide Transitions in Slide Sorter View

1 Switch to Slide Sorter view (see above).

2 Select the slide(s) you wish to add a transition to.

3 Click on Transition icon.

Slide Transition task pane appears.

4 Click on the transition effect you require in the Slide Transition task pane.

13.11.3 Add Sound to Transitions

In the Slide Transition task pane:

1 Select the slide(s) you wish to adjust.

2 Click on the drop-down arrow next to Sound.

3 Select a sound from the list.

Practise this!

Create a copy of an existing presentation. Set all slides to the Box In transition effect. Set the first slide to appear with applause and the last slide to appear with the sound of a click. Save this presentation.

13.12 Adding Sounds

13.12.1 Adding a Sound File to Your Presentation

If you have audio files stored on your computer, it's simple to add them to your presentation.

1 Select the slide to which you wish to add sound.

2 Click on the Insert menu.

3 Click on Movies and Sounds.

4 Click on Sound from File.

5 Navigate to the sound you require and select it.

6 Click OK.

7 Choose if you want the sound to play automatically.

13.12.2 Adding PowerPoint's Sound Clips to your Presentation

PowerPoint 2003 includes a number of sound clips in its gallery. To add one of these to your presentation:

1 Select the slide to which you wish to add sound.

2 Click on the Insert menu.

3 Click on Movies and Sounds.

4 Click on Sound from Clip Organizer.

5 Click once on the sound you want to add to your presentation.

6 Choose whether you want the sound to play automatically.

13.13 Adding Animation Effects

13.13.1 What are Animation Effects?

Animation effects can be applied to any object on your slide, such as text or a picture. Once an object is animated, it will make an entrance onto (or exit from) the screen in some snazzy way. This can be useful for long bulleted lists. Each point can fly in separately, so that your audience does not have to concentrate on the whole list at once.

13.13.2 Applying an Animation Scheme

There are preset animation schemes that you can apply to your presentation and modify. These schemes affect objects in placeholders. The schemes are categorised into Subtle, Moderate and Exciting.

In Normal or Slide Sorter view:

1 Select the slide(s) you wish to apply animation to.

2 Click on Slide Show menu.

3 Click on Animation Schemes

Slide Design task pane appears.

4 Select the effect you require.

A preview of the effect will be seen.

13.14 Printing Slides

13.14.1 Printing all the Slides

Click on the Print icon.

13.14.2 Print Options

1 Click on the File menu.

2 Click Print.

3 Change the Print range options as required:

- Click on All to print all slides, Current slide to print the slide you are on, or Selection to print whatever you have selected.

- Click on Slides and type in the slides you want to print – if you want to print slide 5, type in 5, for slides 4 to 19, type 4-19, for slide 3, slide 12 and slides 15 to 22, type 3,12, 15-22.

4 Change the Copies options as required – type in the number of copies you require, or use the up and down arrows.

5 Click the drop-down arrow by the Print what box and choose what you want to print – e.g. handouts, slides, speaker's notes, or outline.

6 Change any other options as required:

- Grayscale prints out in black and white and shades of grey, Pure black and white prints out in just black and white.

- Scale to fit paper reduces or enlarges the slide to fit the sheet of paper.

- Frame slides prints a border around the slides.

- Collate lets you change the order of pages – if you are not sure, leave it ticked. Ticked it will print out a three-page presentation in this order: 1, 2, 3, then 1, 2, 3. Unticked will print out in this order: 1, 1, 2, 2, 3, 3.

7 Click OK.

13.14.3 Printing Handouts

You can print handouts for your audience to write their notes on. They will include miniatures of the slides in your presentation.

1 Click on the File menu.

2 Click on Print.

3 Click the drop-down arrow under Print what.

4 Click on Handouts.

5 Click the drop-down arrow next to Slides per page and click on the number you require.

6 Choose the order you require.

7 Click OK.

13.14.4 Printing Speaker's Notes or Outline View

If you would just like the outline text of your presentation (as it appears in the outline page), or you would like to print out the notes you have typed in the notes pane:

1 Click on the File menu.

2 Click Print.

3 Click the drop-down arrow underneath the Print what box.

4 Click on the option you require.

5 Click OK.

13.15 Moving, Resizing and Deleting Placeholders

These will work with any placeholder – text, pictures, clip art, and so on.

13.15.1 Moving Placeholders

1 Select the whole placeholder – dotted lines appear around the edge.

2 Position the mouse over the dotted line – mouse pointer will change to a four-headed arrow.

3 Click and drag to a new location.

13.15.2 Resizing Placeholders

1 Select the whole placeholder, making sure that dotted lines appear around the edge – if they are diagonal lines, click on them once to make them dotted.

2 Position the mouse over a resizing handle – it will change to a double-headed arrow.

3 Click and drag to resize – dragging from a corner will resize the box proportionally, and dragging from a middle handle will stretch or squash the shape of the box.

13.15.3 Deleting Placeholders

1 Select the whole placeholder – dotted lines will appear around the edge.

2 Press Delete.

13.16 Moving and Copying Text

13.16.1 Moving Text Using the Icons

1 Select the text you would like to move.

2 Click on the Cut icon – the text is moved to the Windows Clipboard.

3 Position the cursor in the place you would like to move the text to.

4 Click on the Paste icon.

13.16.2 Copying Text Using the Icons

1 Select the text you would like to copy.

2 Click on the Copy icon – the text is copied to the Windows Clipboard.

3 Position the cursor in the place you would like to copy the text to.

4 Click on the Paste icon.

13.16.3 Moving Text Using the Menu

1 Select the text you want to move.

2 Click on the Edit menu.

3 Click on Cut.

4 Click where you want to put your text.

5 Click on the Edit menu.

6 Click on Paste – the text will have moved to the new location.

13.16.4 Copying Text Using the Menu

1 Select the text you want to move.

2 Click on the Edit menu.

3 Click on Copy.

4 Click where you want to put your text.

5 Click on the Edit menu.

6 Click on Paste – the text will be in both the new and the original location.

13.16.5 Viewing the Clipboard

When you either cut or copy text in PowerPoint XP, it is stored on the clipboard. To view the clipboard:

1 Click on the Edit menu.

2 Click on Office Clipboard.

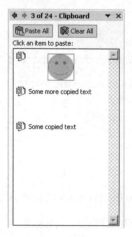

13.16.6 Using the Clipboard

To paste items from the clipboard:

1 Click where you would like to put the item.

2 Place the mouse pointer over the item you want to paste.

3 Click on it.

Eventually the clipboard will get full up

Once you have cut or copied 24 items, the clipboard will get full. Click on the Clear All icon to empty it.

13.16.7 Deleting Text

1 Select the text you wish to delete.

2 Press the Delete or Del key.

13.17 Moving, Copying and Deleting Slides

13.17.1 Moving Slides

You can move slides in Normal view (using the thumbnails pane on the left of the window) or in the Slide Sorter view. Whichever you choose, the process of moving the slides is the same.

1 Click on the slide to move, holding down the mouse button – a blue border will appear around the slide.

2 Drag the slide to its new location – a line indicates where the slide will be placed.

3 Release the mouse button to place the slide.

13.17.2 Selecting Several Slides Next to Each Other

1 Click on the first slide.

2 Hold down the Shift key.

3 Click on the last slide.

13

13.17.3 Selecting Several Slides that are Not Next to Each Other

1 Click on the first slide.

2 Hold down the Ctrl key.

3 Click on all the other slides you want to select.

13.17.4 Copying Slides

1 Go to Slide Sorter view.

2 Click on the slide you wish to copy.

3 Click on the Copy icon.

4 Click between the two slides where you want the copied slide to appear.

5 Click on the Paste icon.

Or

1 Click on the slide you wish to copy.

2 Click on the Edit menu.

3 Click on Copy.

4 Click between the two slides where you want the copied slide to appear.

5 Click on the Edit menu.

6 Click on Paste.

13.17.5 Moving Slides Between Presentations

1 Go to Slide Sorter view.

2 Click on the slide you wish to copy.

3 Click on the Cut (to move) or Copy (to copy) icon.

4 Switch to the window of the presentation you want to move/copy the slide to.

5 Click between the two slides where you want the slide to appear.

6 Click on the Paste icon.

Or

1 Click on the slide you wish to copy.

2 Click on the Edit menu.

3 Click on Cut or Copy.

4 Switch to the window of the presentation you want to move/copy the slide to.

5 Click between the two slides where you want the slide to appear.

6 Click on the Edit menu.

7 Click on Paste.

Shortcut

There are some handy keyboard shortcuts you can use to move or copy items. Simply select whatever you wish to cut or copy and press the Ctrl key and X to cut, or Ctrl and C to copy. Then just press Ctrl and P to paste.

13.17.6 Deleting Slides

1 Go to Slide Sorter view.

2 Click on the slide you wish to delete.

3 Press the Delete or Del key.

13.18 Creating Speaker's Notes

13.18.1 Where Can I Type My Notes?

You can type notes to accompany your presentation, which will only be viewable by you. To do this, you need to be in Normal view. You can type your notes into the Notes pane, which you'll find at the bottom of the screen.

13.18.2 Getting to the Notes Pane

1 Click on the View menu.

2 Click Normal.

3 Click in the Notes pane.

13.18.3 Adding Notes

1 Go to the slide you wish to add notes to.

2 Click inside the Notes pane.

3 Start typing.

Start typing your notes in here

13

13.18.4 Resizing the Notes Pane

If you're typing in a lot of notes, you can easily increase the size of the Notes pane.

1 Position the cursor over the top border of the Notes pane – the cursor will look like a double arrow.

2 Click and drag the Notes pane to the size you want.

13.19 Changing the Appearance of Text

13.19.1 Making Text Bold, Italic, Underlined or Shadowed

1 Select the text or placeholder you want to change.

B *I* <u>U</u> S

2 Click on the icon you require (shown below) – it will look pushed in when clicked.

Going from left to right, here is what each icon does:

- **Bold**.
- *Italic*.
- <u>Underline</u>.
- Shadow.

To remove any of these effects, just click the icon again – it will no longer look pushed in.

13.19.2 Changing the Fonts

1 Select the text or placeholder to change.

2 Click the drop-down arrow next to the Font box.

| Arial | ▼ |

3 Click on the font you require – use the scroll bar to see more fonts if necessary.

13.19.3 Changing the Size of Text

1 Select the text or placeholder to change.

| 10 | ▼ |

2 Click the drop-down arrow next to the Font Size box.

3 Click on the size you require – use the scroll bar to see more sizes if necessary.

Or

1 Select the text or placeholder to change.

A A

2 Click on the Increase or Decrease Font Size icons – the big A increases the size, the small A decreases it.

13.19.4 Changing Font Colour

1 Select the text or placeholder you wish to change.

2 Click on the Format menu.

3 Click Font.

4 Click on the drop-down arrow next to Color.

5 Click on the colour you require.

   Or

   Click on More Colors.

   Click on the Standard tab.

   Click on the colour you require.

6 Click OK.

My text doesn't look the right colour

The text will not look right until you deselect it. If it is still selected, it will look very wrong indeed.

13.19.5 Changing Line Spacing

1 Select the text or placeholder you want to change.

2 Click on the Format menu.

3 Click Line Spacing.

4 Change the options as required:

   ■ **Line spacing**: the amount of space between the lines.

   ■ **Before paragraph**: the amount of space between the paragraphs.

   ■ **After paragraph**: the amount of space after the paragraphs.

5 Click OK.

13

13.19.6 Changing the Alignment

Changing the alignment changes the position of the text inside the placeholder. Text can either be aligned to the left of the placeholder, in the centre of the placeholder, or to the right of the placeholder.

1 Select the text or placeholder to change.

2 Click on the alignment option you require – the first icon aligns the text to the left, the next one centres it, and the last one aligns it to the right.

13.20 Bullets and Numbering

13.20.1 Changing the Style of Bullet Points

1 Select the text or placeholder you want to change.

2 Click on the Format menu.

3 Click Bullets and Numbering.

4 If necessary, click on the Bulleted tab.

5 If required, click on the drop-down arrow underneath Color and click on the colour you require.

6 If required, click into the box underneath Size and choose the size you require.

7 Click on the bullet style you require.

8 Click OK.

13.20.2 Choosing Another Character

If you don't like any of the bullet styles, go to the Bullets and Numbering dialog box, and then:

1 Click on Customize.

2 If required, click the drop-down arrow next to Font and choose the font you require.

3 Click on the symbol you require.

4 Click OK.

5 Click OK.

13.20.3 Removing Bullets

1 Select the paragraph you want to remove bullets from.

2 Click on the Bullets icon to remove bullets.

13.21 Changing the Background

13.21.1 Changing the Colour of the Background

1 If you are in Slide Sorter view, select at least one slide.

2 Click on the Format menu.

3 Click Background.

4 Click the drop-down arrow underneath the preview.

5 Click on a colour from those pictured (these are from the current colour scheme).

Or

Click on More Colors.

Click on a colour from the Standard tab.

Click OK.

6 Click on Apply to All to change all the slides.

Or

Click on Apply to change selected slides.

7 If you are in Slide Sorter view, select at least one slide.

8 Click on the Format menu.

9 Click Background.

10 Click the drop-down arrow underneath the preview.

11 Click on a colour from those pictured (these are from the current colour scheme).

Or

Click on More Colors.

Click on a colour from the Standard tab.

Click OK.

12 Click on Apply to All to change all the slides.

Or

Click on Apply to change selected slides.

13.22 Checking Your Presentation

13.22.1 Checking Spelling

Don't worry if spelling isn't your strongest point. PowerPoint includes a spell checker, so you can easily pick out any errors in your presentation.

1 Click Spelling icon.

PowerPoint highlights the first spelling error.

2 Click on the option you require (see table below).

At the end...

Microsoft PowerPoint

The spelling check is complete.

OK

3 Click OK.

Shortcut

Right click any word which has a red or green line underneath it and a shortcut menu of suggested corrections will appear.

If you have the American dictionary

Try clicking on Tools, Language, Set language, English (UK), OK.

13.22.2 How to Correct Your Mistakes

13.22.2.1 Spelling corrections

If the word is spelt correctly	Click on Ignore
If the word is spelt correctly and occurs several times in the document	Click on Ignore All
If the word is spelt correctly and is a word that you use very commonly, e.g. your name	Click on Add to Dictionary This will add the word to the dictionary so that it is never seen as a misspelling again
If the correct spelling is listed under Suggestions	1 Click on the correct suggestion 2 Click on Change
If the correct spelling is listed under Suggestions and the misspelling occurs commonly in the document	1 Click on the correct suggestion 2 Click on Change All
If PowerPoint has found a duplicate word (e.g. I would like like to see you) and you would like to delete the duplicate	Click on the Delete button (this will appear in place of the Change button when PowerPoint finds a duplicate word)
If the word is spelt incorrectly and the correct suggestion is not listed	1 Click into the large box containing the text 2 Make the correction manually 3 Click on Change

13.22.2.2 Grammar corrections

If there is no grammatical error	Click on Ignore
If there is no grammatical error and similar sentences appear in the rest of your document	Click on Ignore Rule
If the correct grammar appears under Suggestions	1 Highlight the correct suggestion 2 Click on Change
If the grammar is incorrect, but the correct suggestion does not appear	1 Click into the large box containing the text 3 Make the correction manually 4 Click on Change

13

13.22.3 Proofreading Your Presentation

Always proofread your presentation!

It's a good idea to have a checklist of things to check in your presentation, as although it may look perfect to you, there may be errors lurking where you least suspect it. It can also be helpful to get someone to look over it for you.

Go through your presentation with a fine tooth comb before presenting it to your audience. Things to look out for include:

- **Images** – are they the right size and in the right place? How are they aligned?

- **Text** – is the font correct and consistent? Is the text a reasonable size? How easily can it be read?

- **Bullets and numbering** – have you used these correctly? Does the list stop where it should?

- **Slides** – are they in the correct order? Is the colouring consistent?

- **Spelling and grammar** – make sure there are no mistakes (see above).

- **Colour schemes** – does the text contrast clearly with the background? Is the background colour easy on the eye and not too violent! Does the colour scheme suit the message you are trying to convey i.e. serious, fun or urgent?

Practise this!

Write your own checklist of things to check in your presentations. Include any mistakes you frequently make, any house style you should be adhering to and anything from the above list you wouldn't usually think of checking.

13.23 Designing Your Presentation

13.23.1 Don't Use Too Much Text!

It's important to keep your presentation simple and easy to follow. The best way to do this is by using plenty of pictures and not too much text. Remember, it's you who is giving the presentation – not your computer screen. You shouldn't have to rely too much on what it written on your slides, they should be there simply to reinforce what you're saying.

Try to keep the amount of content on each slide consistent. By limiting the number of points or ideas on each slide, you'll make it far easier for your audience to take in the information.

13.23.2 Adding Pictures to Presentations

When you're preparing your presentation, keep in mind the old saying about how many words a picture is worth.

It's far easier for people to absorb information quickly by looking at a picture or chart, than by wading through reams of text. A good amount of relevant pictures and charts will help to make your show far more engaging.

However, don't try to cram too much detail into your graphics. The whole point of a chart is that it gets information across simply. The example below clearly fails at this.

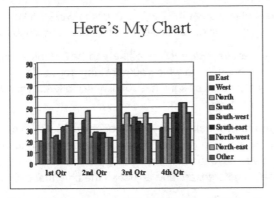

There is simply too much information on this chart. You're better off reducing the amount of detail than losing your audience as they try to decipher what's on the screen.

13.23.3 Using Colours

Using plenty of colour is an easy way to brighten up your presentation. However, try not to get carried away with using colour, as this can make your presentation confusing and detract attention from your main points.

The simplest option is to use a colour scheme. This means your presentation will have a limited number of complementary colours, rather than tons of different hues battling it out on screen.

When using colours, you should also consider how they may affect your audience. For instance, a presentation made up solely of blacks, browns and greys is unlikely to draw in the punters! On the other hand, if you are over-reliant on lots of strong colours like red, purple and orange, your show might be off-putting for your audience. It's normally best to opt for neutral colours that won't overshadow the points you are trying to get across.

Additionally, consider how your show will appear to any colour-blind people in your audience. For instance, if you use blue text on a green background, someone who is colour-blind may find it tricky to make out what is written on the slide. An easy way around this is to use dark text on a pale background.

13

Assessor's tip

Lynne says:

Some colours, such as red, are very difficult to make out when projected. If you are going to use a projector to give your presentation, have a practice before the show so you can check how all the colours look.

13.23.4 Timing Your Presentation

Give plenty of thought to how long your presentation will take. If you have only a short window of time, try cutting some slides from the show.

- **What order should your presentation be in?** Take a good look at your presentation and ask yourself whether it could be organised better. Are the slides in the correct order? Should there be more explanation at the beginning of the show? If your presentation follows a logical sequence, it will be far easier to retain your audience's attention.

- **What is the attention span of your audience likely to be?** Think about how easy it will be to keep your audience engaged in what you're talking about. If you're talking about the company stationery budget, it's likely that you'll need to keep your presentation short and snappy to retain their interest.

- **How much time do you have?** Make sure your presentation fits the time that you have available for delivery. The last thing you want is to spend ages presenting the first half of the show, and then find you have to dash through the second half. You can check this by practising the presentation beforehand, and adjusting the time that each slide is shown for.

13.24 Importing Text from Word

13.24.1 Importing Text from Word

If you have text in a Word document that is very similar to the text you want in a presentation, you can get PowerPoint to import that text.

1 Open the presentation you wish to import into.

2 Move to the slide which will appear before the imported information.

3 Click Insert.

4 Click Slides from Outline.

Look in: Local Disk (C:)

5 Click the down arrow at the end of the Look in box.

6 Click on the folder where the Word document is saved.

7 Click on the Word document to select it.

Insert

8 Click on the Insert button. New slides containing the imported information will appear in your presentation.

My slides look strange!

PowerPoint guesses how you want the imported text to look, based on how the document is formatted. It takes clues from headings, indented text and lists in the document. Sometimes this can produce some rather odd results! However, once the text is imported into the presentation, you're free to format it as you like.

13.25 Importing Charts from Excel

13.25.1 Checking Your Data in Excel

Your Excel spreadsheet must be laid out in exactly the same way as the datasheet in PowerPoint. In other words your data must be at the top left-hand corner, with no titles above or below it.

1 Open the spreadsheet containing the data you wish to chart.

2 Check that your data is in the top left-hand corner, with no extra data above or below it.

	A	B	C	D
1		Mon	Tue	Wed
2	Jaffa Cakes	12	56	36
3	Ice Creams	25	11	55
4	Chocolates	25	56	22

3 Check which sheet your spreadsheet is on.

4 Close and save your spreadsheet.

5 Close Excel.

13.25.2 Importing from Excel into PowerPoint

1 Create a new slide with a layout for a chart.

2 Double click on the chart area.

3 Click on Import file.

4 Change the Look in box to the folder where your spreadsheet is saved.

5 Click on your spreadsheet.

6 Click OK.

Import Data Options

Select sheet from workbook:

Chart1
Chart2
Sheet1
Sheet2
Sheet3

Import:
- ⦿ Entire sheet
- ○ Range:

☑ Overwrite existing cells

[OK]   [Cancel]

7 Click on the sheet you require.

8 Click OK.

13

13.26 Importing Slides from Another Presentation

13.26.1 Inserting Slides from Other Presentations

If you have created slides which you wish to use in several presentations, it's easy to import them.

1 Open the presentation you wish to import into.

2 Move to the slide which will appear before the imported slide.

3 Click Insert.

4 Click Slides from File.

5 Click Browse.

6 Click on the drop-down arrow at the right of the Look in box.

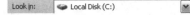

7 Click on the name of the presentation you wish to import slides from.

8 Click Open.

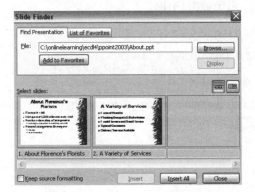

9 Click on the slide you wish to insert.

10 Click Insert.

Or

Click Insert All to insert all the slides.

The box will remain on screen, enabling you to insert other slides.

11 Click Close.

Rudy says:

When you insert a slide from an old presentation, you'll find its design will have changed. That's because inserted slides follow the template of the presentation they are put into. Make any changes as necessary.

13.26.2 Copying Slides Using Slides View

1   Open the presentation you wish to copy from.

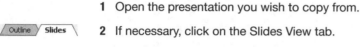

2   If necessary, click on the Slides View tab.

3   Click on the slide you want to copy.

4   Click on the Copy icon.

5   Open the presentation you wish to copy to.

6   Right click on the slide which will appear before the slide you wish to copy.

7   Click on the Paste icon.

13.27 What is an Organisation Chart?

13.27.1 What is an Organisation Chart?

An organisation chart is used to create hierarchical charts which display the structure of an organisation.

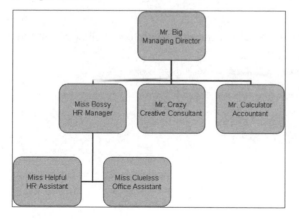

13.27.2 Adding an Organisation Chart Using the Slide Layout

1 Create a new slide.

2 Choose Organisation Chart layout.

3 Click OK.

4 Double click the organisation chart placeholder.

5 Choose the type of chart you want.

6 Click OK.

Or

1 Select the slide you wish to add an organisation chart to.

2 Click on the Insert menu.

3 Click on Diagram.

4 Choose the type of chart you want.

5 Click OK.

When you have inserted an organisation chart, a new toolbar will appear above the chart.

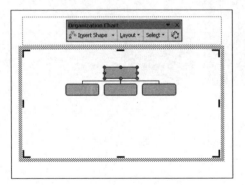

13.27.3 Adding More People to an Organisation Chart

To add more people to an organisation chart:

1 Click into the shape you wish to link from.

2 Click the drop-down arrow next to Insert Shape on the Organization Chart toolbar.

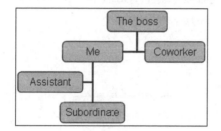

3 Select the type of employee you wish to add. A new shape will appear in the appropriate place.

- Subordinate will add a box directly below.

- Coworker will add an adjacent box on the same level.

- Assistant will appear below but before any subordinates.

4 Click into the next shape and repeat until complete.

13.27.4 Working with an Organisation Chart

Once you have inserted the organisation chart, you'll need to add some information to it.

1 Click into a shape you wish to add type into. Diagonal lines will appear around it.

2 Type in your information.

3 Press Enter to type on the next line.

4 Click into the next shape and repeat until complete.

Practise this!

Create an organisation chart for your company or department. Include employees at different levels of seniority within the company such as subordinates, coworkers and assistants.

13.27.5 Switching from the Organisation Chart to PowerPoint

Once you have finished your chart you will need to come out of the organisation chart and go back into PowerPoint. To do this, just click outside the area of the organisation chart.

13

13.27.6 Switching from PowerPoint to the Organisation Chart

If you need to edit your organisation chart, just click on it once.

13.28 Adding Pictures to Slides

13.28.1 Inserting with a Clipart Slide Layout

To create a new slide:

1 Click on the New Slide icon.

2 Double click the placeholder for clipart. You will be taken to the Clipart gallery (see the next section).

I didn't choose a layout with a Clipart placeholder

It's easy to change the layout of a slide once it's created.

1 Click on View.

2 Click on Task Pane.

3 Choose the Slide Layout pane.

4 Select the slide to change.

5 Choose a layout with clipart.

13.28.2 Inserting Clipart Without a Clipart Placeholder

In Normal view:

1 Select slide.

2 Click on Insert.

3 Click on Picture.

4 Click on Clipart. You will be taken to the Clipart gallery (see the next section).

My layout has changed!

When you insert clipart or pictures this way the layout changes to a title, text and clipart layout.

13.28.3 Inserting Pictures that are not Clipart

If you wish to insert a picture file that is not part of the Clipart collection, such as a logo or a scanned image:

13.28.3.1 Inserting a picture from a file

1 Move to the slide you wish to add a picture to in Slide view.

2 Click on the Insert menu.

3 Click Picture.

4 Click From File.

5 Change the Look in box to the folder where your picture is saved.

6 Click on your picture file.

7 Click Insert.

13.28.3.2 Inserting a picture from a scanner

1 Move to the slide you wish to add a picture to in Slide View.

2 Click on the Insert menu.

3 Click Picture.

4 Click From Scanner or Camera – you will be taken to your scanning software.

5 Scan the picture as normal.

13.29 Using the Clipart Gallery

13.29.1 Inserting a Picture

When you first enter the Clipart gallery you will see this dialog box:

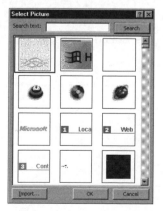

1 Type a word or phrase which describes what you're looking for.

2 Click the Search button.

3 Select the clipart picture you want.

4 Click OK.

Practise this!

On a new slide, insert a picture of something that relates closely to the industry you work in (such as money, a book, computers, travel).

13.29.2 Using the Clipart Task Pane

The Clipart task pane gives you a few more options when selecting clipart. To view the Clipart task pane:

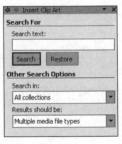

1 Click on Insert.

2 Click on Picture.

3 Click on Clipart.

   The clipart task pane appears.

4 Type a word or phrase describing what you're looking for in the Search text box.

5 Select where to search in Search in box if required.

6 Select type of media (clipart, pictures, movies, sound) in Results should be box.

7 Click on Search.

8 Click on Results icon to expand the view.

9 Click on selected item.

10 Click on Modify to search again.

13.30 Moving, Copying, Resizing and Deleting

13.30.1 Selecting an Object

1 Click on the object.

White 'handles' will appear around the edge.

2 Click away to deselect the picture.

13.30.2 Moving an Object

1 Select the object.

2 Click on the Edit menu.

3 Click Cut.

Or

Click Cut icon.

4 Click your mouse where you want the object to go.

5 Click on the Edit menu.

Click Paste.

Or

Click Paste icon.

Or

1 Select the object.

2 Position the mouse in the middle of the object.

3 Drag to a new location. The mouse pointer should look like a four-headed arrow.

13.30.3 Copying an Object

1 Select the object.

2 Click on the Edit menu.

3 Click Copy.

Or

Click the Copy icon.

13

4 Click your mouse where you want the object to go.

5 Click on the Edit menu.

Click Paste.

Or

Click the Paste icon.

Or

1 Select the object.

2 Hold down the Control key (Ctrl).

3 Position the mouse over the object.

4 Drag to a new location.

Or

1 Right click on the object.

2 Select Copy from the menu.

3 Right click inside the placeholder you wish to add the image to.

4 Select Paste from the menu.

13.30.4 Resizing an Object

1 Select the object.

2 Hover the mouse over a handle. It will change to a double-headed arrow.

3 Click and drag inwards to make the object smaller.

Or

Click and drag outwards to make the object bigger.

Assessor's tip

Sheena says:

If you drag from a corner handle then the picture will stay in proportion. If you drag from a middle handle you will stretch or squash the picture.

13.30.5 Deleting an Object

1 Select the object.

2 Press the Delete key.

If you inserted the object using the placeholder

You will still see the placeholder when your object is deleted. This will not print, and it will not show during an on-screen show. To get rid of it, change the layout, delete the placeholder or add a different object.

13.31 Rotation and Ordering

13.31.1 Flipping an Object

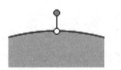

1 Select the shape(s) you require.

2 Click Draw.

3 Click Rotate or Flip.

4 Click Flip Horizontal.

Or

Click Flip Vertical.

13.31.2 Rotating an Object

1 Select the shape(s) you want to rotate.

2 Hover the mouse pointer over the green circle – the rotate symbol will appear.

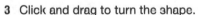

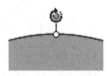

3 Click and drag to turn the shape.

Or

1 Select the shape(s) to rotate.

2 Click Draw.

3 Click Rotate or Flip.

4 Click Rotate Left.

Or

Click Rotate Right.

Or use the menu to rotate a shape more exactly.

1 Select the shape(s) to rotate.

2 Click on the Format menu.

13

3 Click Object or AutoShape.

4 Click on the Size tab.

Rotation: 270°

5 Change the rotation options as required – type in the angle you want to rotate by, or use the up and down arrows.

6 Click OK.

13.31.3 Changing the Ordering

If you have several objects on a page that are on top of each other, they form a kind of 'queue'. Whichever object you can see on top is at the front of the queue, and whichever object you can see underneath all the others, is at the back of the queue. In the diagram below there are three circles, and their number corresponds to their position in the queue:

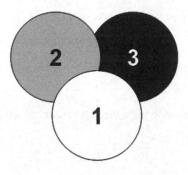

You can change this order using the **send to back/bring to front** commands, or the **send backward/bring forward** commands. Let's imagine that you decide to send the first circle to the back. The circle will go to the back of the queue, behind the other two circles:

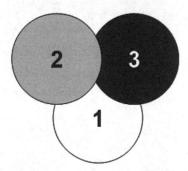

If, however, you sent the same circle backwards it would just go one stage behind in the queue, rather than all the way to the back. In other words, it would go behind the second circle, but not behind the third:

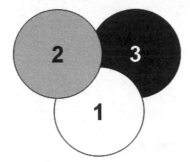

1   Select the object you wish to move.

2   Click Draw.

3   Click on Order.

4   Click Send to Back.

   Or

   Click Bring to Front.

   Or

   Click Send Backward.

   Or

   Click Bring Forward.

13.32 Alignment

13.32.1 Aligning Shapes to Each Other

If you wish to line shapes up on the slide, you can choose to line them up to each other or relative to the slide. Below are some diagrams of two shapes aligned to each other in different ways.

Horizontal alignment for shapes that are side by side:

Vertical alignment for shapes that are above each other:

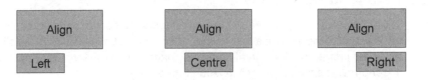

1 Select the shapes you wish to align to each other.

2 Click Draw.

3 Click Align and Distribute.

4 Make sure the Relative to slide option is not ticked.

5 Click on the Alignment you require.

Assessor's tip

Rudy says:

If all your shapes have appeared on top of each other, it means you've chosen the wrong type of alignment. If your shapes are side by side you need align top, align middle or align bottom. If your shapes are above each other, you need align left, align centre, or align right.

If I align two shapes to each other, which one will move?

If you align top, the shapes will line up to whichever shape is higher up on the slide. If you align left, the shapes will line up to whichever shape is furthest left on the slide etc.

13.32.2 Aligning Shapes Relative to the Slide

Sometimes you may want to line shapes up to the left of the slide, or with the top of the slide etc., rather than lining them up to another shape. In these instances, you need to turn on Relative to Slide.

1 Select the shapes you wish to align.

2 Click Draw.

3 Click Align or Distribute.

4 If Relative to Slide is ticked, go on to step 8.

  If Relative to Slide is *not* ticked, go on to step 5.

5 Click Relative to Slide.

6 Click Draw.

7 Click Align or Distribute.

8 Click on the Alignment you require.

13.32.3 Distributing Objects Evenly

The Distribute Evenly feature allows you to space objects out evenly. The spacing can be even between the shapes at either end, or spaced out evenly across the slide. In the following image, the first row of arrows is spaced evenly in relation to each other. The second row is spaced evenly in relation to the slide.

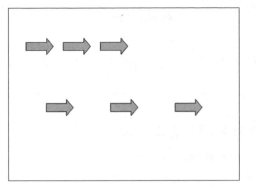

1 Select the shapes to distribute evenly.

2 Click Draw.

3 Click Align or Distribute.

4 Tick Relative to Slide if you wish the shapes to be distributed relative to the slide.

   Or

   Leave Relative to Slide unticked if you wish the shapes to be distributed relative to each other.

   Click Distribute Horizontally if your shapes are side by side.

   Or

   Click Distribute Vertically if your shapes are above each other.

13.33 Using the Drawing Toolbar

13.33.1 Displaying the Drawing Toolbar

If the Drawing toolbar is not displayed:

1 Click on View.

2 Click on Toolbars.

3 Click on Drawing.

13.33.2 Drawing Shapes and Lines

1 Click on the shape you wish to draw.

2 Click and drag over the slide to create the shape.

3 Click away from the shape to finish.

13.33.3 Creating a Perfect Shape or a Straight Line

1 Click on the shape you wish to draw.

2 Hold down the Shift key.

3 Click and drag over the slide to create the shape.

13.33.4 Drawing a Text Box

If you wish to add extra text onto your slide, you can draw a text box.

1 Click on the Text Box icon.

2 Click and drag over the slide to create the text box.

3 Type your text into the box.

4 Click away from the box to finish.

13.34 Test Your Knowledge

The questions below will test what you know of the knowledge and understanding requirements of this unit. All the answers to these questions are contained or referred to within this chapter.

1 What different types of images could you include in a presentation?

2 Where could you get images to put in your presentation?

3 How you would go about inserting still images onto a slide?

4 What sort of chart would you insert if you wanted to display the staff members and their roles at your company?

5 Name four ways that PowerPoint can display presentations.

6 What could you add to make objects in your presentation appear in an interesting way?

7 What other materials can you produce with PowerPoint that will assist your presentation?

8 What are important things to consider when designing your presentation?

9 What could you add to your presentation to help you remember what to say?

10 What are animation effects?

13.35 Evidence

The tasks you undertake as evidence for your ITQ should be work-related. Therefore, your supervisor at work should be able to give you guidance on the type of tasks you should take on. Below are some ideas of possible tasks for this unit. Consider how you can adapt these ideas to make them more relevant for your own workplace and to ensure you cover all the skills requirements.

- Write a report detailing why it is important to proofread and check your presentation. Highlight the major things to be aware of and specific items that need to be checked.

- Write a report explaining what design features you would consider when producing a presentation that communicates clearly and effectively with the audience. What factors would you take into account and implement?

- Create a presentation about what needs to be done in an emergency at your workplace. Include any photos or images of fire exits and equipment. Create lists of dos and don'ts, details of first aid officers and other relevant information. Make sure the design of the presentation gets the key points across clearly.

- Create a simple presentation that explains your main tasks and responsibilities in your job. Be sure to include images, a chart and appropriate colours and formatting. You can manipulate and resize these as necessary, taking screenshots at each stage. Create speaker's notes for each slide. Save the presentation as a slide show and print the speaker's notes.

CHAPTER 14

Specialist or Bespoke Software

14.1 About This Unit

What you need to know

To gain ITQ Level 2 in this unit, you should demonstrate the following competency:
Use specialist or bespoke software effectively for more complex tasks.
　　To achieve this you should know about:

1　What the purposes for using IT are and the capabilities of the software.

2　What most tools and functions can be used for and how to use them for more complex tasks.

You should also be able to display the following skills and techniques:

1　Handling files appropriately.

2　Combining information of different types.

3　Entering, editing and processing information for more complex tasks.

4　Checking information for more complex tasks.

How to prove your skills

You need to carry out at least two work-based tasks which demonstrate the skills and knowledge listed above. In order to show your competency, it may well be necessary for you to complete more tasks than this.
　　Make sure you have plenty of evidence that shows how you completed each task, such as a copy of the file you worked on, or a document with screenshots of the processes you followed. You can back this up by producing a report which shows your knowledge of the subjects covered within the unit.

14

This module may be available to you if your company makes extensive use of specialist or bespoke software.

- Specialist software: a program with functions outside of the general packages covered in the other ITQ units. For example, specialist accounting software.

- Bespoke software: a program written specifically for your company or organisation. For example, a stock control system.

Given the sheer range of software that could be used for this unit, it is not possible to go into detail about specific tools and features you should use. However, you should ensure the software is reasonably complex, since Level 2 requires you to use some more advanced features. The rest of this chapter gives you further pointers to ensure the evidence you produce covers the necessary areas.

14.2 Using the Software

14.2.1 Why is the Software Right for the Task?

Whatever task you are completing, a key requirement of this unit is your ability to explain why you need to use a specialist or bespoke package. Think about the following things.

- What can you do with the software that you can't do with other programs?

- What features are available in the software that aren't available elsewhere?

- How does using this software make it faster and/or easier for you to complete this task?

You also need to understand the tools and functions available in the software. What do these tools do? How do you use them?

Assessor's tip

Lynne says:

If you are new to the software you are using in this unit, consider getting some further training on it. You will be expected to be able to use all the main tools and features of the program you're working with.

14.2.2 Working with the Software

There are four key skills you need to be able to demonstrate in this unit. Make sure the software you are using gives you the opportunity to show your ability in these areas.

- **Handling files**. You need to be able to perform basic file management, such as opening and closing files and creating new ones. You should also be able to organise your files by saving them into specific folders, saving them as different file types and so on.

Practise this!

Open your software and go through all the main file handling techniques. Take plenty of screenshots to show that you are able to use all the relevant features in this area.

- **Combining information**. The key here is that you need to be combining information **of different types**. For example, you might be using a product-ordering database which has the capacity to display images of the various products. Adding image files to the database would be a perfect way to show your capability in this area.

  Alternatively, the information in your software may need to go online. Adding this information to a website would also be a good option.

  Make sure you are able to use the tools in your software package that enable you to insert external files, and that you are then able to work on them once they are imported.

Practise this!

Open a new file in your chosen software. Import information from another package into this new file.

- **Entering, editing and processing information**. This is all about the bread and butter of the software's usage. Think about the following:

  1 What kind of data does it produce?

  2 How do you enter this data?

  3 What can you do with the data once it has been entered?

  4 Of the tools available to you, which do you use on a regular basis? Why?

Practise this!

Use the features of your software package to add new data. Ensure this data is processed properly (for example, you may need to save the data in a particular way in order for it to be useable).

- **Checking information**. Consider the tools available in the software for checking the information you add. Perhaps there is a spell checker, or a function you can use to ensure the numbers you have entered are correct? What information do you need to check manually? Why is this important?

14

Practise this!

Make a list of all the things you need to check when entering information into this piece of software. List also how you run these checks.

14.3 Test Your Knowledge

The questions below will test what you know of the knowledge and understanding requirements of this unit. The answers to these questions are referred to within this chapter, but will be dependent on the software you are using.

1 Name two features of your specialist software that are not included in more mainstream packages.

2 Explain one way in which using this software saves time in your working day.

3 Why is it easier to complete the task using this software, rather than using a non-IT-based approach?

4 List the steps you would take to open a file (or view data) in this package.

5 List the steps you would take to save your work. If the package saves your work automatically, describe how you ensure this has happened.

6 What kind of external files you can import into this software? How do you do this?

7 What kind of information is input into this software? How do you input the information?

8 List at least two checks that you make to ensure your work is accurate.

9 Which one feature of the software do you use most often?

10 What drawbacks are there to using this software (if any)?

14.4 Evidence

The tasks you undertake as evidence for your ITQ should be work-related. Therefore, your supervisor at work should be able to give you guidance on the type of tasks you should take on. Below are some ideas of possible tasks for this unit. Consider how you can adapt these ideas to make them more relevant for your own workplace and to ensure you cover all the skills requirements.

- Create a document that explains how to open a file in your chosen software. Explain how you would print that file, make changes to it, save it and then close it. Include any other common file management techniques you would use in your day-to-day work.

- Keep a record of the next time you need to import external data into a file in your chosen software. Make a note of what functions you used and any difficulties you came across. Support the document with plenty of screenshots.

- Compile a short manual that explains how to enter information into your chosen software. Discuss how you can edit this information, and why using the software makes the whole task easier.

- Create a list of checks you need to make whenever you enter new information into the software. Detail which checks can be made automatically using the software and which must be performed manually. Include screenshots where appropriate.

14

CHAPTER 15

Evaluate the Impact of IT

15.1 About This Unit

What you need to know

To gain ITQ Level 2 in this unit, you should demonstrate the following competency:
Analyse information and draw fair conclusions about the benefits and drawbacks of using IT.
  To achieve this you should know:

1 How IT changes what individuals and organisations do.

2 How to improve access to using IT.

3 How to identify health and safety issues in using IT.

4 What common security risks there may be.

5 Benefits and drawbacks to improving learning.

You should also be able to use the following skills and techniques:

1 Analysing and evaluating the impact of IT use.

2 Planning and learning IT skills.

How to prove your skills

You need to carry out at least two work-based tasks which demonstrate the skills and knowledge listed above. In order to show your competency, it may well be necessary for you to complete more tasks than this.
  Make sure you have plenty of evidence that shows how you completed each task, such as a copy of the file you worked on, or a document with screenshots of the processes you followed. You can back this up by producing a report which shows your knowledge of the subjects covered within the unit.

15

15.2 IT and Society

15.2.1 How Has IT Changed Our Lives?

IT is now a part of almost everything we do, whether you are setting the microwave to warm up your baked beans or programming a space probe to explore the outer reaches of the solar system. Both processes – and everything in between – utilise the functionality of computers.

The key to this unit is that you show an understanding of how information technology has changed our lives.

Think about what life was like before computers and what it is like now. There are many examples, a few are listed in the table below.

| At home | | |
Process	Then	Now
Withdraw money from the bank	Stand in line at your local branch, waiting for your turn. The cashier makes a note of how much you have withdrawn and updates their paper records accordingly.	Use your plastic card to withdraw money from any of the cash machines all over the world. All are linked by computer systems which automatically update your bank account.
Pay your telephone bill	Fill in a form with the details of your payment, then send it to the phone company along with a cheque.	Log onto your online bank account and set up a direct debit so your bill is settled automatically each month.
Communicate with your friend in Australia	Use the phone to make an expensive call or write a letter that will probably take at least a week to arrive.	Send an email that arrives in their inbox instantly. Or chat using an instant messaging program. Or make a free phone call using voice-over IP.
Listen to the latest chart-topping album	Buy a cassette tape for your brand new personal stereo, which is slightly smaller than a house brick.	Download it from a music website onto your personal mp3 player, which also holds another 400 albums and is smaller than a matchbox.

At work		
Process	**Then**	**Now**
Send an important document to a customer	Type out the document, put it in the post and wait for them to receive it a couple of days later.	Attach the document to an email and send it to the customer, who receives the file immediately.
Find out more information about a company	Look through phonebooks, newspapers and records.	Click on the company's 'About Us' link on their website.
Work out a monthly budget	Create a series of calculations in a ledger. All the calculations need to be worked out by hand.	Create a spreadsheet using a program such as Excel. All the calculations are worked out automatically by the computer.
Create a list of customers' details	Write details by hand, with each record stored in a filing cabinet.	Create a database using software such as Access. You can type in new records and edit existing ones in seconds.

These are just a few examples and of course there are many more. You may not think all changes are for the better, but what is important in this unit is that you can prove you recognise how things have changed.

Changing jobs

IT hasn't just changed the way we do our jobs – it's changed the type of jobs we have in the first place. An entire industry has built up around computers, with people working in jobs such as technical support staff, website designers, IT trainers and so on. Even for those whose jobs are not specifically focused on the use of computers, IT skills are still desirable – and often a requirement.

Practise this!

Make a list of five activities in your own life that have been affected by the advent of IT. How have things changed with the involvement of computers?

15.2.2 How Has IT Changed the Way Your Company Works?

The easiest way to see how IT has changed the way organisations work is to look at your own company. How dependent is it on IT? What would happen if your company's entire IT network evaporated overnight? Chances are everything would grind to a very sudden halt.

Consider the following points:

- How important is email to your company? What daily tasks are dependent on the use of email?

- What IT-related issues are there at your company? Perhaps your computers are old and slow. Perhaps the software you use could do with updating.

15

- How much time does your company save by using computers?

- How would common tasks have been completed before your company had computers?

What other ways can you think of in which IT affects the company you work for?

15.2.3 How Has IT Changed Other Companies?

Companies have made many changes as the use of IT has become more widespread.

Consider some of the following examples:

- Storing customer details. Instead of keeping reams of paperwork on each customer, businesses can now create a database that can store records of all customers. This can be instantly updated when necessary.

- Staff training. Staff can now learn at their own pace from their own computer using e-learning.

- Manufacturing. Computers can be used to control robotic set-ups which can manufacture anything from cars to chocolate bars in a fraction of the time it used to take.

- Staff working patterns. Staff can now work easily from outside of the office. Workers may be working at home, on the train, even on the beach. All of this is possible because of laptops and wireless Internet connections.

- Communication. Email has transformed the way we communicate. It is now possible to send important documents instantly using email, rather than sending them via the postal system, which could take several days.

- Job types. The very jobs that people have are now different because of IT. This is an entirely new industry and as such it has created new jobs. Similarly, some jobs have become obsolete.

Practise this!

Consider how other companies have evolved as IT has become more useful. What changes have you seen in the way your bank works? How about your local supermarket? How many companies can you think of that *don't* have their own website?

15.2.4 The Information Revolution

Many would argue that the most important effect of the IT boom has been the spread of the Internet. For this unit, you need to think about how the ever-increasing use of the Internet has affected how people can access information. It's now possible to have information at your fingertips 24 hours a day.

Some examples for you to consider:

- Checking your bank balance. You can now use the Internet to log onto your bank account. From there you can not only check your bank balance, but also make payments to companies and individuals, set up overdraft extensions, apply for a mortgage, and so on.

- Online shopping. If you're allergic to the weekly shop, you no longer have to set foot in a supermarket. You can do all your grocery shopping online and have it delivered to your door. Everything else from music CDs to cars can also be bought online. Price comparison sites enable you to quickly find out which shop is offering the cheapest deal.

- Reading the latest news. You can log onto your favourite news site to read the headlines as they happen, instead of waiting for the next morning's paper. These sites offer additional features, such as the option to click through to related stories, write comments about what you've read, or to watch video footage of the story.

- Signing up for email lists. When you find a site you like, you can sign up to their mailing list. The site can then send useful information straight to your email inbox.

- Finding the film times at your local cinema. Cinema showing times are listed online, which saves you searching through the local paper. When you find a film that's being shown, you can click on its name to go straight to a review which tells you whether it's worth watching. You can then book your cinema ticket online.

- Checking the weather report. Instead of waiting for the *Six o'Clock News* to finish, you can go straight to a weather site to find a weather report specifically for your town. If you're about to go on holiday, you can also look up a weather report for that place – and for wherever else you fancy, for that matter.

What other ways can you think of in which you can more easily access information than in the days before the Internet?

Finding out more information

In this unit, you should also be able to gather your own information on how IT has changed our lives. The best place to keep in touch with the latest developments is online, but you can also keep an eye out for specialist computing magazines and books.

On the Internet you'll find reviews of new gadgets, the latest IT news, information on software updates and more. Try the following sites for starters.

IT Week: www.itweek.co.uk

ZDNet: www.zdnet.co.uk

Download.com: www.download.com

PC Review: www.pcreview.co.uk

Computer Buyer: www.computerbuyer.co.uk

15.3 IT Issues

15.3.1 Accessibility Options

It's easy to take IT for granted, but those with physical disabilities often face difficulties when using standard computers. Specialised hardware and software such as the examples listed below can improve accessibility.

Screen reader software. Designed for those with visual impairments, this software reads out what is written on the screen. Similar software can be used to magnify what's on screen.

Microsoft Windows tools. Windows comes bundled with a range of accessibility tools. You can find these in the Accessibility Options folder in the Control Panel. For example, those with visual impairment can switch on a high-contrast display, which makes text easier to read. There are also a range of keyboard functions which can make the keyboard easier to use.

Specialised hardware. There are all sorts of products that can make it easier to communicate with a computer. For instance, you can buy keyboards with larger keys, or pointing devices that are operated with the feet instead of the hands. For more examples of specialised computer hardware, take a look at sites such as www.keytools.co.uk and www.connectsys.co.uk.

Speech recognition software. This enables the user to talk to the computer, instead of using the keyboard. The software recognises the user's words and automatically types them onto the screen.

Additional software options. Users who cannot use pointing devices such as mice and trackballs can generally use the keyboard instead. All major programs support keyboard-only use.

Accessible web pages

Website creators are now required to make their pages accessible to all. That means people should be able to access the information, regardless of any disabilities they may have.

Take a look at the following links for more information:

Web Accessibility Initiative: www.w3.org

BBC – My Web My Way: www.bbc.co.uk/accessibility

Accessibility at Microsoft: www.microsoft.com/enable

15.3.2 Health and Safety

You need to consider health and safety issues when using computers. For information on this aspect of computing, take a look at Chapter 2, Operate a computer.

15.3.3 IT and Security

The use of IT opens up a whole new level of security issues. If someone wants to steal from your company, they no longer have to physically break into the premises. Instead, they might try to hack into your company's server, where they may find banking details, records of your customers and other sensitive information. Take a look at Chapter 5 on security for more information on keeping data safe.

15.3.4 Better or Worse?

There's no denying information technology has changed all our lives for ever, but is that a good thing?

For this unit, you have to think about the drawbacks to using IT, as well as the benefits.

- Is it always quicker to use a computer? Not all tasks are best suited to the IT approach. What tasks do you prefer to do without using a computer?

- What difficulties do you face when using a computer in your work? Computers don't always run smoothly. Perhaps you come up against a recurrent problem when using yours? Perhaps you find a certain piece of software hard to use?

- How safe do you think your computer-stored information is? We trust a lot of important information to computers, but this can be vulnerable if security is not high enough. What would happen if a hacker was able to gain access to the information on your company's server?

What other drawbacks to using IT can you think of?

15.4 Learning More About IT

15.4.1 Understanding Your Limitations

One of the skills you need to have for this unit is 'planning and learning IT skills'. At the root of this is the necessity of understanding what skills you already have and which you need to develop further.

Take an objective look at what you can currently achieve using IT and then think about what things you would like to be able to achieve. It may be useful to compile this as a document. You can then discuss your existing skills with your supervisor and create a plan of further learning.

15.4.2 Improving Your Skills

There are many ways you can learn new IT skills. The simplest way is to learn 'on the job' – also known as being thrown in at the deep end. This has the advantage of giving you hands-on experience of the new skill straight away, but it does mean you are effectively teaching yourself.

Classroom-based training is another traditional option. The main advantage of this is that you are led by a classroom tutor who can give you individual guidance. However, you may not find this option ideal if you are short on time. Attending a classroom course may take a day or two out of your working week. Also, if you are being taught in a group you may find the pace too slow or too fast.

15

15.4.3 Using IT for Learning

IT opens up new ways of learning. You can use training software on your computer, or you can go online and use e-learning.

15.4.4 Training Software

Advantages: Can be taken whenever you have spare time. You can work at your own pace.

Disadvantages: Requires willpower from the student to stick with it. Some users can find it a lonely way of learning.

15.4.5 E-learning

Advantages: Can be accessed from any computer. Can be accessed whenever you have a spare few moments.

Disadvantages: Requires willpower from the student to stick with it. Can be affected by the speed of your Internet connection.

15.5 Test Your Knowledge

The questions below will test what you know of the knowledge and understanding requirements of this unit. All the answers to these questions are contained or referred to within this chapter.

1 Name two ways that IT has changed the way you spend your time out of work.

2 Name two ways that IT has changed the way you work.

3 How might it benefit a company to store its customers' details on computer?

4 What hardware/software might a visually impaired person use to make computing easier?

5 List two office-based health and safety risks.

6 How could you keep the risks you specified to a minimum?

7 What risks might be attached to downloading software from the Internet?

8 What benefits are there to e-learning compared to other types of learning?

9 What is a computer virus?

10 What risks are there to your data if your computer hardware is malfunctioning?

15.6 Evidence

The tasks you undertake as evidence for your ITQ should be work-related. Therefore, your supervisor at work should be able to give you guidance on the type of tasks you should take on. Below are some ideas of possible tasks for this unit. Consider how you can adapt these ideas to make them more relevant for your own workplace and to ensure you cover all the skills requirements.

- Produce a document that discusses how IT affects the way you do your job. In what ways does IT make your job easier? What difficulties does it produce?

- Make a list of the IT skills you already have, then pinpoint where you need to develop further skills. Find out how you could learn these skills and list which method you prefer and why.

- Create a list of five work-based tasks and five tasks from outside work. List how IT helps you do each task, then list what you would have to do if you did not have access to IT.

- Create a checklist of IT safety concerns. Include health and safety considerations as well as risks to data. Next to each, list a way to minimise the risk.

15

CHAPTER 16

Use IT Systems

16.1 About This Unit

What you need to know

To gain ITQ Level 2 in this unit, you should demonstrate the following competency:
Set up and use hardware safely and protect software and data appropriately.

To achieve this you should know about:

1 What most types of computer hardware are and how to use them.

2 Errors on most types of hardware and software and with data.

3 How to identify health and safety issues in using IT.

4 What common security risks there may be.

5 What advice is available and how to get it.

You should also be able to display the following skills and techniques:

1 Setting up different types of hardware safely.

2 Accessing data from networks.

3 Protecting software and data in different ways.

How to prove your skills

You need to carry out at least two work-based tasks which demonstrate the skills and knowledge listed above. In order to show your competency, it may well be necessary for you to complete more tasks than this.

Make sure you have plenty of evidence that shows how you completed each task, such as a copy of the file you worked on, or a document with screenshots of the processes you followed. You can back this up by producing a report which shows your knowledge of the subjects covered within the unit.

16

16.2 Choosing This Unit

16.2.1 Which Option to Choose

This is a unit that overlaps with four other ITQ units – Operate a computer, IT troubleshooting for users, IT maintenance for users and IT security for users. If you intend to include any of those units in your ITQ, you should not also use this unit as there is a lot of similar content.

16.2.2 What You Need to Know

All the information you need for this unit is contained within the following: Chapter 2, Operate a computer, Chapter 3, IT troubleshooting for users, Chapter 4, IT maintenance for users and Chapter 5, IT security for users.

In particular, you should focus on (but not limit yourself to) the following areas of those chapters:

- Types of hardware and storage media, how to connect them up and how to use them.
- Common errors, how to deal with them and how to find advice on fixing them.
- Keeping risks to people and hardware at a minimum.
- Understanding security risks and keeping your computer and data safe.
- Accessing files, either on your computer or on a network.

16.3 Test Your Knowledge

The questions below will test what you know of the knowledge and understanding requirements of this unit. All the answers to these questions are contained or referred to within Chapter 2, Operate a computer, Chapter 3, IT troubleshooting for users, Chapter 4, IT maintenance for users and Chapter 5, IT security for users.

1 What would you use a scanner for?

2 Which of the following can store more data: floppy disk, hard drive, CD-ROM?

3 How would you use a flash drive?

4 Why might you need to open the Task Manager utility?

5 You are going to call technical support with a query about Microsoft Word. How would you find out which version you are using?

6 Why might you need to change the way your office chair is set up?

7 Name one risk of downloading software from the Internet.

8 Why should you be wary if you receive an email attachment from someone you don't know?

9 What would you use the Windows XP Backup utility for?

10 What use would you have for a software patch?

16.4 Evidence

The tasks you undertake as evidence for your ITQ should be work-related. Therefore, your supervisor at work should be able to give you guidance on the type of tasks you should take on. Below are some ideas of possible tasks for this unit. Consider how you can adapt these ideas to make them more relevant for your own workplace and to ensure you cover all the skills requirements.

- Write a set of instructions detailing how you would connect up your PC if you had to move it across the office. Include steps on how to safely connect any piece of hardware to your computer.

- Create a spreadsheet to log any errors you come across during your working day. In the spreadsheet, list the error, what your initial thoughts were, whether you needed to seek additional help and how the problem was resolved.

- Carry out a risk analysis of your workstation. Compile a document that lists all the areas of your workstation, showing which are safe and which (if any) are not. List possible changes that could make your workstation safer.

- Create a document that describes how you reduce the chances of a virus infecting your computer. Take screenshots of the process of updating your anti-virus software and running a virus check with it.

16

CHAPTER 17

Use IT to Exchange Information

17.1 About This Unit

What you need to know

To gain ITQ Level 2 in this unit, you should demonstrate the following competencies:

Use more advanced email software facilities. Access and retrieve relevant information using browser software.

To achieve this you should know about:

1 More advanced email facilities.

2 Common problems with exchanging information and how to sort them out.

3 What laws and guidelines affect using IT and how they affect it.

You should also be able to display the following skills and techniques:

1 Sending and receiving emails using more advanced facilities.

2 Searching for relevant information efficiently.

How to prove your skills

You need to carry out at least two work based tasks which demonstrate the skills and knowledge listed above. In order to show your competency, it may well be necessary for you to complete more tasks than this.

Make sure you have plenty of evidence that shows how you completed each task, such as a copy of the file you worked on, or a document with screenshots of the processes you followed. You can back this up by producing a report which shows your knowledge of the subjects covered within the unit.

17.2 Choosing This Unit

17.2.1 Which Option to Choose

This is a unit that overlaps with two other ITQ units: Internet and intranets, and Email. If you intend to include either of those units in your selection, you should not also use this unit as you will be going over a lot of common ground.

17

17.2.2 What You Need to Know

The information you need to complete this unit is already covered in the Internet and intranets and Email chapters of this book. The unit focuses more heavily on the uses of email. The main skills you need in relation to using the Web are in being able to use search engines.

In particular, you should focus on (but not limit yourself to) the following areas of those chapters:

- Sending and replying to email messages.
- Attachments (including compressing and decompressing them).
- Using an address book (including sending to groups).
- Using additional email features, such as adding a signature.
- Viruses and how to avoid them.
- Spam emails and what to do about them.
- Laws relevant to email and the Internet.
- Using search engines efficiently.

17.3 Test Your Knowledge

The questions below will test what you know of the knowledge and understanding requirements of this unit. All the answers to these questions are contained or referred to within Chapter 6, Internet and intranets and Chapter 7, Email.

1 What does a distribution list enable you to do?

2 Give one reason why you should be aware of the size of attachments on emails you are sending.

3 What could happen to your computer if it became infected by a virus?

4 What is a spam email?

5 What law deals with the sending of spam emails?

6 Why should you be wary if you receive an email with an attached file from someone you don't know?

7 A customer of your company gets in touch to request a copy of any personal data you hold on them. Why must you comply with this request?

8 What does it mean to forward a message?

9 How would you search the Internet for pages containing this exact phrase: much ado about nothing?

10 Name one software program you could use to compress an attachment before sending it.

17.4 Evidence

The tasks you undertake as evidence for your ITQ should be work-related. Therefore, your supervisor at work should be able to give you guidance on the type of tasks you should take on. Below are some ideas of possible tasks for this unit. Consider how you can adapt these ideas to make them more relevant for your own workplace and to ensure you cover all the skills requirements.

- Send an email to your line manager with an attached document. Ensure that this attachment is compressed before sending.

- Using a distribution list that you have either created or that exists at your workplace, send an appropriate email to your colleagues. Adjust the message to high priority, if necessary, and make any formatting changes that need to be done.

- Write a short report on how you would deal with spam and viruses when using email or instant messaging. Detail what you could do to avoid these things and how to deal with them when they arrive in your inbox.

- Create a document that describes a time when you had the search the Internet for information for a work project. Describe the information you had to find, how you decided where to look, what information you discovered and how you narrowed it down to what you needed. Make sure you use advanced search techniques such as phrase searching and Boolean searching. Include screenshots of the whole search process.

17

Index